DOMESTIC INTERIORS

DOMESTIC INTERIORS

REPRESENTING HOMES FROM THE VICTORIANS TO THE MODERNS

edited by
georgina downey

BLOOMSBURY
LONDON • NEW DELHI • NEW YORK • SYDNEY

Bloomsbury Academic

An imprint of Bloomsbury Publishing Plc

50 Bedford Square
London
WC1B 3DP
UK

175 Fifth Avenue
New York
NY 10010
USA

www.bloomsbury.com

First published 2013

British Library Cataloguing-in-Publication Data

A catalogue record for this book is available from the British Library.

ISBN: 978 1 84788 932 4 (Cloth)
978 1 84788 931 7 (Paper)
e-ISBN: 978 1 84788 933 1 (epub)

Library of Congress Cataloging-in-Publication Data

A catalogue record for this book is available from the Library of Congress.

Typeset by Apex CoVantage, LLC, Madison, WI, USA.

Printed and bound in Great Britain

This book is dedicated to my mother
Catherine Downey-Armstrong
1939–2012

CONTENTS

LIST OF ILLUSTRATIONS

CHAPTER 1

CHAPTER 2

CHAPTER 3

CHAPTER 4

CHAPTER 5

CHAPTER 6

CHAPTER 7

CHAPTER 8

CHAPTER 9

NOTES ON CONTRIBUTORS

Anne Anderson is an Honorary Research Fellow at the University of Exeter. She is working on *Aesthetic Materialities: Constructing Taste from Whistler to Wilde*. She has published in the *Journal of Design History*, *Women's History Review*, and the *Journal of the William Morris Society*.

Francesca Berry is Lecturer in History of Art at the University of Birmingham. Her publications include, 'Lived Perspectives: The Art of the French Nineteenth-Century Interior', in *Imagined Interiors: Representing the Domestic Interior since the Renaissance* (V&A Publications 2006); and 'Designing the Reader's Interior: Subjectivity and the Woman's Magazine in Early Twentieth-Century France', *Journal of Design History* (2005). Her research can also be found in the 3000-entry online research database, Domestic Interiors Database: *Representing the Domestic Interior since the Renaissance*, published by the AHRC Centre for the Study of the Domestic Interior.

Georgina Downey is a Visiting Research Fellow in Art History at the University of Adelaide. She has been involved with the Graduate Program in Art History since 2001. Her writings have appeared in *ANZJA, the Journal of Australian Studies, the Journal of Australian Cultural History, Broadsheet, Artlink* and *Photofile* and she has contributed to catalogues and symposia for the Art Gallery of South Australia, the Queensland Art Gallery, and the Lawrence Wilson Art Gallery at the University of Western Australia.

Imma Forino, Arch and PhD, is Associate Professor of Interior Architecture at Politecnico di Milano. She is member of the PhD Board in Interior Architecture & Design (Politecnico di Milano) and the International PhD Board in Philosophy of Interior Architecture (Università degli Studi di Napoli-Italy & Universidad Autónoma de Aguascalientes-México). Her publications include *Uffici: Interni arredi oggetti* (Einaudi 2011), *George Nelson: Thinking* (Testo&immagine 2004), *Eames: Design totale* (Testo&immagine 2002), and *L'interno nell'interno: Una fenomenologia dell'arredamento* (Alinea 2001).

Trevor Keeble is an Associate Dean of the Faculty of Art & Design & Architecture at Kingston University, London. Along with colleagues from the Modern Interiors Research Centre, he is a co-editor of *Designing the Modern Interior: From the Victorians to Today* (Berg, 2009). He has also contributed essays on the history of domestic interiors to a number of publications, including *The Modern Period Room* (Routledge 2006), *The Imagined Interior* (V&A Publications 2006), *Women and the Making of Built Space in England 1870–1950* (Ashgate 2007) and *Design and Culture* (Sage forthcoming).

Brenda Martin is Curator of the Dorich House Museum at Kingston University. Her publications include 'A House of Her Own: Dora Gordine and Dorich House' in *Women's Places: Architecture and Design, 1890-1960* (Routledge 2003); 'Photographs of a Legacy,' in *The Modern Period Room* (Routledge 2006); and 'An Artist at Home: Studio Residences and Dora Gordine,' in *Embracing the Exotic: Jacob Epstein and Dora Gordine* (Papadakis 2006). She contributed to *Dora Gordine: Sculptor, Artist, Designer* (Philip Wilson 2007) and she was the curator of the Dora Gordine retrospective at the Dorich House Museum in 2009.

Julieanna Preston is an Associate Professor and Director of Research and Postgraduate Studies for the Institute of Design for Industry and Environment at Massey University, Wellington, New Zealand. Her notable recent works include *Intimus: Interior Design Theory Reader* (co-edited with Mark Taylor; Wiley, 2006), *Interior Atmospheres* (Architectural Design, Wiley 2008) and 'Wedges and Shims: Levering a Feminist Interior Practice' (Interior Tools, Interior Tactics Conference, Edinburgh, 2008).

Mark Taylor is Professor of Architecture at University of Newcastle, Australia, where he teaches and researches on architecture and the interior. He regularly reviews manuscripts for international publishers and is editor of *Surface Consciousness* (Wiley 2003), co-editor of (with Julieanna Preston) *Intimus: Interior Design Theory Reader* (Wiley 2006), and is editor of *Interior Design & Architecture: Critical & Primary Sources* (Berg 2013). He has published papers in *Architectural Design, Interiors: Design Architecture Culture and IDEA Journal*, and has contributed essays on the interior to a number of publications, including *Diagrams of Architecture* (Wiley 2010) and *Performance Fashion and the Modern Interior* (Berg 2011).

John C. Turpin is Professor of Interior Design and Dean of the School of Art and Design at High Point University North Carolina. His explorations of the history of interior design in America concentrate on the work of Dorothy Draper (1888–1969). His publications include 'Risk as a Window to Agency: A Case Study of Three Decorators', *Journal of Interior Design* (2008), 'The History of Women in Interior Design: A Review of Literature', *Journal of Interior Design* (2007); 'Interiors: Cultural Blueprints of Human Existence', in *The Built Environment: A Creative Inquiry into Design and Planning* (Crisp/WKI 1994); and 'Domestic Doyennes: Purveyors of Atmospheres Spoken and Visual,' in *Intimus: Interior Design Theory Reader* (Wiley 2006). He is the current co-editor with Anne Massey of the journal *Interiors: Design, Architecture, Culture*, published by Berg.

INTRODUCTION

georgina downey

> Let us therefore compare the system of the unconscious to a large entrance hall, in which the mental impulses jostle one another like separate individuals. Adjoining this entrance hall there is a second, narrower, room—a kind of drawing room—in which consciousness too, resides. But on the threshold between these two rooms a watchman performs his function. (Freud 1917: 336–7)

In the lecture from which the above quote comes, Sigmund Freud explained how the unconscious works using a simple analogy to rooms. The great communicator knew that his audience would immediately conjure internal mental pictures not only of their own entrance halls and drawing rooms but also the familiar uses and social activities associated with each of these rooms. Through this analogy to a 'chain of command' between rooms, with the entrance hall, or 'usher', reporting to the drawing room, overseen by 'the watchman on the threshold', Freud made his points about how the tripartite structure of the unconscious operates. He knew that he only had to name the rooms and his comparison between *real* space and the spaces of the mind would be made clear. Similarly, the aim of this book is to probe, on a room-by-room basis, the relations between interior and image in the early modern home so that the relationships between rooms in terms of occupation and culture are explained clearly and legibly.

Domestic Interiors is structured as an architectural ensemble—a book made up of rooms. Each chapter reflects current experiential approaches to the representation of a particular room in the modern interior. The essays here, by scholars from the United Kingdom, Italy, the United States, New Zealand and Australia, explore the dominant conceptual frameworks that underpin each room, and their unique history and development, while supporting the overall argument that the domestic interior was a key location of modernity from the Victorian to the modern period.

Organizing a table of contents *as* an architectural ensemble seemed an obvious approach for bringing together new and original essays from the disciplines most concerned with the interior;

architecture, interior design and art history. This structure—while serving readers interested in a particular room—also simulates previous models: the room-by-room approach taken by décor advice manuals from the late nineteenth century, the floor plan (a primary conceptual tool in both architecture and interior design), and the board on which *Cluedo* is played, a game invented in England in 1944 by Anthony E. Pratt to amuse a population confined indoors during long air raids and blackout nights.

Scant scholarly attention has been paid to how the rooms of the modern domestic interior worked together in terms of their different histories of occupation and significance. This is surprising because the room plan for the small domestic house or apartment is such a basic fundamental structuring principle in the ordering of private life. Rooms are the units of space we think in, and dream in. The consistency with which rooms are assigned their roles in the modern home is among other things a boon to the absent-minded. Who hasn't walked into a room and stopped in one's tracks, having completely forgotten the reason for entering? One recalls one's purpose from working logically back from the room's function.

We seem compelled to sort undifferentiated space into parts, into zones where the same kinds of rituals can occur, usually on a daily basis. We then categorize, order, archive, arrange and *ornament* on a room-by-room basis. The most dramatic changes in how we have done this in Anglo European cultures occurred in the eighteenth and early nineteenth centuries. During this period, not only did an abstract language for describing interiors develop in terms of space and décor, but, more importantly, a connection between actual interior space and psychological interiority began to develop; people began to realize that these spaces could and should be designed to harmonize with, nay create, certain mood states in the occupant.

Since then, and from the vantage point of the twenty-first century, it is unclear whether we stand again at a watershed moment in terms of notions of domestic space. Certainly, emerging scholarship is suggesting that the digital screens (smart phones, iPads, iPods, virtual space technology, TV and cinema) through which we negotiate so much of life permit us to occupy a multiplicity of spaces simultaneously, which will certainly affect long-held beliefs about home as a 'refuge' from the external world. Luca Basso Peressut has written that:

> technological devices . . . create an internal-interior whose boundaries are represented by as many shells which compress or dilate our interior space while we move: from the *iPod* with its headphones through the *iPhone*, to the glasses (which in the near future will let us watch TV and the personal computer by isolating [us], on command, from [our] surroundings. (Basso Peressut 2012: 1)

Architecturally, however, we have retained a fairly consistent 'family' of rooms that has not changed in essence since the Victorian era, give or take the advent of the computer nook, or the amelioration of the kitchen, dining room and drawing room into one space. This suggests that the rooms of our lives have evolved but slowly, while the technology underpinning them, the wires, cables and ether clouds that connect us to the outside world, have evolved very fast. We are thus left with a kind of jet lag—the cure for which is often, in the twenty-first century house, the adoption of consoling Victorian or other historic décor, which, combined with digital appliances and conveniences, creates a hectic, hybrid and deeply important zone.

How we make rooms expresses who we are to the world, décor has indeed been construed as a 'second layer' of clothing, and this performative aspect of the interior is an important aspect of this volume's rationale. *Domestic Interiors* contributes to what British design historian Penny Sparke has called the 'resurrection of the interior', a resurrection that, she notes, particularly emphasizes the domestic (Sparke 2009: 2). Consequently, our focus here is on domestic interiors, on typical rooms (both elite and average), with the addition of studios and hidden spaces that hark back to the commencement of our chronology in Victorian times. Thus this book doesn't address those public interiors (offices, prisons, airports, shopping malls, etc.) where people have spent as much if not more time than at home.

Moreover, this book's field of focus is on the *represented* room. Rooms obviously invite a particular decorum, sets of behaviours, rituals and expectations—but how do we know, in the past, how these were conducted if not through the visual media? Our focus, then, is on the visual qualities of representations of domestic space, whether paintings, works on paper, illustrations, photographs or film stills, which allow us to move freely and theoretically between ideal and actual spaces. It means that as well as discussing the occupational and spatial qualities of each room, contributors will address the representation of their room 'qua' image: who made it? When? Why? What are its formal qualities? How is it composed? What are its iconographical qualities? And what kind of viewer does it imagine? This book includes representations of domestic spaces that imagine all kinds of viewers—in the main, these tend to be art audiences—but some chapters discuss 'trade' or commercial images in early home advice journals, in which the 'address' is to a consumer. Other chapters draw upon a repertoire of illustrations, advertisements and film stills, indicating that we are looking across a wide range of media representing the interior.

In this sense, we take the methodologies of the 'new' art history, along with some of its intellectual core, to give significance to the forms of things *depicted* (meaning the thematic preoccupation known as the visual, or alternatively, as the pictorial turn which was so central in the development of 'new' art history of the mid-1990s). But while images have primacy, art history is not the lead discipline in this multidisciplinary volume; instead, it is hoped that its convergence with architectural history, design history and interior architecture will provide readers with a range of complementary methods and approaches to the domestic interior.

WHAT IS THE INTERIOR?

Charles Rice has considered the emergence of domestic space from the nineteenth century as important because it was experienced by modern individuals as both material and immaterial, spatial and imagistic, and he points to the paradox that these two 'interiorities' don't necessarily converge. It is the tension between these two registers that produces the experience of the interior; put simply, it is four walls, and the notion of shelter, as well as an inner entirely conceptual world (Rice 2004: 276). That is, the interior is at once both spatial and conceptual. Rice's argument is a sophisticated addition to the privileging of the visual. His notion of the 'doubled interior' has been deeply influential; indeed, it, along with Penny Sparke's work on the gendered modern interior, seeded the recent critical/theoretical turf from which this volume grows. However, perhaps the concept of a doubled interior tells only half the story, and, from our research, this omits the sensual and emotional effects of space on the body and, indeed, the body's relationship to space as a material, psychical and spatial event. This latter expanded notion of the interior informs the chapters within this volume in ways that, it is hoped, will prove critical to the next phase of scholarship on the interior.

Notwithstanding, from the cultural and gender studies viewpoint, through the act of enclosing space and making rooms, we remake ourselves. I suggest 'remake' because the rooms in which we dwell offer us the crucial chance to honour, or to defy, the inborn genetic, familial, gendered, racial conditions that we otherwise cannot control. Through making our rooms, we display to ourselves and others where we fit in the social and material world. Images of domestic spaces reflect back to us the attitudes and material and bodily arrangements we call interiority. How the occupied interior does this is an important question since home is the key space through which individual subjectivity is fundamentally constituted.

How do we understand *represented* interiors? Well, with difficulty, for what room is exactly like its portrait? Each representation in art or design or illustration of a domestic interior is essentially, if not a lie, then an artificial fixing of something so fluidly mobile it can change perceptually with the removal of an object or a shift in the light. Not only do 'regimes' within rooms over time filter in and out various objects, but ambient variables—light, temperature, noise and the surrounding environment (social, political)—change how rooms feel and look. Single-point perspective figurative systems cannot show a whole house or room at once—they cannot show all the spaces. Even in one room, there are always corners one cannot see, unless of course one is a cubist. Room pictures also contain hot spots—fixtures, zones and spaces that carry more symbolic cargo than other parts. For the Romantic painters and poets, open windows were powerful symbols for the process of longing and yearning, and of the tension between freedom and societal constraints. For the Decadents and symbolists in fin-de-siècle Paris, doorways and corridors were made to function, in both art and literature, as portals to the 'mysterious unknown'. Around the same time (early 1890s), textures and textile-based wallcoverings blurred boundaries between interior and exterior, culture and nature; in particular, they linked the garden to the interior.

These subtleties created issues for artists and designers wanting to represent the interior. Stefan Muthesius also points out that the nineteenth century was period that witnessed a greater desire for 'immediacy' in the representations of interiors. Illustrators borrowed techniques from the fine arts to accommodate this need such as partial views, *chiaroscuro* (light and dark), textures, angled viewpoints, a certain sketchiness to better convey an impression of a room (Muthesius 2009: 61–2). Muthesius goes on to say that, in this period also, 'a room was increasingly understood "like a picture"' (Muthesius 2009: 140).

Thus a field of vision filled with 'room-ness' is also full of tags, hooks, ellipses, gaps and mysteries for the eye and mind of the viewer. The eye cannot 'take it all in' in one glance; this is due to how the eye flickers (saccades) between scan-paths accommodating foveal, para-foveal and peripheral vision. This means an image of a room is more like a montage or 'slice' than a solid, single, smoothly perceived entity. So why start with something that was never there in the first place? Because it is *interesting* that representations of interiors are always already mediated, even as they document room appearances and suggest habitation practices.

Thus each chapter reasserts the importance of our approach to the interior *as pictured,* not merely as a stage or backdrop, with the 'right' ornaments to indicate class and sex, but as an active 'agent of feeling' and a constituent space of modernity. Each chapter recasts images and ideas in substantially new ways, with a view to how the modern interior has been staged and the spatial relations lived, engendered and represented. We can also work the interpretive process from the opposite direction; in several instances, chapters probe the spatial dynamics and occupational practices of categories of domestic space and how they contribute to developing deeper and more nuanced interpretations of well-known artist's depictions of space from new viewpoints.

Why is our time period, the late nineteenth century to the early twentieth century (the 1880s through 1940s, to be specific), significant? This period witnessed the emergence of the domestic interior as a generative space for modernity. 'Interiority' entered the language and became the focus of images and texts around domestic space that began to proliferate in the period. In fact, specialist in nineteenth-century decorative arts Charlotte Gere considers, 'The art of depicting the interior reached its highest point of refinement in the nineteenth century' (quoted in Muthesius 2009: 58).

Increasing value was placed on privacy, and architects and urban planners developed the single person's dwelling, the studio apartment, and the small family home, which reflected modern peoples' needs and expectations. The scope of the book concludes with the 1940s, thus incorporating all the modernist notions of technologies in the home (modern conveniences), modern 'style', a streamlined aesthetic, and 'good design for all'. We halt before the postwar explosion of consumer culture and the much more rapid cycling of styles, which have resulted in throwaway and waste regimes.

From the last third of the nineteenth century, contemporary representations of the domestic interior exposed the new relations of men and women to the new intimate spaces of modernity. Taste makers, critics, designers, artists and men and women of letters began to explore the notion that the best setting for portraying modern individuals was in the home—and that portraits should be made through the acute observation of how a person arranges and inhabits his or her domestic space.

Private life thus began to generate sites for literary and artistic modernism. Much that is most significant in art and literature in the period was produced by those who grew up in dark, repressive Victorian rooms where there was a strict separation of masculine and feminine spheres of influence, and genteel conformity was reflected in strict hierarchical orders between rooms, furnishings and associated propriety. They thus embraced modernity as liberation from the morals, values and tastes of their parents. It is no surprise that our best-known 'literary' interiors now emerge: Proust's grandmother's house in Cambrai, *Mandelay*, Gordon Square, Howard's End, and the Ramsays' house in *To the Lighthouse*, the houses of Edith Wharton, Henry James, Lawrence Durrell and so forth. The writing of these rooms conveys a pervasive sense of modern psychological interiority.

From the 1880s, visual cultures became increasingly saturated with images of domestic interiors intensified by the psychological ambiguities and tensions urban individuals carried into their homes, which were being analysed and taxonomized both by Freud, who noted the importance of house symbolism in dreams, and by the French neurologist Charcot at the Pitié-Salpêtrière Hospital. Both found that the workings of heredity and the mysterious inner drives constituted another form of interiority. This period culminated artistically in what Susan Sidlauskas has called 'expressive' interiors; compositional analogies that elicit sympathy or empathy in the viewer for the figures in the painting (Sidlauskas 1994: 671–96).

Thus it can be seen how representations of modern life were underscored by new psychosocial formulations on which a number of disciplines have focused. Therefore, our understanding of modernism and the modern domestic interior is much more multifaceted than seeing it as just a style or as an artistic response to modernity.

In fact, the notion of differentiating rooms and assigning them different uses is deeply ingrained in our modern sense of interiority. Opening up this notion, Penny Sparke writes:

> The emergence of the private domestic interior, and its capacity to facilitate self-reflection, or 'interiority' on the part of its inhabitants, was also part of that same historical moment. Following Benjamin's logic to its conclusion, the interior itself was therefore, an integral component of modernity and by definition, modern. (Sparke 2008: 12)

Gender is likewise a central category of enquiry and present as a primary framework in conceptions of the interior in each chapter. Historically, the time period in focus saw increased opportunities for women to exercise taste and control over the modern interior through increasingly intense levels of production, consumption and display in the metropoles of Europe, her colonies and the Americas. Women even began setting up their own dwellings outside of marriage and family. In 1933, Virginia Woolf called on women writers to take 'rooms of their own' (and 500 pounds a year). The interior became the outward and visible sign of an inward and invisible feminine subjectivity.

The reforms of domestic space seemed to offer the opportunities to move beyond the reflexive equations of femininity with 'home' that were so prevalent. Gilbert and Gubar sum up the dangers of this identification when they quote Simone de Beauvoir's warning: 'To become literally a house, after all, is to be denied the hope of that spiritual transcendence of the body', which is after all what makes humanity distinctly human (Gilbert and Gubar 1984: 87–92). In fact, in many cases, the modern interior led to women becoming 'early adopters' of its precepts, and in this period we see women creating public reputations as designers, artists and taste leaders.

The exercise of feminine taste was marginalized in the reform of the interior by modern architecture's rejection of ornament. Yet in practical terms, this 'continual turnover of goods and images created by marketing aimed at arousing women's "consumer desire" led to 'opportunities for women to engage in the aesthetic experience of modernism' (Sparke 2008: 12).

How the domestic interior was codified in representation according to notions of function, comfort, class, prestige and performance of self, and how cultural and social values were embodied in changing spatial configurations in the late nineteenth and early twentieth centuries will be explored through the following chapters.

Working spatially from the outside in, from the most public to the most private of rooms, we start with the veranda or porch. In 'Verandas: Spaces without Walls—the Veranda in Colonial Singapore', Brenda Martin explores this 'liminal space on the margins'. With its shade and cooling breezes, this zone of the house drew occupants away from those stifling rooms at the heart of the house, thus becoming a multifunctional space for relaxing, socializing, meeting, doing business and performing household duties in the far flung colonial territories of the empire. The veranda was also a space of contact and exchange between expatriate ruling classes and imperial subjects and, as such, was a space charged with desire and bilateral exchange.

It was a space, Martin explains, that in the 1920s and 1930s in Singapore house design and decoration that was *modified* by art deco, a style imported from Europe; nonetheless, the veranda itself modified the foreign occupants' tastes, lifestyles and behaviours; it created new social rituals (the drinking of 'sun-downers' there), and it encouraged greater physical informality than at 'home' with its cane/bamboo recliners. Then, in a deft and original contribution, Martin explores the progress of modernist styles. Oriental furniture, fabrics and decorative arts transferred well to the open-plan living and clean styling of the modern colonial house, and they were also shipped back to Europe commercially, for markets there as well as brought back as keepsakes with families returning home. Thus rather than the usual simplistic assumption of formal stylistic responses to modernity forever travelling from metropolitan centre to rustic periphery, Martin shows how the influence went both ways—with Singapore modern style being promoted back to English consumers through the Daily Mail Ideal Homes exhibitions of the 1920s and 1930s.

In 'Halls and Corridors: Spaces between and Beyond', Trevor Keeble argues that the hall and its younger relative, the corridor, were 'key spaces through which late Victorian models of domesticity gave way to early modernist revisions of domestic space, function and movement'. Thinking about the legacy of this Victorian typology, Keeble focuses on halls in typical London domestic terraces, and he demonstrates that 'though these [halls and corridors] varied considerably in scale, . . . the hall and the corridor of the London terrace performed a largely conventional duty'. They did this by articulating Englishness; mediating between cosy interior and the 'wildness' beyond the front door (whether that be actual 'wild nature' or the urban jungle). Halls and corridors thus provided a 'backbone' for a whole set of crucial ideas about the planning of the modern dwelling.

Thus Keeble takes us a long way from the original hall of architectural history—a medieval single, open space, in constant use, with furniture and effects being brought in and out as needed—to its role in Victorian times, which was to establish social position and to create an almost exaggerated sense of privacy and protection for the family, to its return in a sense to a dynamic free flowing medieval form again in Le Corbusier's Villa Savoye. The representations Keeble uses to take us on this journey down the hall include photographs of a Victorian-era hall corbel, used to hang a curtain separating public front spaces from private ones in the centre of the home; an illustration from Rhoda and Agnes Garrett's *Suggestions for House Decoration* (1877) of a hall table and chair; and an image of the hallway at Wickham Hall, Kent (1897).

Moving into the drawing room/sitting room from the hall, in 'Drawing Rooms: A Backwards Glance: Fashioning an Individual Drawing Room', Anne Anderson explores this essential room that links the daily life of the occupant(s) with invited guests. It was also, more strongly than other rooms, construed as a feminine space. In the period in question, it was where, Anderson explains, the '"lady of the house" [was] at the centre of her universe'; where her roles of wife, mother, household manager and hostess were each enacted in turn. While reaffirming the position of women to, in some cases, a suffocating degree, it was also a space where, paradoxically, women became free to exercise their own taste and control, and to fashion distinctive identities. In her chapter, Anderson considers how the psychological shift to individualism was reflected in the décor of the drawing room. Antiques offered the ideal vehicle for demonstrating discrimination and individuality, quickly becoming 'a marker of refined sensibility'. Anderson draws on the idea that the woman's task was to personalize drawing rooms by creating modern feminine aspirational identities. This required women to consume material goods, which in turn had the consequence of bringing women into a particular relationship with modernism as purchasers, advocates, translators, interpreters and, in significant numbers, active agents in design, production and the provision of advice. And this power in turn was of deep concern to male taste arbiters who published at length on 'good' as opposed to 'feminine' taste.

The result was the drawing room as a self-conscious statement—arranged with 'discriminating eclecticism'. The modern drawing room was lighter and brighter and artfully strewn with objets and art that refreshed and reaffirmed its owner's 'subject-object' relations—it was a more meaningful space in every way than the very formal drawing rooms of the early Victorian period, those into which 'no one wished to withdraw'. Into this modern mix came the antique; Anderson aptly quotes Marshall Berman who pithily said in 1983, 'An important part of being modern was being anti-modern'; this explains how, in creating liveable modernism, the antique paradoxically became an important expressive element in the room. Antiques constituted (and still do) the tasteful 'backward glance' to the best of the past. Thus, in concluding this detailed reading of the space, Anderson reveals the paradox of how glancing backwards moved the drawing room forward.

In 'Dining Rooms: Measuring the Gap between the Edwardians and the Moderns', John C. Turpin looks at the dining room in terms of what he calls its evolution as a 'physical manifestation of social expectations'—through the Edwardian period and into the modern. He explores this unique space where the visceral activities of conversation and dining collide. Through Charles Dana Gibson's *Castles in the Sky* (1903), he reads the Edwardian-era dinner as a highpoint of formal dining etiquette in which aspiring American upper classes imitated European customs. Turpin takes his argument through to Norman Rockwell's *Freedom from Want* (1943), which he describes in terms of the cultural ascendancy of the American middle class, with the associated rise in more relaxed and informal social relations. His method draws on visual analysis and material, as well as social studies—with the focus throughout remaining on decoration *and* decorum, both of the dining room itself and of table settings, and how these demarcated the socially prescribed distance between diners. His notion of the 'space between' becomes the defining metaphor throughout the chapter, referring to many spaces between: the actual physical space between diners prescribed by place settings; the metaphoric space between the Europeanized American upper class and the middle classes; and also the metaphoric space between the legendary twelve-course Edwardian banquets and the more modest family meals in new modern suburban homes in the 1940s.

In 'Studios: Live (red) Matter; Matisse's *l'Atelier Rouge*', Julieanna Preston explores the studio via the speculative and tentative method of actor network theory. This focus on the home studio is a critical addition as the studio was conceived by modern architects as an integral part of the small, modern home or apartment. It could be used for the making or display of art, as a home office, for music practice, or as a library—but it's the room that brings together the relationship with self and the world as this is interceded through the creative imagination. The studio is a private space and yet, at the same time, a social and commercial space, where creative products are not only made but considered and reworked and shown to family, friends, dealers, patrons and clients. Preston extends theories of the studio in innovative potential directions, specifically with her premise that the objects, furniture and textiles of the studio are not simply the 'hapless bearers of symbolic projection' but rather, they may be construed as 'co-dwellers in the generative space of the home-studio'. Her exemplar is Henri Matisse's well-known *The Red Studio* of 1911, a painting loved, loathed and mused over endlessly for the astonishing use of pure red pigments in it, which wash across the entire surface, on which, seemingly carved into the pigment, we see paintings, curtains, plants, chairs, tables and Matisse's collection of personal artefacts arrayed within this rubicund space.

Preston's reading takes us on a journey into the painting and thence into Matisse's own 1911 studio. Here her method privileges sensation as a means to unlocking how the painting works *as* a depiction of a studio. She emphasizes how, for any artist who works at home, the studio is a liminal space that serves both work and socializing, the requirements of the outside world and the pleasures of meeting oneself on paper or canvas.

In 'Kitchens: From Warm Workshop to Kitchenscape', Imma Forino affirms that in the history of interiors, the kitchen is the most traditional room in the house. Less likely to be on public view, it has evolved more slowly over the centuries than other spaces in the house. In peasant homes, it was the heart of everyday family life: it was where meals were cooked, where domestic chores were done, where children were tended, and even where sleeping pallets were spread on the floor. In nobles' dwellings the kitchen was occupied by servants and later by other staff. Until the nineteenth century, it was far removed from the living and entertaining areas since its smells and noises were not welcome in polite society. As the middle classes became established, it became the scene of the housewife's activities.

Forino focuses on the intimacy, furnishing and equipment of the kitchen. She handles the subject chronologically, but with a narrative emphazis on the visual sequence of the kitchen as an 'interior-scape'. After a brief outline of the kitchen's evolution from antiquity to the seventeenth century, the chapter proper begins with the concept of intimacy as the Dutch of that century gave the kitchen modern expression: kitchens in Flemish painting portray a vivid scene of interiority. Later, the 'warm workshop' of chefs and housekeepers in the early nineteenth century turns into the woman's realm of the Victorian era. From 1860 to 1890, a series of inventions simplified the life of the housewife. Forino finds a 'serene interiority', linking *The Kitchen* (1895) by Carl Larsson with the Gamble House (1907–8) by Greene & Greene. She goes on to state:

> A diluted art nouveau informs a tranquil domestic world. In the first decade of the twentieth century, on the other hand, Christine Frederick's scientific kitchen (1912), with its standardized labour and the 'mechanical bride' idea derived from Taylorism, anticipated the fragmentation of the soul in Ludwig Kirchner's *Alpine Kitchen* (1918). In Europe, the experimental designs of the 1920s and 1930s prefigured a minimal and wholly functional kitchen. In America, on the other hand, the next decade saw designs for 'the kitchen of tomorrow'—to paraphrase the title of a book on the home by Henry Wright and George Nelson (1946). Before 'easier living' arrives, the Streamline interlude represents the idea of the Future with the aerodynamic styling of utensils [and white goods].

Forino concludes by examining George Nelson's essays, articles and designs which focus on the need for practicality in the American kitchen; this brings us fully into the modern era with the concept of the 'continuous kitchen . . . an idea that has lasted—though with many transformations—until the present day'.

In my own chapter, 'Bathrooms: Plumbing the Canon: The Bathtub Nudes of Alfred Stevens, Edgar Degas and Pierre Bonnard Reconsidered', I contend that certain well-known nineteenth and twentieth-century paintings of female bath time have a lot to tell us about attitudes to the advances of modernity, as these are encoded in bathing technologies. I investigate well-known representations of female bath time *through* the mechanics of bathing to see what these might suggest about progressive attitudes towards the space of the bathroom, hygiene and the feminine body. The bathrooms in focus here are those in Alfred Stevens' *The Bath* (1873–4), Edgar Degas's *Woman in a bath sponging her leg,* 1884, and Pierre Bonnard's *The Bath* 1925. Through these works I argue that the tub was a site of transformation from the Victorian to the modern age thus signalling the arrival of the modern bathroom, its technologies, and its regimes of hygiene and bodily care.

In 'Bedrooms: Corporeality and Subjectivity', Francesca Berry explores the proposition that the 'in bed' scene and the intimate staging of the female body as erotic object within it did not hold the allure for early-twentieth-century artists and their audiences that it had held for their nineteenth-century predecessors. The artist's studio usurped the bedroom as the preferred erotic setting as early-twentieth-century avant-gardists rejected the notions of domestic sexuality and commodified femininity that had been signified and disavowed in the bedroom scene. At the same time, the bedroom or bedsit scene attained a new currency as a space of subjective experience and potentiality in the work of female artists; a place in which to live and work as an individual. These images tended to share with illustrations for design a marked absence of the body, whilst everywhere signalling subjective presence. Berry's chapter thus maps the changing representational uses of the bedroom through the late nineteenth and early twentieth centuries. She analyses the meanings and implications of these representational types and pays particular attention to the bed as a recurrent physical presence and stage for the body. The chapter culminates with an analysis of the representation of the child's bedroom across a range of artistic and visual cultures. Her case study images include Frederico Zandomeneghi's *In Bed*, 1878; Édouard Vuillard's, *In Bed*, 1891; Mary Elliott Brown's drawing of her 'bedsitter' in Paris, *Towards the Window with a Washstand*, circa 1912; and Willebeek Le Mair's *Miss Waterlow in Bed* circa 1920s. Berry argues that these images of being 'in bed' bring new implications regarding the issues of intimacy, eroticism, corporeality and subjectivity to the modern bedroom scene.

In 'Hidden Spaces: Cavities, Attics and Cellars: Morbid Secrets and Threatening Discoveries', Mark Taylor explores the modern home in terms of its hidden rooms and secret passages. The identification of the mind with space is examined through the architectural literary devices of nineteenth-century novelists, in conjunction with the accounts of detectives of real spaces of horror in the nineteenth century. His examples include poetry and fiction in which character and narrative are developed through the occupation of concealed spaces. Additionally, he draws on actual built spaces of the nineteenth century that featured an ominous overabundance of these spaces of concealment, including the infamous Holmes Castle in Chicago, which was renovated for murderous ends by its owner Herman Webster Mudgett, alias Henry Howard Holmes. Taylor reappraises the domestic interior as both a psychological and topographical encounter, and a place where the inanimate is made animate. He does so through an exploration of 'house fiction' in which fictive and real concealed architectural structures become mutually imbricated as horror stories unfold. Thus he shows how hidden rooms operate as metaphors of the mind that are subsequently mirrored in the physical spaces of the domestic environment.

This book is for students, scholars and anyone interested in the domestic interior in modern times. It has been conceived with the passionate conviction that the study of domestic space is a global, collaborative and cross-disciplinary process, and it is intended to take its readers, whoever and wherever they be, on an engaging and informative room-by-room journey towards a deeper understanding of the interior and interiority.

REFERENCES

Basso Peressut, L. (2012), 'Nomadic Interiors', paper presented to Flow[2] A Conference in Two Parts, Melbourne School of Design, University of Melbourne, 8–10 February 2012 [conference proceedings], <http://www.msd.unimelb.edu.au/events/conferences/flow2012/> accessed 22 March 2012.

Freud, S. (1917) 'Introductory Lectures on Psycho-Analysis,' in *The Standard Edition of the Complete Psychological Works of Sigmund Freud*, vol. 16, trans. James Strachey, 1974, London: The Hogarth Press.

Gilbert, S. M., and Gubar, S. (1984), *The Madwoman in the Attic: The Woman Writer and the Nineteenth Century Literary Imagination*, New Haven: Yale University Press.

Muthesius, S. (2009), *The Poetic Home: Design the 19th-Century Domestic Interior*, London: Thames & Hudson.

Rice, C. (2004), 'Rethinking Histories of the Interior', *The Journal of Architecture*, 9/3: 276.

Sidlauskas, S. (1994), 'Resisting Narrative: the Problem of Edgar Degas's *Interior*', *The Art Bulletin*, 75/4: 671–96.

Sparke, P. (2008), *The Modern Interior*, London: Reaktion Books.

Sparke, P., Massey, A., Keeble, T., and Martin, B., eds. (2009) *Designing the Modern Interior: From the Victorians to Today*, London: Berg.

1.

VERANDAS: SPACES WITHOUT WALLS— THE VERANDA IN COLONIAL SINGAPORE

brenda martin

> VERANDA: In architecture, most frequently, an open-walled, roofed porch at to the exterior of a domestic structure and usually surrounded by a railing. The word came into English through the Hindi verandā, but it is related to the Spanish baranda, meaning "railing," and thus most likely entered Hindi via Portuguese explorers of India. (Oxford English Dictionary n.d.)

The subject of this chapter is the changing use of the veranda in colonial bungalows in Singapore in the twentieth century. Originally a necessary barrier against the fierce tropical heat and rain, by the twentieth century the veranda had arguably replaced the English parlour and the Chinese ancestral hall as the main space of welcome. From the British colonials homes to those of the wealthy Chinese elite, it was the first part of the home that the visitor, guest or tradesman saw. Its arrangement and furnishings were therefore of the greatest importance and portrayed the nationality, status and identity of the owners of the house. The veranda evolved in the late nineteenth and early twentieth century from more than just a threshold and a barrier; as such, the possibilities for social interaction in this cool, shady space became ambiguous. It was both inside and outside, both a formal reception space and a casual domestic space for relaxation. The veranda was an enigmatic liminal space surrounding the inner private sanctum of the tropical home. For everyone, it provided a welcome respite from the weather. It was used as a trading space for hawkers and as a place to do household chores by servants, and in clubs and hotels such as Raffles, it became an extension of the ballroom and other function rooms.

Contemporary cultural discourse has seen the European home in the colonies as a significant expression of an imperial power, and the creation of a particularly English home culture abroad as way of imposing an alien value system and European social rituals (Jones 2007: 16).[1] William Glover sets out the argument, with regard to the nineteenth-century Indian colonial bungalow, for the importance of maintaining moral standards and the difficulty of keeping up familiar styles of dress and social patterns in a tropical climate. Glover writes that 'if the bungalow was, in part, a setting for the cultivation and display of refined manners and taste, then its physical appearance played a role in the pervasive sense of anxiety about the effects on human character of living in a colony highlighted in European writings' (Glover 2004: 73). Popular conception was that living in a tropical climate had a debilitating effect on both health and morals, expressed in classic novels such as Joseph Conrad's *Heart of Darkness* (published in 1899 and set in the African Congo) and later in the short stories of W. Somerset Maugham, who visited Malaya, Singapore and other British colonial outposts during the 1920s. In contrast, the interwar years in Singapore and Malaya were regarded as a golden age, rewarding in material and social terms to those who lived there (Shennan 2004: 130).

Domestic housing for British colonials in Singapore until the 1880s was mostly provided by the Public Works Department (PWD) and was based on a basic model of tropical housing in India. The casual recreational nature of the large veranda which surrounded the formal reception and living rooms was described in a *History of India* as

> the one place the imperialists [mostly men at this time] had just for messing around on. Everything was easygoing about the veranda. Its furniture was meant for lounging; its pictures and trophies were beloved rather than precious. Secondly, the veranda was the place where the British woman, in particular, could feel some tentative personal contact with the 'alien world' of India outside. In short, the veranda was a sort of bridge built cleverly to fulfil absolute desires in British domestic architecture. The construction linked the rigid and conventional life of the imperialist with the lost liberties of home. (Indianetzone 2011)

More ambiguous images of the veranda in Singapore and Malaya in the twentieth century were described by Guy Madoc in the oral history documentaries of Britain's colonial past recorded by Charles Allen for BBC Radio in 1983:

> Now in these old-fashioned bungalows at the front of the house was the veranda. You lived on the veranda, which was probably big enough to have played a game of badminton in. It had no windows or walls, just a balustrade about three foot [sic] high and otherwise open to the elements. The only protection when the wind blew and the rain beat were the roller blinds, which were called *chicks*, which your cookboy was expected to lower when things became unpleasant. These *chicks* were often lined with blue canvas cloth which cast 'a very attractive, bluish, subdued light that was extremely pleasant; it was such a relief to the eyes to come from the glare outside into the gentle blue-green lighting that suffused the bungalow'. (Allen 1983: 126)

Allen's recordings show that young wives arriving from the United Kingdom trying to make homes in the colonies, especially if they were living on plantations 'up-country' in Malaya, were faced with standard bungalows filled with standard Public Works Department furniture. Government employees moved often, and 'beyond putting up her own curtains "which were never pulled but looked very pretty", installing her own plant pots on the stairs and veranda, adding one or two of her own pieces of furniture and her own pictures on the walls there was little a *mem* could do to make a real home for herself and her husband' (Allen 1983: 218).

It can be concluded from the above that in the mid-nineteenth century in these transient and anonymous surroundings, the most important sense of identity was not that of an individual, but as a member of the British colonial administration of Malaya. However, this changed during the rapid economic expansion of the late nineteenth and early twentieth centuries. For the new employees of large companies such as British American Tobacco and the Firestone Tyre Company, cultural traditions and the cultivation of an identity of authority was based on rural nineteenth century England, and a more personal sense of 'Britishness'.

Conversely, for people leaving Britain to work in the colonies, images of what one might expect of life in the tropics were provided by stories from people from India returning on leave, and by cartoons and print illustrations in newspapers such as the *Illustrated London News, The Graphic, The Bystander* and *Empire Illustrated. The Graphic*, a weekly illustrated newspaper published from 1869 to 1932, carried advertising and a special column entitled 'Home: A summary of news in Britain' for its huge overseas readership. The Singapore Harbour Board and government employees arriving after 1900 were likely to be allocated one of the 'black and white' houses designed by the PWD or European architects such as R.A.J. Bidwell at Swan & Maclaren, the leading architectural practice at that time. These were built in the English mock Tudor architectural style with black beams patterning a white infill, hence the nickname 'black and white'. They had large overhanging eaves, deep porches and wide verandas, a cross between the English country house and the colonial bungalows of India. Typically, the house was a sequence of large and small rooms set around a large central reception room, punctuated with many doors and window openings placed opposite each other for a cooling through breeze. In a typical arrangement, four or five bedrooms would be at the back of the house with steps up from the outside to each, for the night soil removal before proper sanitation arrived. The receptions and dining rooms were ranged along the front and sides of the houses, with large verandas on all sides which increased the living space. The kitchen and servants sleeping quarters were separate from the main house.

The abundance of local servants and cheap consumer goods contributed to a higher standard of living than was possible at home, compensating somewhat for the debilitating heat of the tropical climate. Gone were the internal corridors, back stairs and the green baize door to the warren of small household rooms and pantries of the wealthy English home, and bungalow design evolved with few internal corridors and large open airy spaces. The veranda with its cooling breezes became an important hybrid exterior/interior living space which was not designated for one activity, or indeed class. Social gatherings which might take place at 'home' in morning rooms and parlours, such as breakfast, afternoon tea and cocktails before dinner, were transferred to the veranda, as seen in Figure 1.1. Rituals such as these, when held in the semi-outdoor spaces of the veranda, took on new names: 'cocktails' became 'sundowners'; lunch or afternoon tea became 'tiffin'.

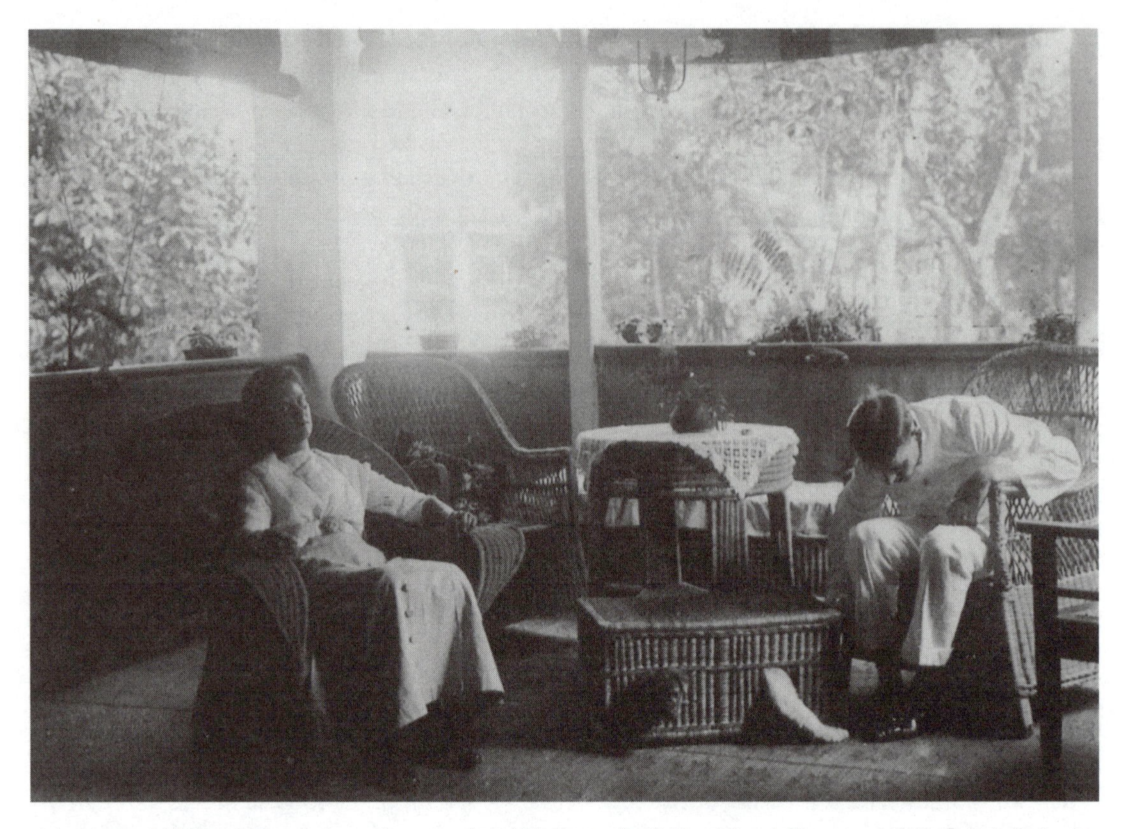

1.1. Mrs and Mr Jan de Jong-Lels on the veranda at Villa Austerlitz, 2 Lloyd Road, Singapore, 1913. © Bels Collection. Courtesy of National Archives of Singapore.

Where there was an opportunity for choice and the expression of personal identity, the interior decoration of this liminal space at the height of the British Empire, around the turn of the century, was based on historical styles from the past—from classical Greek and Roman styles, to Jacobean, Victorian and Edwardian English country house styles. Images of the time, most of them black-and-white photographs, show that cane or rattan furniture was popular, as it offered a cool alternative to upholstered chairs and was less prone to pests and mildew which attacked the fabrics of cushions and covers.

The better-off could furnish their homes with quality furniture and wares from mail-order catalogues sent over by English department stores such as Harrods, Maples and Waring and Gillows, and for the less well off, the Army & Navy store supplied absolutely everything, from food to the smallest household item. The catalogues for the Export and Shipping Departments advertised prominently that they delivered goods to the London docks. These were then shipped to agents in Singapore, usually Guthrie & Co., Patersons or Simons & Co. who had warehouses, locally called 'godowns', at the Singapore ports, which received the goods. The excellence of the service is illustrated by the telegraphic address of Harrods, which was given as 'Everything, Harrods, London'. In 1929, the Harrods catalogue advertised a range of 'finely constructed Cane Furniture for the House, Conservatory or Garden', and although the terminology relates more to the home market, the furniture had exotic names that evoked the countries it was intended for such as the

Cairo chair, the *Malacca Kingsdown*, the *Bungalow*, the *Mecca* and the *Lotus*—all different designs made of pulp cane (Harrods Catalogue 1929: 350. Maples also supplied cane furniture suitable for the tropics (see Figure 1.2), which could be chosen from a special catalogue for 'Wicker and Cane Furniture and Screens' which was considered suitable for 'winter gardens, lounges, gallery and verandas, loggias and similar spaces in hotels and clubs', a clear reference to the colonial market. Furniture manufacturers such as Harris Lebus and Shoolbreds in the East End also made deliveries to the London docks for shipment abroad. The advertising blurb describes the light cane chairs in distinctly feminine terms, as 'dainty and easily portable' and also as 'comfortable and not costly'.

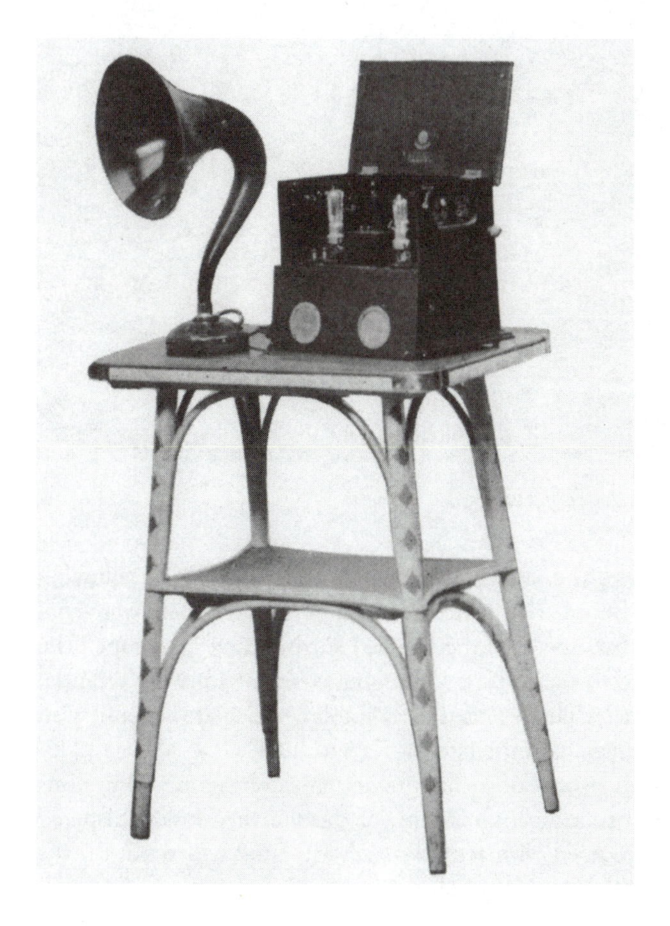

1.2. Cane table in art deco style with glass top with a radio. No. W111, 1922 Maples catalogue, p. 29. Source: Geffrye Museum, London.

This was a clever marketing ploy in response to the evolution of the verandas of clubs and hotels as the main spaces for modern women to socialize, providing an alternative to the more masculine clubhouse. Figure 1.3 shows the newly built Singapore Turf Club, which opened in 1930, with the Ladies Tea Room on the veranda. The formal nature of this meeting space is revealed in the women's dress, which includes hats in a hot climate, and the formal arrangement of the furniture in a setting reminiscent of an indoor parlour tea. The veranda here has clearly become another

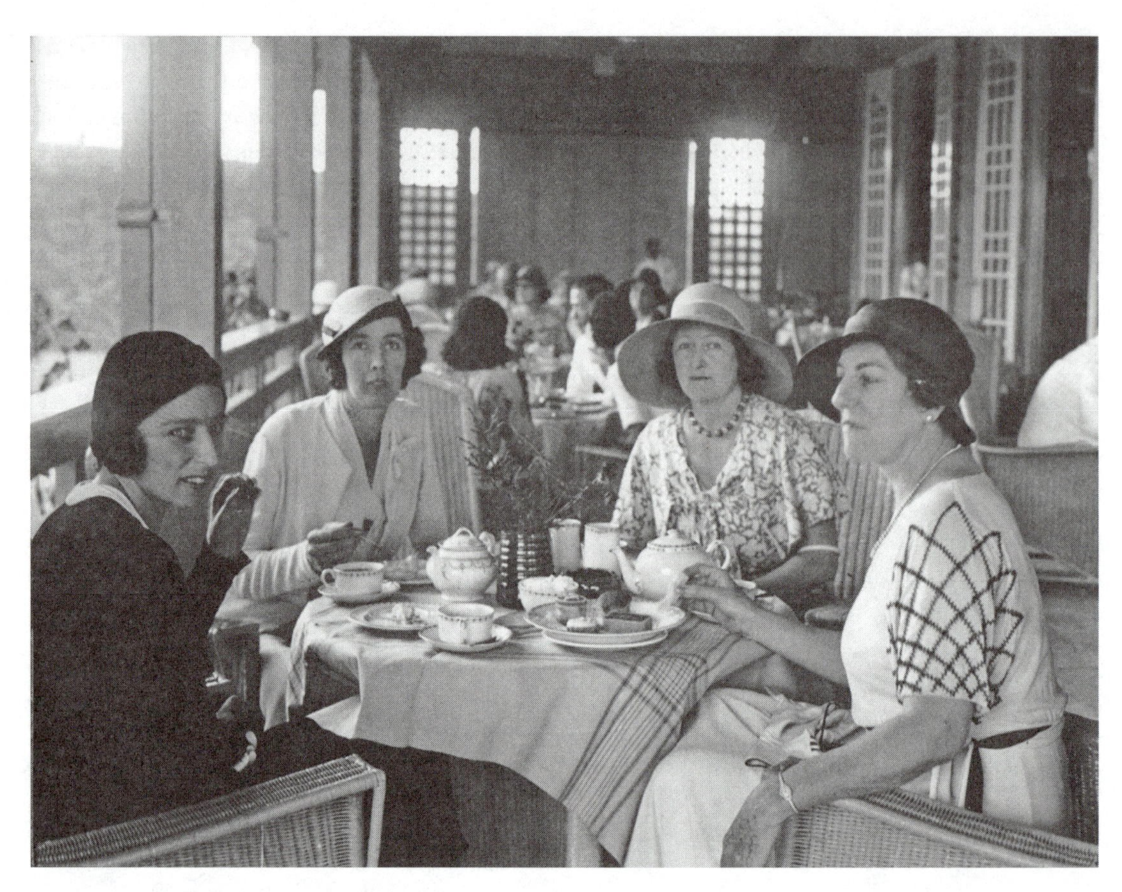

1.3. Ladies Tea Room, Singapore Turf Club, 1930. Private collection.

room, not an ambiguous unformulated space, and it is enclosed with latticework panels, allowing the visitors to be outside but within secure boundaries. Situated on the first floor, there were cool breezes and a chance to connect at a safe distance with the tropical surrounding landscape. The formal arrangement of furniture, as opposed to the scattered lounging chairs of a private veranda, is mirrored in the upright style of the light cane chairs and the café tables, which are covered with checked tablecloths in light pink and pale green, and the latest art deco china.

The more flexible nature of the veranda as a scene of social interaction can be glimpsed in films and books, where the veranda is the site of social transgressions, of the snatched kiss, whispered confidence or dramatic revelation, often preceded with remarks such as, 'Shall we go out on the veranda?'; like the garden or the wood in Shakespearian plays, it is used as a location where the normal rules of society do not apply.

In parallel, in the late nineteenth and early twentieth centuries, the wealthy Chinese community who wished to emulate the British upper strata of Singaporean society were also building houses based on the Western model with large deep verandas and looking to cast off traditions in favour of a more modern and relaxed lifestyle. Here the verandas were taking the place not of the parlour, but the ancestral hall, the very formal room in a traditional Chinese home where visitors were welcomed. Herbie Lim Eng Kwan described the arrival of visitors in his grandmother's time at Mandalay Villa, one of four holiday villas built in 1902 by Lermit & Westerhout for his grandfather Lee Cheng Yan, a wealthy property, trading and financial businessman. 'Cars would roll to a stop outside the arched entrance porch or veranda. There were no doors to any of the three arches of the semicircular veranda, which was furnished with a round marble table and comfortable rattan armchairs. Flanking this were long garden benches that were placed against the columns of the veranda' (Lee and Chen 2006: 27). Lim recalls that his grandmother welcomed people to the house on the veranda and that up to fourteen people could be seated in this area, which was placed to catch the sea breezes. The house also had an 'inner veranda' where the occupants sat if the weather was hot or very rainy, but this was furnished in a more formal way with a marble-topped teak table and teak chairs. The inner part of the deep veranda was also used by Lim's grandmother as an office space, and photographs were taken posed on the veranda.

In an article on Raffles Hotel in Singapore, the sociologist Daniel Goh observes, 'Sitting in the extended veranda, the white colonial male could gaze safely at the sensual manifestations of the imperial networks traversing the public verandas of the colonial city' (Goh 2010: 177–95). Yet for the white female, newly arrived from Edwardian England, the veranda was not a comfortable space, as it was inhabited also by servants coming and going from the interior of the house, haggling with hawkers and chatting while doing the washing and cooking tasks. Guy Madoc recalls that when 'on duty in the bungalow, servants were always immaculately turned out in starched clothes' but that 'in the kitchen and servants areas at the back of the house the boy the cook and the water carrier would lounge about on their veranda in fairly casual clothes. When summoned they would quickly put on the starched trousers and jacket and come in' (Allen 1983: 214). For the women especially, the sense of interiority and haven, which had its high point in the Victorian parlour—a cosy refuge from the outside world and a cold climate—was disrupted by the constant presence of servants, and the veranda represented for some a threatening open space where the invisible boundaries of domestic interior spaces were challenged (Glover 2004). For the Victorian and Edwardian colonial wife especially, the loneliness of life on a rubber plantation and the sense of being watched through open windows and doors caused anxiety, and seemed to transgress the invisible safe boundaries between servant and master, male and female, and British and 'native' (see also Clancy-Smith and Gouda 1998; Collingham 2001; Stoler 2002).

A decade later, in the 1920s, this was no longer the case. New arrivals to the colonies felt no desire to relate to the parlours of the past generations who were associated in their minds with a war and the destruction of society. Although still regarding themselves as part of the British Empire abroad, they identified themselves with the modern progressive world epitomized by the 1925 'Arts Decoratifs and Industriels Moderne' exhibition (later called the 'Art Deco' exhibition) in Paris. The mass slaughter of men in the war and the liberation of women from service to work in factories, offices and shops meant there were fewer servants to be had, and those who remained in service had a more general role and more personal contact with their employers. However, the colonies still provided a lifestyle supported by numerous native servants and for less money than would be paid back home. According to Margaret Shennan, a typical household would contain amongst other servants

> a syce or chauffeur to drive and look after the car, an amah or ayah as a nursemaid for the children, . . . a gardener or kebun, a dhobi or laundryman, and a tukan ayer to take care of water and sanitary needs—all for a salary bill in 1930 of no more than $150 to $180 a month, less than an average monthly budget for food and drink. (Shennan 2004: 114–15)

All of these servants also used the veranda for work, rest and socializing, their oriental rugs and textiles adding to the eclectic mix of furnishings.

By the 1920s in Europe, modern housing design was changing to accommodate the lack of armies of servants and simpler lifestyles. Modern villas for the wealthy, such as the Villa Savoye in Poissy, France, built in 1928–9 by the architect Le Corbusier, were open plan in layout, with functional social and leisure spaces seen as one, the rooms corresponding to each other through open doorways and archways rather than as boxes divided by corridors. The sparse arrangements of furnishings inside the house and the use of the outside roof terrace for exercise and relaxation in the fresh air mimicked the spaces of the tropical bungalow and the use of the inside/outside veranda as living and recreational space.

The young couples arriving to set up home in Singapore and Malaya were therefore more familiar with open-plan living, and the ambiguity of shared living spaces with servants, through innovations such as rational planning and scientific management in modern labour-saving settings, promoted by women designers such as Dorothy Braddell, Caroline Haslett, Anne Shaw, Edna Moseley and Elizabeth Denby. Braddell, for example, showed a combined kitchen and living room for a small country house at the 1933 Daily Mail Ideal Home Exhibition in London, which was designed to cope with the absence of a cook. The new materials of concrete and steel construction, the flowing lines of the glamorous international and art deco styles and open-plan interiors transferred to the tropics well. If you had the money to build your own villa, it was imperative to appear modern in a small colonial society. Outside living, using the roof terrace and balconies, was now an accepted part of modern home design, and the veranda no longer appeared as a threatening open space, but as a place to show off modern credentials. It had become the 'best room', its first impression giving a clue to the modern identity of those within. W. Somerset Maugham, in a short story set in 1930s Malaya, describes how Anne, wife of Alban, a 'lowly District Officer' in the colonies, is proud of the way she has furnished their veranda in the latest modern style and the one-upmanship she feels over her less fashionable neighbours:

> It was getting on towards tiffin time and in a few minutes Alban would be back from the office. It gave her pleasure to reflect that it was an attractive room for him to come back to, the large veranda which was their parlour, and she knew that though they had been there eighteen months he was still alive to the success she had made of it. The jalousies were drawn now against the midday sun and the mellowed light filtering through them gave an impression of cool silence . . . Visitors were surprised because there were no knick-knacks. They were taken aback by the bold colour of her curtains and could not at all make out the tinted reproductions of pictures by Marie Laurencin and Gauguin in silvered frames which were placed on the walls with such cunning skill. She was conscious that few of them quite approved and the good ladies of Port Wallace and Pemberton thought such arrangements odd, affected and out of place; but this left her calm. They would learn. It did them good to get a bit of a jolt. And now she looked round the long, spacious veranda with the complacent sigh of the artist satisfied with his work. It was gay. It was bare. It was restful . . . Three immense bowls of yellow cannas completed the colour scheme. (Somerset Maugham 2000: 89)

Now that traditional boundaries between 'British' and 'native' cultures were breaking down, the furniture on the veranda could include Chinese, Malay and oriental furniture, which had originally inspired much of the art deco styling. This was transferred home with returning colonials, so that the bare spaces of European modernism were enlivened by a traditional Burmese fabric, or the deep glow of tropical hardwood furniture, doors and other decorative items. This wealth of information and choice was helped by the fact that Singapore was connected to cities all around the world by sea. There were regular services by the P&O British Indian and Apcar lines which were the official London and Far East mail service; the Glen and Shire Line service to London, Rotterdam, Hamburg, Hong Kong, Changhai and Japan, charging 600 Singapore dollars in 1932 for the fare to London; the Burns Philip Line which sailed to Brisbane, Sydney and Melbourne via Java, Darwin and Thursday island; Canadian Pacific, sailing Hong Kong to England via Shanghai, Nagasaki and Yokohama; the Blue Funnell line to Java and Western Australia; and the Swedish East Asiatic Company, through Algiers, Oran, Amsterdam and Gothenburg. The more local China Navigation and Siam Steam Navigation and Straits Steamship sailed every alternate Tuesday to South China ports such as Penang, Belawan, Port Swetenham, Malacca, Muar, Port Dickson, Lumut and Telek Anson and Batu Pahat, charging for a round trip to Bangkok 160 Singapore dollars.

Leslie Froggatt, an experienced superintendent engineer for the Straits Steamship (1934–48), recalls in his unpublished memoir *Nothing Lasts for Ever*:

> If you had money to spend, you had the finest selection of English, American and oriental merchandise imaginable, embroidered silks and tapestries, carved teak furniture, and leering black wood Buddha's, fine egg-shell china hand painted in the most extravagant designs, long ivory back-scratchers and masses of ornaments and curios in ebony jade and moonstone, pewter mugs, bright hand carved silver from Siam, and skin bags of every kind. We had everything we could want from East and West. (quoted in Shennan 2004: 116)

The home and style magazines now shipped regularly to Singapore and brought news of the latest styles, marketed in model room settings, similar to those shown at the 1925 'Art Deco' exhibition, by design studios of the big department stores such as Primavera for Printemps, la Maîtrise for Galeries Lafayette, and Pomone for the Bon Marché store. Perhaps inspired by this example, two women living in Singapore in the 1930s put on their own model room exhibition. They were typical of the new breed of colonial arrivals, and had been intensely influenced and involved with art and interior design in Paris and London during the 1920s. One was Dora Gordine (1895–1991), a rising sculptor (Figure 1.4) who had been commissioned by the British government in Singapore to produce sculpture for the new town hall. Gordine was married to Dr. G.H. Garlick, a doctor in the Malay civil service to Sultan Ibrahim of Johore, and was at the centre of colonial society. The other was Evelyn Doris Laing (nee McIntosh), wife of Philip Laing, whose company was building, at the time, the grandstand and racecourse of the Singapore Turf Club (1930) for the major building contractors Swan & Maclaren (Liu 1999). Gordine had been hugely influenced by the 1925 Paris exhibition when she had worked on a mural in the British Pavilion, and, in 1929, she had commissioned a modern studio/house from August Perret in Paris at 21 rue du Belvédère. Laing was a painter trained at St. Martins School of Art, London; she had exhibited at the 78th New England Art Club exhibition in London, in 1928, which is where she may have met Gordine, also an exhibitor, for the first time. Laing was also keenly interested in modern design, and was the designer of the Ladies Tea Room (on the veranda) of the Turf Club.

The model room exhibition, which was of a 'sitting room in the modern style', was in a small shop in the Capitol Buildings in the centre of town. It contained armchairs, tables, furniture and

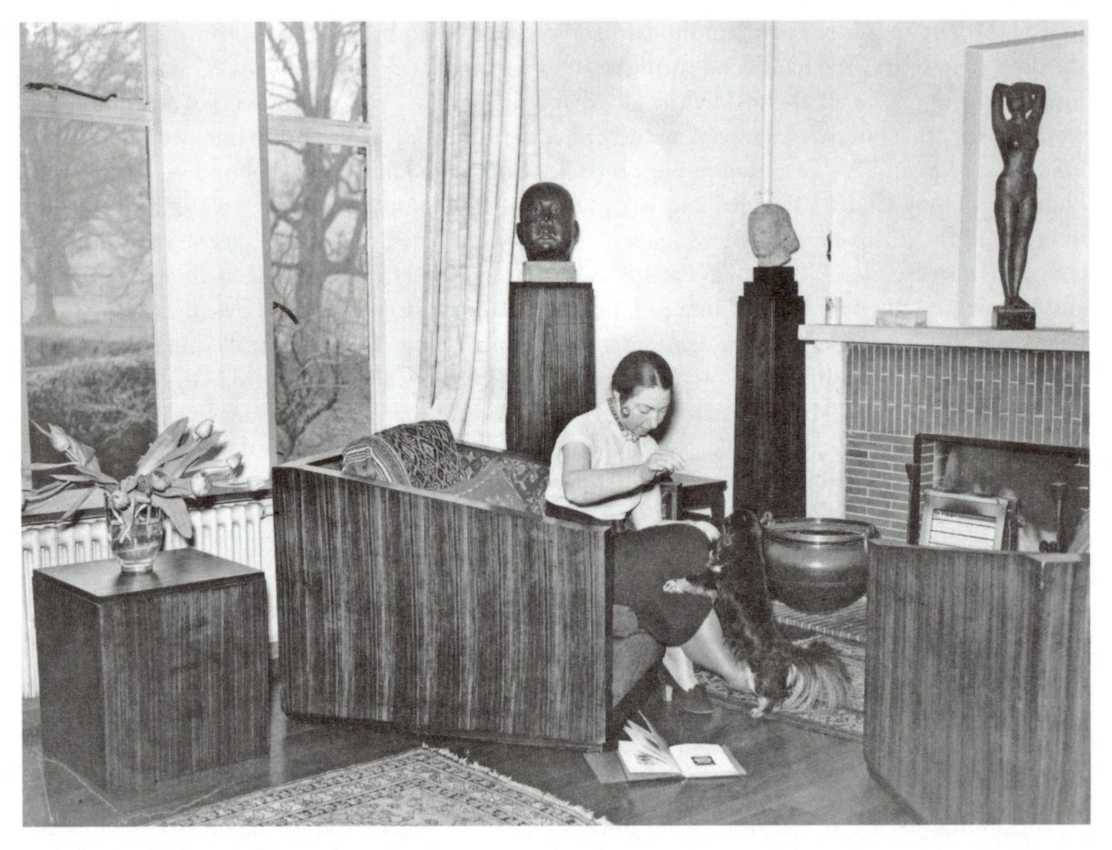

1.4. Dora Gordine sitting in her London home, Dorich House, on a modern Parisian-style chair covered with a Burmese fabric. Her house also included Chinese couli hats as lampshades, traditional Chinese furniture, altar tables, stools and dining set in ebony. Source: Dorich House Museum Archives.

rugs in the modern style and a bronze sculpture by Gordine, which was set on a sideboard. The *Straits Times* exhorted the young wives of the community to visit the exhibition:

> Much has been heard of the art of interior decoration and various magazines make a great feature of photographs of rooms furnished in the modern manner. Singapore wives who have wondered wistfully whether they could do something of the kind with their houses or flats will do well to visit the exhibition of modern interior decoration which Mrs. Evelyn Laing has opened. ('Interior Decorations Mrs. Evelyn Laing's Exhibition in Singapore' 1931)

The article went on to praise the conservatism of the exhibition as a restrained example of good taste and modern design, which was still regarded with suspicion and a possible source of a social gaff:

> It is modern in design, but at the same time there is nothing about it of the extreme, an error into which the enthusiastic amateur decorator can easily fall, for the cult of the straight line can be overdone and some designs of tapestries and carpets which are arresting at first sight would be tiring to live with. Mrs. Laing shows that a room can be in the modern style and yet restful to the eye. ('Interior Decorations Mrs. Evelyn Laing's Exhibition in Singapore' 1931)

Figure 1.5 shows how the latest modern art deco style furnishings had reached Singapore from Paris and London in the 1930s. The modern sofa and square furniture resembled closely those designed by the French decorator and rationalist designer Djo Bourgeois in 1930 (Sparke 2007: 158). The cupboard in the background is possibly by the English designer Betty Joel, and the panther ornament is also reminiscent of her ensembles. The glass just visible in the windows and doors show that electric air conditioning had been installed. The open-plan staircase, wide archways, high ceilings and arrangement of the furniture around a centrepiece rug designed by Laing all show how the modernist open plan and clean lines of the art deco style transferred so well to the tropical climate. The integral relationship of the veranda and the living spaces can clearly be seen in the left of the image. The wall lights and chandeliers were designed by Gordine; they also appeared in her London home of a similar style, which she had built when she returned in 1936. This was typical of the spread of the modern style in the 1920s and 1930s.[2] Ironically, the simple forms of modern furniture had been based on Chinese forms, as Raymond Koechlin noted in 1925: 'Modern furniture in our houses would not be understandable in its search for a noble simplicity and rare materials if it were not linked to Chinese models' (Koechlin 2003: 73).

A problem in furnishing the veranda in the latest style if you were on a limited budget was the impermanence of life in the imperial colonies, the constant moving on from post to post. If you

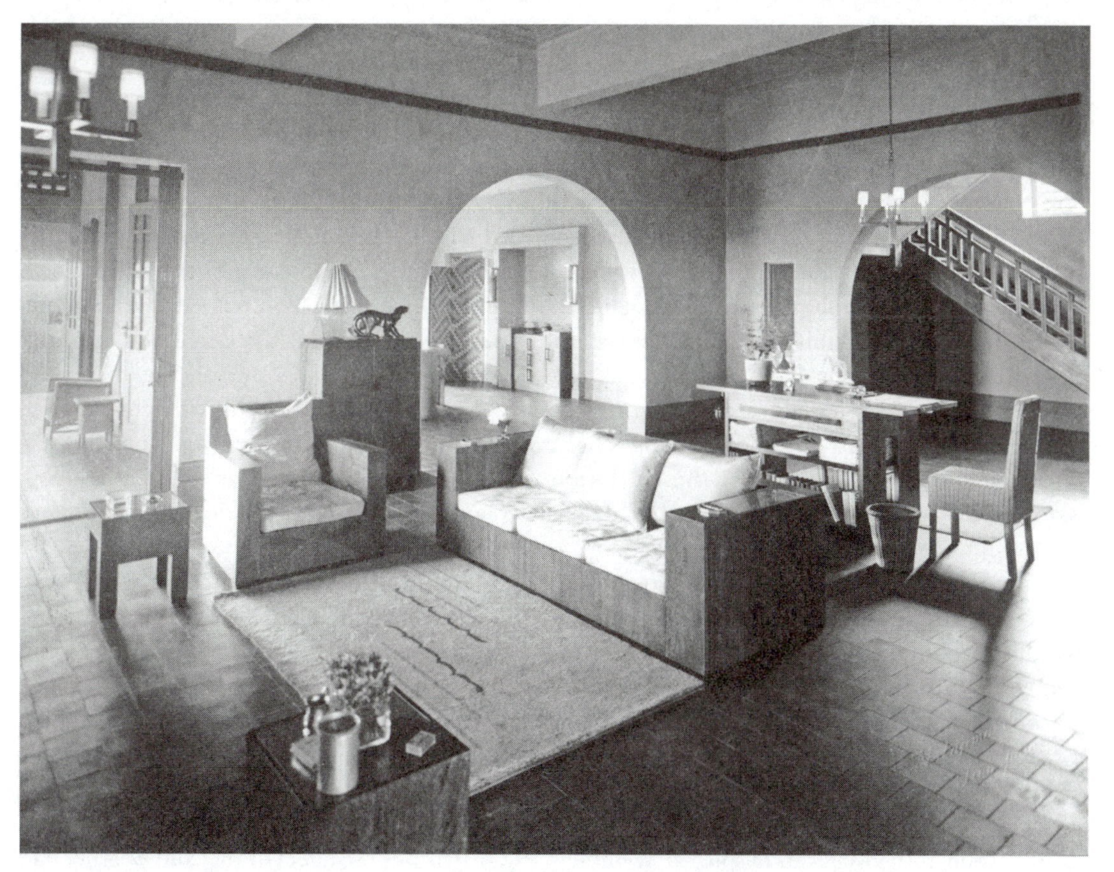

1.5. Modern room in Singapore, 1930s. Private collection.

could not afford expensive items, it was best to buy furnishings and screens from the Holland Road market in Singapore and paint them. But still favoured was rattan furniture, which was light and easily portable. Adverts in the *Straits Times* in the 1930s show that any number of Kelvinator refrigerators, furniture and other items were on sale when people were at the end of their posting, 'returning to England'. By 1940, the end of British rule in Malaya was not far off. The eclectic nature and integration of colonial furnishings in Malaya are described in a letter from Nancy Wynne in 1940, who advised, 'Simple "rotan" [sic] furniture is favoured in Malaya; it is light and cool and easily replaced and it can be made to look very dainty if painted with bright paint . . . pictures are a care, and need constant attention . . . the same may be said of carpets, although bright which are brought from India . . . lend a touch of colour to rooms, and are easily taken up and shaken' (quoted in Shennan 2004: 196).

The use of the veranda as prime living space was of course entirely dependent on the hot climate, so 'veranda living' did not transfer to the United Kingdom, where south-facing balconies and roof terraces were becoming popular, but were not warm enough to become an integral part of the living space. However, the novelty of the veranda and colonnaded refreshment area of the Malaya Pavilion at the 1924 British Empire exhibition in London proved unexpectedly popular. It was decorated in cream with bands of royal yellow and with names of settlements and states written in umber in panels above, and taking refreshments in this inside/outside space became so profitable that in the second year of the exhibition the exhibition organizers cashed in by building two similar cafes on either side, taking most of the trade and profits from the Malay Pavilion. The refreshment veranda covered about 3,000 square feet and was built in the traditional 'Malay vernacular school' with a curved and shingled roof and open sides screened by bamboo chick blinds. It was called, picturesquely, the 'chalet'. Large panoramic views of Malaya were hung on the colonnades giving an impression of a surrounding tropical landscape. The cane and rattan chairs with striped cushions, and enamelled and tiled top bamboo tables, delineated this space as exotic, modern and forward looking, different from the mock Tudor style of the Old English House erected by Maples & Co. at the same exhibition, which was accompanied by the quote, 'The object of the exhibit is to illustrate the Tudor period, a style which is essentially English.' The official report considered that the exterior of the romantic Malay Pavilion was lit by bad floodlighting, which looked 'artistic and cheap', but the inside was lit by electric light bulbs in Chinese lanterns from Singapore, giving a lighting effect which was 'unsurpassed from the aesthetic standpoint in any part of the exhibition' (*Report on the Malaya Pavilion* 1926: 5). Silk sarongs were exhibited in the Arts and Crafts Gallery, and tiny one-volt electric lamps lit models of tin mines.

John Little's shop from Singapore took orders for exotic furniture and exhibited forty-eight rattan chairs, twelve couches, eight tables, eight waste-paper baskets and eight teak flowerpot stands. Hecht Levis and Kahn (later the British Cane Furniture company) exhibited rattan chairs and rented up to 200 for visitor use. The tropical landscape was simulated by thirty-six artificial palms in ornamental tubs due to lack of fuel for hothouses. In the second year, artificial ferns were added, but they required constant cleaning because of the smut of London. After the exhibition, the whole exhibit, with its cane chairs and tables so reminiscent of a life of leisure in the tropics, was sold off to a country club. *The Times* described the pavilion in May 1924, as an 'encyclopaedia of Imperial Information' ('The Malayan Display at Wembley' 1924: 10). But the effect of the cold weather had been underestimated. The roof was blown off the 'chalet' and the kitchen was gutted by fire. The grey interiors were too drab for the gloomy weather, and in the second year of the exhibition a light green was substituted to give the desired effect of a tropical interior. While the British experienced this authentic Malay culture safely at home, the British summer of 1924 was so damp and cold the poor Malays in their traditional clothes suffered ill health and in one case death from double pneumonia (*Report on the Malaya Pavilion* 1926).

The last few years of colonial rule, before the Japanese occupied Singapore in 1942, saw the transfer of exotic styles and patterns from Asia to the United Kingdom with returning colonials and travellers. *Vogue* was reporting on Chinese fashion modes in February 1936, colours such as Manchu brown were being advertised, and Gardiners of Selkirk was selling fabrics with exotic Indian names such as Ruelga, Angar, Angarfil, Nevega, Travela and Starga, which were sold through the London stores of Marshall & Snelgrove, Dickins & Jones, Harvey Nichols, Harrods, and Peter Robinson (*Vogue* 1936: 13). The Chinese exhibition at Burlington House showed Chinese Chippendale and used a 'photomural' of a Chinese figure in a display of a room with 'Chinese accents' (*Vogue* 1936: 17). The decorator Syrie Maugham produced a tea service of etched opaque white glass to look like white carved jade, and Claridge's in London updated its carriage entrance and ballroom in the 1930s with a design by Basil Ionides and Oswald P. Milne which drew heavily on Chinese patterns.

But aside from the material goods of Singapore and Malayan cultures, it was impossible to recreate in England the easy-going lifestyle lived out on the veranda. Many who returned missed the landscape and colour of local life. Gaston Bachelard in *The Poetics of Space* put forward the argument that the spaces of human inhabitation are experienced through memory and experience and their relationship with their natural surroundings. Through the inhabitant's perceptions of light, smells and sounds peculiar to that place, the house becomes more than just walls and the objects within, allowing human consciousness to enliven the whole, as an experienced or lived-in space (Bachelard 1994: 38–73). Considered in this context, the verandas provided a sensual romantic link to the natural world for the inhabitants of the tropical colonial house, enabling them to be at once inside and outside, mixing memories of home and the exotic landscape of Singapore. This sensory perception often became very poignant for long term residents such as Roland Braddell, who wrote of his emotional reaction on opening a camphor box from Singapore when he was in England as follows, 'a strange smell of mould and damp hot earth sweating after rain, that unforgettable smell which arises when any box is opened that has lain long in the tropics . . . it brings a great lump into his throat, and tears stream down his face . . . It is the scent of the East' (Braddell 1934: 2, 13).

NOTES

1. See also John M. MacKenzie, ed., (1986), *Imperialism and Popular Culture*, Manchester: Manchester University Press; and Edward Said (1978), *Orientalism: Western Conceptions of the Orient*, London: Penguin. For construction of culture through material objects see Daniel Miller (1987), *Material Culture and Mass Consumption*, Oxford: Basil Blackwell; and Marius Kwint, C. Breward and J. Aynsley, eds., (1999), *Material Memories: Design and Evocation*, Oxford: Berg.
2. Dorich House Museum, www.dorichhousemuseum.co.uk

REFERENCES

Primary Sources: Geffrye Museum, London. Department store catalogues: Harrods Catalogues, 1929. Tumery Dept. Maples Modern Furniture, 1910–1952. Maples Wicker and Cane Furniture and Screws Catalogue, 1925. Ham's Lebus catalogue, n.d. Army and Navy Stores 1929–1940. Schoolbreads Store Catalogues of Furniture, Household Goods, Clothing, Garden Supplies, 1930–1939.

Allen, C., ed., (1983), *Tales from the South China Seas,* London: Andre Deutsch & BBC.

Bachelard, G. (1994), *The Poetics of Space*, tr. Maria Jolas, Boston: Beacon Press.

Braddell, R. (1934), *The Lights of Singapore*, 6th edn, London: Methuen & Co.

Caldecott, A. *Report on the Malaya Pavilion, British Empire Exhibition* (1926), Government Printing Office, Singapore. LSE Library, London, UK.

Clancy-Smith, J., and Gouda, F., eds, (1998), *Domesticating the Empire: Race, Gender, and Family Life in French and Dutch Colonialism*, Charlottesville: University Press of Virginia.

Collingham, E.M. (2001), *Imperial Bodies: The Physical Experience of the Raj, c. 1800–1947*, Cambridge: Polity Press.

Glover, W. (2004), '"A Feeling of Absence from Old England" the Colonial Bungalow', *Home Cultures*, 1/1: 61–82.

Goh, D. P. S. (2010), 'Capital and the Transfiguring Monumentality of Raffles Hotel', *Mobilities*, 5/2: 177–95.

Indianetzone, 'British Architecture', *History of India*, <http://www.indianetzone.com/38/british_domestic_architecture.htm> accessed 28 Aug. 2011.

Jones, R. D. (2007), *Interiors of Empire, Objects, Space and Identity within the Indian Subcontinent c. 1800–1947*, Manchester: Manchester University Press.

Koechlin, R. (1925), 'Le Bronzes Chinois', *Art et Decoration*, 47, quoted in A. Jackson (2003), 'Art Deco in East Asia', *Art Deco 1910–1939*, London: V&A Publications.

Lee, P., and Chen, J. (2006), *The Straits Chinese House*, Singapore: Editions Didier Millet Pte Ltd/National Museum of Singapore.

Liu, G. (1999), *Singapore—A Pictorial History 1819–2000*, Singapore: National Heritage Board.

'Malayan Display At Wembley' (1924). *Times [London, England]*, 5 May 1924: 12. Available online: The Times Digital Archive, accessed 17 Aug. 2012.

Shennan, M. (2004), 'Halcyon Days', *Out in the Midday Sun—The British In Malaya 1880–1960*, John Murray.

Somerset Maugham, W. (2000), 'The Door of Opportunity', *Far Eastern Tales*, London: Vintage.

Sparke, P. (2007), 'A Modern Decorator in the French Tradition', in J. Black and B. Martin, eds., *Dora Gordine: Sculptor Artist Designer*, London: Philip Wilson.

Stoler, A. L. (2002), *Carnal Knowledge and Imperial Power: Race and the Intimate in Colonial Rule*, Berkeley: University of California Press.

Vogue. Spring Fashions Double Number, 19 Feb. 1936

2.

HALLS AND CORRIDORS: SPACES BETWEEN AND BEYOND

trevor keeble

Halls and corridors are arguably some of the key spaces through which late Victorian models of domesticity gave way to early modernist revisions of domestic space, function and movement. This chapter considers the legacy of this Victorian domestic typology as it engaged new modes of thinking about, and representations of, domestic space during the first decades of the twentieth century. In recognition of the fact that the hall and corridor have constituted different spaces in different places throughout time, this chapter will focus on their role in the terraced and semi-detached houses typical of London in the late-nineteenth and early-twentieth centuries. Although these spaces varied considerably in scale, this chapter will demonstrate that within their specific contexts and locations, the halls and corridors of these urban and suburban London homes performed a largely conventional duty.

Whilst the hall and corridor have often constituted a fundamental feature of domestic space, perhaps more specifically the divisions between domestic spaces, the representational and presentational contexts of the hall and corridor offer an insight into the ways in which the space of the home negotiated the boundary between public and private worlds. Situated as it is upon the threshold of that boundary, the hall is often presented within the representational discourses of domestic design advice as a space of both transition and presentation, staged as both a prelude to the spaces beyond and an outward image to the world. In this sense, the chapter is concerned less with what people were advised to do and more with how this advice articulated ideas and assumptions about these spaces.

Exploring this representational discourse, this chapter proposes that the hall and its perhaps more explicitly purposeful relation, the corridor, constitute representational spaces in their own right, and that examination of the changing representational and discursive character of these spaces offers insight into the ways in which domesticity and its interior were made modern during the nineteenth and twentieth centuries. Whilst the chapter begins by considering the explicitly modernist articulation of domesticity and space made during the early years of the twentieth century, it proposes that the domestic form typical of later Victorian London was in itself an explicitly modern formulation, one at the heart of which lay the hall and the corridor.

THE EVOLUTION OF THE HALL AND CORRIDOR

> The Villa Savoye is, at first sight simple and clear in its overall form: a cubic volume raised up on pilotis, freestanding in an apparently verdant landscape. Entered from the road by a double driveway, the ground floor is given over to the turning circle of a car, the entrance hall, a three-car garage, and quarters for servants. A ramp at the center of the square plan leads to the main level, as does a bull-nosed stair. Arriving at the *piano nobile*, the ramp and stair give onto, respectively, the large living room which takes up the entire north side of the villa, and itself gives onto the partially enclosed terrace and the kitchen-bedroom wing, to the east and south. Above, on the third floor, the ramp and stair end in a private solarium, protected to the north and open to the south. (Vidler 2012: 74–5)

When, in the late 1920s, the Parisian architect Le Corbusier finally got the chance to put his polemical ideas into practice, he offered to the world a new and entirely modern form of domestic life. Realizing his five-point vision of a new architecture, Le Corbusier created a dynamic model of domesticity which, through architectural promenade and open, fluid spaces, fundamentally challenged the private world of the nineteenth century home (Frampton 2001: 79). At its most polemical, the project to reform architectural language for the twentieth century entailed a deconstruction of the place and spaces of the home in such a way as to challenge the very notion of the room.

Adrian Forty has described how contested notions of 'space' were key to architectural discourses during the 1920s. Though terms often used to describe different ideas and propositions during this period, *space* and *spatiality* were concepts used both to mark the modernity of the new architectural project, and as a means to reject metaphorical, referential ways of talking about architecture (Forty 2000: 265). Forty has suggested three specific uses of the term *space*: space as enclosure; space as continuum; and space as extension of the body (Forty 2000: 266). Whilst Le Corbusier's Villa Savoye (1928–31) most clearly typifies an understanding of space as continuum, it is worth noting that other contemporary architects, most notably the Viennese architect Adolf Loos, chose not to reject the notion of the enclosed room quite so readily. Behind bare facades, Loos-designed houses such as the Moller House (1927–8) in Vienna and the Müller House (1929–30) in Prague retained a more traditional notion of the compact plan of distinct yet related volumetric spaces as rooms.

Notwithstanding the differences between these two models of avant-garde living for the twentieth century, the continental project to usher in a new age of modern living fundamentally, and not for the first time, challenged the design and experience of domesticity across the English Channel. In her comparative history of nineteenth century Parisian and London homes, Sharon Marcus described how:

> Victorian developers designed terraces that conformed more to the new ideals of social and spatial privacy: they gated and locked formerly communal gardens in squares, set terraced houses far back from the road and used architectural treatments that rendered the individual house within a row more distinct. (Marcus 1999: 97)

In short, Marcus argued that Englishmen were characterized by their allegiance to 'personal individuality' and 'architectural individuation'. Nevertheless, the pattern of urban domesticity in England conformed quite remarkably to a set plan, which favoured a horizontal spread of private single-family dwellings in comparison to the more densely populated apartment blocks of the French capital.

In an 1878 lecture entitled 'On Middle-class Houses in Paris and Central London', English architect William H. White presented an argument to the Royal Institute of British Architects in favour of the Parisian rather than the English model of urban domestic design (Marcus 1999: 83). Though contriving some rather untenable arguments in favour of the Parisian apartment over the London terrace, White offered his listeners the highly revealing reassurance that the apartment block did not violate the chief tenets of British domestic architecture: 'the separation of different households into noncommunicating buildings, and the separation of different household members and functions into distinct rooms' (Marcus 1999: 84). The idea that architectural forms and sensibilities might be so deeply rooted within national concepts of social identity is something which the early twentieth-century modernist architects and writers chose wilfully to reject. However, the study of English domesticity in the nineteenth and twentieth centuries demonstrates how deeply embedded social and cultural ideas of family, privacy and identity have been in the fabric and form of the built environment, and, as this chapter argues, the changing spaces of the hall and corridor lay quite literally at the heart of this.

In his study *The Invention of Comfort*, John Crowley noted that the hall was a common feature of European domestic space from the early Middle Ages through to the sixteenth century (Crowley 2001: 8). As the principal space of the house, the hall was used for domestic, social, productive and administrative purposes. Yet in spite of this relatively undefined functional designation of the space, the hall did establish a longitudinal axis upon which social hierarchy was performed. The creation of a top table in relation to a central hearth offered a spatialization of hierarchy, which Crowley has argued constituted from Carolingian times onwards 'a symmetry of spatial and domestic organisation of aristocratic households [which] schematized the personal service of lesser nobles in attendance on their lord—at the dining table, and in the bedchamber, cellar (for drinks), and stables' (Crowley 2001: 11).

The implication of the hall within the hierarchical planning of domestic space is one characteristic, which, as this chapter will show, does not diminish throughout its changing history. Perhaps the other is its pivotal role in the negotiation of the public and private nature of domesticity. Witold Rybczynski also described the medieval hall as a single open space in which people cooked, ate, entertained and slept, and in so doing characterized it as a place of impermanence and improvisation which was in constant use (Rybczynski 1988: 25–6). Both writers clearly characterized the hall as a public space used for hospitality, and indeed Crowley went so far as to suggest that its door remained open throughout the day to indicate and welcome this (Crowley 2001: 11).

Over time, the hall changed its form and purpose as other, initially subsidiary, spaces opened up around it. Initially a single chamber was simply divided into functional areas for activities, such as cooking and food preparation; these functional areas eventually developed into more clearly designated rooms, which removed their activities from the hall. Naturally this changed both the social and physical position of the hall. Discussing the emergence of the English 'bourgeois' home in the eighteenth century, Rybczynski noted that 'although aristocratic homes were often organized around a medieval-style centrally located hall, the hall in a middle-class house was a room adjacent to the entrance, located so that doors led from it to the main common rooms' (Rybczynski 1988: 108). The eventual outcome of this proliferation of rooms was that the house became less compact and in an increasing bid for 'privacy' developed long wings. These wings, Rybczynski argued, 'required corridors for movement and inevitably produced a greater measure of privacy for the individual rooms'(1988: 119). A consequence of this was that the hall was no longer required to give access to the rooms and became smaller (Rybczynski 1988: 119). In a footnote to his discussion, Rybczynski qualified his connection of the hall and the corridor by suggesting that 'with time, the once-grand hall became little more than a large vestibule'. The outcome of this, he found, was that in modern homes 'the hallway—has been reduced to a utilitarian corridor' (Rybczynski 1988: 108).

Of course the corridor has its own developmental history, often linked to that of the hall. In his essay 'Corridor Spaces', Mark Jarzombek documented the physical and cultural evolution of the corridor, and in so doing detailed a fascinating etymological development of the word *corridor* which offers a deeply meaningful insight into its specific spatial character. Coming originally from fourteenth-century Spanish and Italian, he explained, the word *corridor* 'referred not to a space but to a courier, someone who as the word's Latin root suggests could run fast' (Jarzombek 2010: 731). This elision of the courier and the space through which he travelled articulates a quintessential aspect of the corridor's character as a space through which people move as opposed to a space for repose.

In his seminal essay, 'Figures, Doors and Passages', Robin Evans suggests that the first corridor in England was designed as 'a longe entry through all' by John Thorpe at Beaufort House, Chelsea, in 1597 (Evans 1978: 48). He goes on to explain that whilst an 'enfilade' arrangement remained for the social rooms, passages became 'very evident in houses built for the rich' after 1630. These offered the 'the innovation of independent access' thus separating the rich and the poor inhabitants of a building, and dividing the house into two domains, 'an inner sanctuary of inhabited space, sometimes disconnected rooms, and unoccupied circulation space' (Evans 1978: 49).

Undoubtedly the most significant aspect of these early examples of corridors is the fundamental way in which they were designed to separate both difference spaces and, perhaps more importantly, the people within them. Whilst it is clear that early definitions of the corridor, such as that offered by William Chambers in *A Treatise on the Decorative Part of Civil Architecture*, identified it as a feature of domestic architecture (Jarzombek 2010: 728), it must be noted that domesticity did not have the explicitly 'private' character that it would develop during the nineteenth century, and that these large, aristocratic buildings were considerably more public than we would understand the word *domestic* to signify today.

Irrespective of this, however, the corridor did come to be used more fundamentally in public buildings during the nineteenth century, as Jarzombek has shown, and in this the corridor effectively modernized these buildings. Giving the example of Barry and Pugin's Houses of Parliament, Jarzombek argued that whilst 'the outside of the building is purposefully historicist, the spatial planning of the interior is all modern' (Jarzombek 2010: 753). In this sense, whether public or domestic, the corridor must be understood as a phenomenon of nineteenth-century modernity.

THE SPACE OF THE HALL AND CORRIDOR

In the aforementioned essay, 'Figures, Doors and Passages', Evans offered insightful observation into the spatial organization of domesticity:

> At first it is difficult to see in the conventional layout of a contemporary house anything but the crystalization of cold reason, necessity and the obvious, and because of this we are easily led into thinking that a commodity so transparently unexceptional must have been wrought directly from the stuff of basic human needs. (Evans 1978: 43)

Explaining that the organization of domestic space tends to hide its power, origins and purpose, Evans identified its development throughout the nineteenth and twentieth centuries as a modernisation undertaken in pursuit of 'privacy, comfort and independence' (Evans 1978: 43).

The centrality of the hall to British domestic planning was plainly evident to the architect Mervyn Macartney when he began his 1904 essay 'The Home and its Halls' by stating, 'In England the history of the hall is practically the history of house planning' (Macartney 1904: Ei). He was certainly not alone in ascribing national characteristics to the hall. Hermann Muthesius, writing in the same year, stated, 'Of all the rooms in the English house, the hall is the one that we are accustomed to think of as most English' (Muthesius 1979: 203). Whilst acknowledging that the hall was as varied as each of the English houses in which it might be found, Muthesius's exposition of why it was so redolently English, suggests that 'it has been, in the main its sentimental qualities that have been valued and imitated' (Muthesius 1979: 203):

> But whatever the form of the Hall, the English always try to make it more than a mere anteroom, believing that it should create a homely impression. It represents one of the most attractive assets of the English house. One steps out of wild nature straight into a warm, friendly atmosphere. Even as one crosses the threshold, one is surrounded by a sense of comforting hospitality and open-armed welcome. This sense results from the cosy furnishing of the room, a faint echo of which is apparent in our own small suburban house. (Muthesius 1979: 203)

This rather romanticized vision of the hall expresses a division fundamental to our understanding of the modern hall: the separation of the inside and outside of the house. Though it is hard to imagine the public sphere of the early twentieth century as quite the wilderness Muthesius suggests, the conceptual and physical separation of the public and the private was fundamental to the understanding of modern domesticity, which evolved throughout the nineteenth century.

Martin Daunton's *House and Home in the Victorian City* argues that developments in nineteenth-century housing 'modified both the nature of the house, and the manner in which it related to the wider urban environment' (Daunton 1983: 11). Daunton continues:

> The important question becomes the nature, placement and permeability of the barrier or threshold between the internal private domain and the external, public domain. (Daunton 1983: 11)

As such, the hall and its thresholds became key to the demarcation of the public and private realms, a demarcation at the heart of middle-class identity in the nineteenth century, and subsequently at the heart of working-class respectability in the twentieth.

An understanding of nineteenth-century domesticity as a private realm relative to the public world beyond its threshold, so clearly articulated by Davidoff and Hall in their study *Family Fortunes. Men and Women of the English Middle-class 1780–1850*, remains the principal conceptual means for investigating and understanding the role domesticity played in the formation of class and identity during this period. This understanding of the home and domesticity as a private refuge from the public realm affords the opportunity to consider how the home was, at times, also public and open to people beyond the family.

The designation of a masculine public space and a feminine private space underpinned much of the representational discourse offered by authors of domestic design advice during the second half of the nineteenth century, and whether these designations actually shaped and formed the domestic behaviour of readers or not, this discourse certainly coloured popular understanding of domestic and social propriety. This led to highly conventional understandings of domestic spaces and their interrelation with one another, which, in addition to testifying to the privacy, comfort and independence that middle-class wealth could buy, began to associate more explicitly gendered characteristics to domestic spaces (Kinchin 1996). In this manner, the masculine/feminine binary, so integral to the discourse and understanding of the separate spheres, began to impress itself more fundamentally upon the decoration, design and use of different rooms (Kinchin 1996).

For the working classes of the period, these domestic opportunities were beyond their reach. Nevertheless the second half of the nineteenth century did witness the increasing privatisation of working-class domestic life, as government and philanthropic bodies began to recognize and address the crisis of life and living standards at the lower end of the social scale. As Daunton has noted:

> The bulk of working-class housing in England up to the mid nineteenth century had been located in self-contained little worlds of enclosed courts and alleys; but within each cell, the residents shared space and facilities in a communal way. There was an ambiguous boundary, an uncertain threshold, between the private and the public. Each group of houses formed its own private world within the city but within that private world, space was a shared asset. (Daunton 1983: 12)

In this context, it is clear to see that the project to regulate and reform working-class domesticity was indeed also a project to regulate the life outside of it. Through examination of changing laws and regulation, the change of design from high-density slums, tenement buildings and courts to well-planned streets, and the changing practices of policing, Daunton has shown the ways in which 'public' spaces became regulated and 'neutralized' (Daunton 1983: 266–73). The effect of this was that 'the emergence of the private, encapsulated dwelling was a physical demonstration of the social value which attached to the conjugal family and domestic life' (Daunton 1983: 37). The emphazis upon neutralizing the public space of the street did tend to reinforce the delineation of the house into front and back, a characteristic absorbed from the middle classes. This distinction went beyond simply the designation of rooms to characterize the use of entrances. The 'front' door constituted a formal entrance used for special occasions and formal visitors whilst the 'back' door leading on to a yard, alley or lane provided an informal and habitual entrance for friends, family and neighbours (Daunton 1983: 280–1). In this sense, the solidly middle-class understanding of domestic presentation can be seen to have infiltrated working-class domesticity.

Alison Ravetz has suggested that the early twentieth century witnessed a 'convergence of middle and working-class standards' (Ravetz 1995: 165), and it is important to understand this development in terms of the deeply functional and symbolic needs combined in this convergence. Just as the middle classes of the nineteenth century had formed domesticity in such a way as to present their status to the world, both without and within, so the widening of middle-class domestic conventions, which emphasized distinction between front and back, upstairs and downstairs, and the functional determination of rooms, also brought about the formal codification of working-class domestic life that went symbolically beyond mere need and function (Ravetz 1995: 149). This had far-reaching effects for those working-class people lucky enough to be housed in new, contemporary homes, and the inclusion of a hall or passage within these homes was highly significant for inhabitants in the expression of their respectable status:

> A depth of two rooms allowed a functional and symbolic separation between house front and back. A further critical distinction was whether or not the ground floor accommodated a 'hall'; for even if this were no more than a narrow passage, it separated the front door from the front room of the house, which could then become a parlour, a room crucial to social status. A hall passage could also give independent access to the rear room and, if it also contained a staircase, to the upper level of the house. This then enabled the rear room to develop its own functions. (Ravetz 1995: 63–4)

The further intervention of the state changed the nature of working-class housing during the early decades of the twentieth century, and, as John Burnett has shown, the modernising programme of council house development regulated the plan and scale of working-class domestic life (Burnett 1986). Ravetz has argued that, in spite of the deeply held codification of the home and its activities, these changes brought about a 'subtle transition from status to function, in which ancient dichotomies of front: back, formal: informal, public: private, leisure: work, and clean: dirty, were at least partially dissolved' (Ravetz 1995: 166). Notwithstanding this, the hall as a transitional space between inside and outside remained essential to the home, even if it constituted little more than a mere lobby.

The designation of the hall and corridor as functional spaces which afford the symbolism of nineteenth- and twentieth-century domestic life is central to Evans's argument which draws on the work of the nineteenth-century writer Robert Kerr to suggest that 'thoroughfares' became the backbone of a plan in the nineteenth century, a plan that offered a network of routes (Evans 1978: 51). Few Victorian authors wrote as extensively on the role and significance of the thoroughfare as Robert Kerr did in his seminal text of 1864, *The Gentleman's House*. Written to lead its reader through a step-by-step consideration of the social and technical formation of the house, *The Gentleman's House* offers a culturally resonant prescription of how the spaces of the home should both inform and respond to the society within it. In the context of the nineteenth-century gentleman's home, this society may be broadly divided into two distinct groups, the family and the servants, and the role of the thoroughfare was identified as the critical device through which to ensure that each member of this domestic society kept to his or her own 'department'. The maintenance of this socio-spatial distinction was fundamental to what Kerr described as the qualities valued by a gentleman of the day:

> Quiet comfort for his family and guests, -
> Thorough convenience for his domestics, -
> Elegance and importance without ostentation. (Kerr 1864: 66)

Interestingly, Kerr qualified his use of use of the terms 'comfort' and 'convenience' by suggesting that the former refers to the 'passive' whilst the latter to the 'active' (Kerr 1864: 71). This distinction, so easily mapped onto notions of consumption and production, offers insight into the ways in which the domesticity created by these spaces might be understood as modern in its strategy. Not surprisingly, the distance between the family and the servants afforded by a house was entirely dependent on social standing and scale, yet as Kerr noted:

> In short, whether in a small house or a large one, let the family have free passage-way without encountering the servants unexpectedly; and let the servants have access to all their duties without coming unexpectedly upon the family or visitors. On both sides this privacy is highly valued. (Kerr 1864: 68)

Throughout his discussion of thoroughfares, Kerr repeatedly suggests that they constitute a mode of 'communication' within and between spaces (Kerr 1864: 76–7). Perhaps echoing the etymological foundations of the 'corridor' discussed previously, this understanding of the thoroughfare as communication imposed an interesting demand upon its design in that, whilst it was required to 'distance', it was also required to 'connect', a demand articulated by Kerr as a delicate balance between 'spaciousness' and 'compactness' (Kerr 1864: 77). It is perhaps this explicitly relative configuration of space which led to Kerr's understanding of the thoroughfare as the 'skeleton of the plan', as noted by Evans. In explanation of this proposition, Kerr suggested that it was within the thoroughfare that the 'relations of the rooms' were expressed by the 'relation of their doors', a 'system', he suggested, if done well, that could be understood 'instinctively' (Kerr 1864: 155).

THE DECORATION OF THE HALL AND CORRIDOR

When it comes to the decoration of the hall and corridor, it becomes clear that from the late nineteenth century on that there is an increasing emphazis upon the purposeful nature of these spaces and upon modest taste rather than ostentatious statement and display. In their 1921 book *Furnishing the House*, R. Randall Phillips and Ellen Woolrich, however, still attached great importance to the furnishing of the hall:

> Seeing that one's first impressions of the furnishing of a house are given at once upon entering, it is important on this account, if on no other, to bestow careful attention to the hall. (Randall Phillips and Woolrich 1921: 5)

Throughout Kerr's discussion of the thoroughfare, he made repeated allusions to the fact that too frequently its design, decoration and general environment were simply not given the consideration they deserved. This was of particular concern in regard to lighting and ventilation which, he noted, were often compromised, and lacked 'cheerfulness', the chief element of which he identified as 'sunshine'(Kerr 1864: 84). This was a concern expressed some years later by Rhoda and Agnes Garrett in their *Suggestions for House Decoration in Painting, Woodwork, and Furniture* (Garrett and Garrett 1876). Though concerned with the design and decoration of a house considerably more modest than that often discussed by Kerr, the Garretts championed the need for light:

> 'In the arrangement of a London house it is a matter of primary importance to avoid as much as possible darkening the rooms, and in the hall the difficulty of obtaining sufficient daylight is greater than in any other part of the house. (Garrett and Garrett 1876: 38)

One 'unusual' and potentially challenging suggestion made by the Garretts was to remove the panels of the street door and replace them with 'cathedral glass' (Garrett and Garrett 1876: 38).

What is clear from reading the Garretts' commentary on both halls and passageways is that in the more modest sized home, the distinction between the two was often difficult to maintain; the spaces often blurring into one another. Describing the hall in these homes as a 'narrow strip' dignified by its name, the authors suggested little room for furniture beyond 'a table, hat and umbrella stand, and a seat of some kind' (Garrett and Garrett 1876: 40). Emphasizing the purposeful modesty of these furnishings, they stressed that the furniture should not make 'any obtrusive demands upon the attention of every passer-by' (Figure 2.1). Should a hall not be large enough even for these small items, the Garretts proposed 'a simple brass rail fixed on the wall with pegs' for hats, coats and umbrellas (Garrett and Garrett 1876: 40).

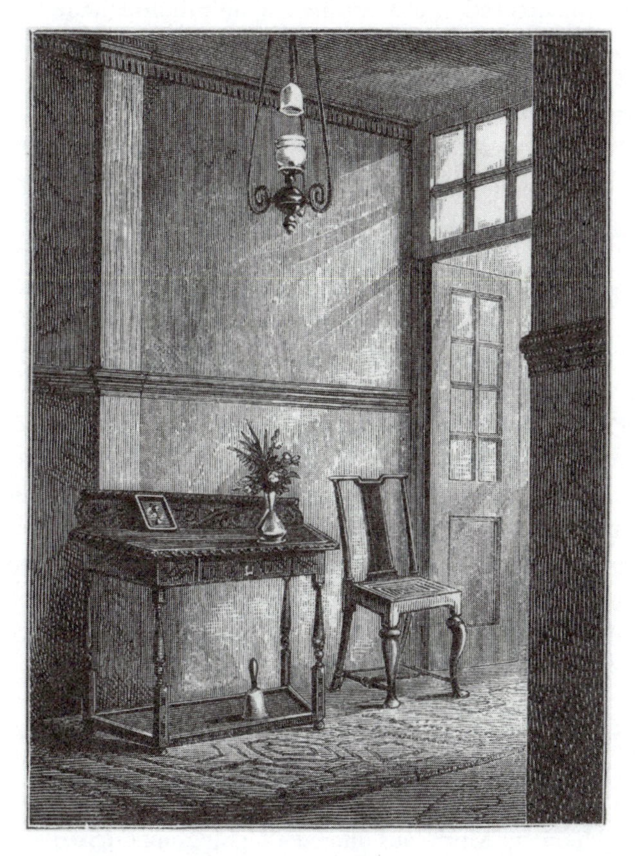

2.1. *Illustration of a Hall Table and Chair*, Rhoda and Agnes Garrett, in *Suggestions for House Decoration* (1876). Out of Copyright: Original owned by private collection.

The furnishing of a small hall constitutes something of a perennial challenge in the discussion of the hall furnishing and was addressed some decades after the Garretts by Randall Phillips and Woolrich in their book *Furnishing the House*. Much like their predecessors, Randall Phillips and Woolrich advocated rather modest requirements for a small hall, merely somewhere to place letters, cards and gloves, and proposed that the best method of treating the hall is 'not to furnish it at all'. Instead, they proposed a simple flap-shelf 'with moulded edges and rounded corners . . . in oak or mahogany, or painted to match the rest of the woodwork' (Randall Phillips and Woolrich 1921: 6–7). This position articulates a further shift in the sensibility that hall decoration and furnishing should focus upon the efficiency of its workings. Describing the need for a shelf for hats and coats, *Furnishing the House* proposed a plain moulded oak, mahogany or painted batten, but warned against too many hooks:

> Most housewives will agree that the fewer the hooks for our visitors' use the better, otherwise the spare over-coats, raincoats, and hats of the family are apt to remain in the hall for unlimited periods. (Randall Phillips and Woolrich 1921: 8–9)

Advice concerning the decoration of both the hall and thoroughfare went beyond the expression of a purposeful and utilitarian character for these spaces, to express a more ambiguous sense of identity for these spaces as interiors. In *Suggestions for House Decoration*, the Garretts advised against the artifice and imitation of marbled papers and oak- and walnut-grain finishes (Garrett and Garrett 1876: 25). Mervyn Macartney suggested a number of reasons for modesty in the decoration of the hall and corridor, as 'rooms in common can never have the same interest as those planned and decorated for an individual' (Macartney 1904: Evi). In addition to this, he warned his reader to remember that it is the hall which gives the keynote to the whole house; so 'if you start with panels in your hall, in the style of Boucher, let us say, do not introduce an open-timber dining room, or a billiard-room with a dado of Lincrusta' (Macartney 1904: Evii). The Garratts articulated a similar approach but on the grounds of economy and the fact that 'we must put out of the question any very costly mode of dealing with the hall' (Garrett and Garrett 1876: 37). Instead, they offered a moulded dado rail running around the wall and up the staircase below which the wall and woodwork might be painted a 'warm brown' or 'soft tint of green'.

The sense that the hall was in some way a depersonalized space was echoed by Randall Phillips and Woolrich who advocated that 'if there is a shelf, two or three good ornaments will be ample, and quite out of place in this situation are photographs and miscellaneous things of a personal kind' (Randall Phillips and Woolrich 1921: 17). This begins to suggest that, unlike the other spaces of the home, the hall and its associated corridor had lost their identity as domestic spaces at all. Now they were simply spaces between and beyond the more defined rooms of the home. Yet in this context, they were also explicitly linked to the public world outside, and in the writings of some authors there is suggestion that the hall retains some more primitive and enduring character than the private home and the neutralized street might allow.

Already noted for his rather sensational view of the 'wild nature' that lay beyond the security of the domestic sphere, Hermann Muthesius offered a highly romanticized view of the hall:

> Not only is the hall a centre of great memories of a proud past but the particular form of the hall, which is the outcome of its position in the ground-plan and of the elaboration of a romantic chain of thought, weaves a special magic round this room. (Muthesius 1904: 203)

Against this backdrop, advice such as that offered by Macartney, that 'in the country it should accord with country life, and be fitted for the needs of people who hunt, shoot and ride' (Macartney 1904: Evii), might articulate a longing for the hall as a romanticized space of earlier, more simple times, and one which suggested the possibility of rejecting domesticity itself. Certainly the iconography of a masculine, rural past was thought to be fitting for the country hall, even at the very end of the nineteenth century (Figure 2.2), and it might be argued that the last vestige of this longing was the barometer which hung in the hall of the mid-twentieth-century suburban semi which, as Paul Oliver argued in *Dunroamin*, 'symbolized contact with nature; a sailor's or farmer's concern with the vagaries of the weather' (Oliver, Davis and Bentley 1981: 173).

Whilst it is impossible to establish some linear history of the hall and corridor as they developed from the nineteenth into the twentieth century, it is clear that the function of these spaces remained essential to British domesticity and that, beyond this, they were the two essential spaces of the nineteenth-century middle-class home which brought modern domesticity to the working classes in the later century. In the context of the entire house, the hall and corridor were spaces 'in common' and as such gradually became defined by what they were not: drawings rooms, dining rooms, kitchens, bathrooms or bedrooms. Nevertheless, whilst those rooms articulated and

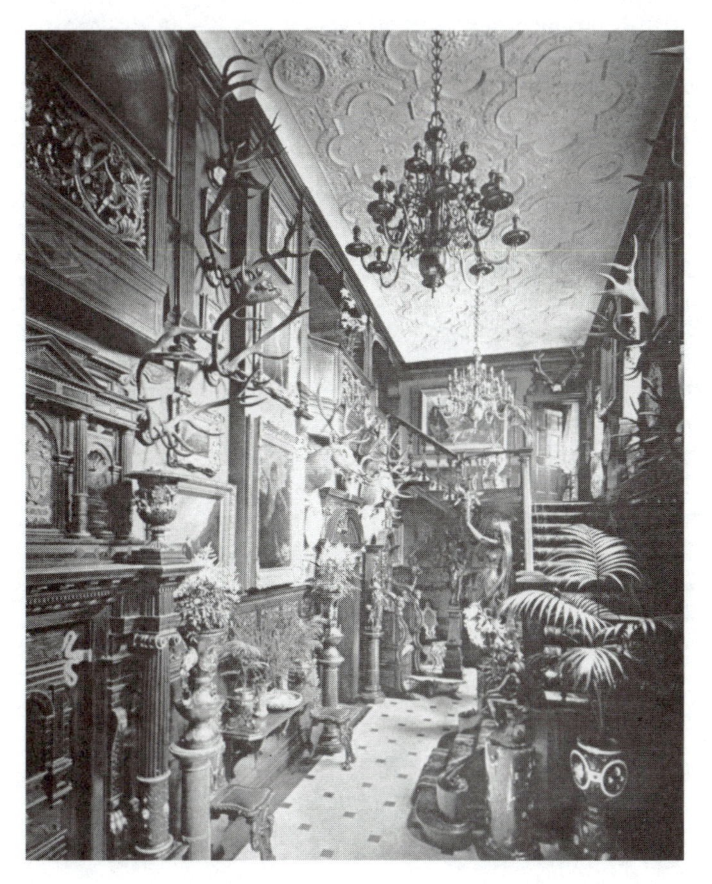

2.2. Photographic view of the hall at Wickham Hall, West Wickham, Kent (1897). Out of Copyright: Original owned by private collection.

expressed the habits, manners and workings of the domestic interior, they did so around the backbone of the hall and corridor.

REFERENCES

Burnett, J. (1986), *A Social History of Housing 1815–1985*, London: Methuen & Co.

Crowley, J. E. (2001), *The Invention of Comfort: Sensibility and Design in Early Modern Britain and Early America*, Baltimore: Johns Hopkins University Press.

Daunton, M. J. (1983), *House and Home in the Victorian City. Working-Class Housing 1850–1914*, London: Edward Arnold.

Davidoff, L., and Hall, C. (1987), *Family Fortunes. Men and Women of the English Middle-class 1780–1850*, London: Hutchison.

Evans, R. (1978), 'Figures, Doors and Passages', repr. in R. Evans, ed., *Translations from Drawing to Building and Other Essays* (1997), London: AA Publications: 42–57.

Forty, A. (2000), *Words and Buildings. A Vocabulary of Modern Architecture*, London: Thames & Hudson.

Frampton, K. (2001), *Le Corbusier*, London: Thames and Hudson.

Garrett, R., and Garrett, A. (1876), *Suggestions for Home Decoration in Painting, Woodwork, and Furniture*, London: Macmillan & Co.

Jarzombek, M. (2010), 'Corridor Spaces', *Critical Inquiry*, 36: 728–70.

Kerr, R. (1864), *The Gentleman's House*, London: John Murray.

Kinchin, J. (1996), 'The Gendered Interior: Nineteenth Century Essays on the Masculine and Feminine Room', in P. Kirkham, ed., *The Gendered Object*, Manchester: Manchester University Press.

Macartney, M. (1904), 'The Home and its Halls', in W. S. Sparrow, ed., *The British Home of Today*, London: Hodder & Stoughton.

Marcus, S. (1999), *Apartment Stories. City and Home in Nineteenth-Century Paris and London*, Berkeley: University of California Press.

Muthesius, H. (1979), *The English House*, London: Granada Publishing.

Randall Phillips, R., and Woolrich, E. (1921), *Furnishing the House*, London: George Newnes.

Ravetz, A. (1995), *The Place of Home: English Domestic Environments, 1914–2000*, London: E & FN Spon.

Rybczynski, W. (1988), *Home: A Short History of an Idea*, London: Heinemann

Vidler, A. (2012), 'Outside In / Inside Out: A short History of (Modern) Interiority', in K. Kleinman, J. Merwood-Salisbury and L. Weinthal, eds., *After Taste: Expanded Practice in Interior Design,* New York: Princeton Architectural Press.

3. DRAWING ROOMS: A BACKWARD GLANCE—FASHIONING AN INDIVIDUAL DRAWING ROOM

anne anderson

A lady has to spend her life in the drawing room. (Oliphant 1866)

The drawing room symbolized the essence of home life in the middle-class Victorian house; a private-public space, connecting the daily life of the family with invited guests, it was a staged space in which 'character' and 'respectability' were enacted. In art, the drawing room framed domestic melodramas and emotional conflict as well as conjured an idyll, a retreat from the cares of the outer world. From George Elgar Hicks's *Changing Homes* (1862), picturing a happy bridal party, to William Quiller Orchardson's *Le Mariage de Convenance* (1883), this space was seen to circumscribe women's lives. Beatriz Colomina argues that architecture does more than accommodate the subject, being 'a viewing mechanism that produces the subject. It precedes and frames its occupant' (1996: 250). As a gendered space, it generates complicated relationships between consumption, display and exchange (Logan 2000; Hamlett 2010a, 2010b; Tange 2010).

Picturing the drawing room means placing the 'lady of the house' at the centre of her universe; in *The Gentleman's House*, architect Robert Kerr pronounced it 'the Lady's Apartment essentially' as it symbolically unified disparate roles, locating her function as wife, mother, household manager and hostess within a single space (1865: 107). The 'unquestioned locus of her realm' (Tange 2008: 167), the drawing room defined cultural notions of feminine identity, a physical and ideological space that framed a woman's actions and thoughts. Here family and guests were to judge the 'respectability' of the house, a place empowered 'to make the ideals of domesticity a physical reality by actualising all that a woman was supposed to embody for her home' (Tange 2008: 167). Reflecting the best qualities of its mistress—moral righteousness, propriety, grace and a concern for other's comfort—the drawing room possessed an agency of its own, extending those qualities to all those who inhabited or visited.

Guided by advice manuals, which opined that each room should suit its primary occupant, women assumed authority for domestic decor; for art critic John Ruskin, a woman's intellect was for 'sweet ordering, arrangement and decision'—her task was to comfort and beautify (1910: 117). Fashioning a House Beautiful[1] was a 'Woman's Aesthetic Mission', proclaimed museum curator Jacob von Falke, as a tasteful home provided a civilising environment (1878: 311). Decorating was even lauded as a duty, for beautifying one's drawing room with 'artistic' needlework or wall stencilling was seen as a worthy means of enhancing a space that played the vital role of improving family life. Decoration established a connection between a woman's duty and the drawing room, the place where she discharged those duties.

The drawing room was a culturally sanctioned space for women, reaffirming their 'proper' position but it was also a site where contemporary assumptions about their role and position in society could be challenged. It was inevitably an ambivalent space, complex and contradictory. Pictorial and literary fictions may value women's domestic labour, with domesticity marking the limit of a woman's existence, or critique poet Coventry Patmore's 'Angel in the House' (1854). Following the moralizing of the 1850s, pictorial renderings of women increasingly objectified them as beautiful possessions. The Aesthetic Cult of Beauty, led by Dante Gabriel Rossetti (1828–82), placed women, now deemed 'stunners', on a pedestal but also condemned them to imprisonment, a 'work of art' in a gilded cage; for those caught in the web of their carpets and wallpapers the consequences could be disastrous, ultimately leading to hallucinations and madness as in Charlotte Perkins Gilman's *The Yellow Wallpaper* (1892; Anderson, 2010). Although a woman might be yet another 'thing' in the drawing room, she could challenge female passivity by fashioning a distinctive environment that expressed her personality: 'a matter of individual idiosyncrasies, personal needs, and interests' (Halttunen 1989: 187). As an extension of her persona, the drawing room was 'a place of her own'; Miss Marjoribanks, the heroine of Mrs Oliphant's novel (1866), effected a

> fundamental duty of women . . . [she] harmonised the rooms by . . . rearranging half the chairs and covering the tables with trifles of her own . . . which converted the apartment from an abstract English drawing room of the old school into Miss Marjoribanks's drawing room, an individual spot of ground revealing something of the character of its mistress. (1969: 47–8)

This chapter considers how the psychological shift to individualization impacted on the décor of the drawing room.[2] Mass-produced and standardized, new furniture would be denounced as tasteless and vulgar. Conversely antiques and handcrafted products would be lauded as 'one of a kind'.

Being old and rare, antiques were inimitable and increasingly unattainable; related to interior décor and 'minor touches which might give a room the charm of completeness' (Saisselin 1984: 71), antiques offered an ideal vehicle for demonstrating discrimination. It is argued here that the shift to individualization transformed the 'abstract' drawing room into the modern 'living room'; this new social purpose was recognized by H. J. Cooper in *The Art of Furnishing on Rational and Aesthetic Principles*:

> The purpose of the drawing room is relaxation and social enjoyment, hence all the powers of our art and mind may be lavished upon this room, which should be the embodiment of our finer nature and often does most faithfully represent us in our individual characteristics, our tastes, and capacities. (Cooper 1876: 11)

As Penny Sparke observes, decorating was a means of self-expression and self-realization; women were encouraged to 'embrace modernity' by exerting control and 'creating a domestic space which would express their own individuality' (2008: 132). This could be read as a feminine version of modernity; it allowed a 'conservative style', seen in the use of family heirlooms, antiques and reproductions, but it was done a 'modern way for modern women' (Sparke 2008: 137, note 2).[3] Women were not expected to create standardized drawing rooms but rather to participate in the creative process of fashioning a room of their own. Through this process, they were constructing 'modern, feminine, aspirational identities' (Sparke 2008: 136) in a world that appeared to threatened individualism and the 'self' through standardization and homogenization. Women aspired to the ideal of Elsie de Wolfe's *House in Good Taste* (1913), a 'fantasy' that embodied both individualization and distinction. In America, this need to imprint the personality of the owner on the home was recognized in the 'personal look': 'No stylish house could be without it, and the effort to have it was made in both the plainest cabins of the Dakota farmers and the big-city houses of Manhattan' (Seale 1975: 20).

Antiques became a marker of refined sensibility on both sides of the Atlantic; for American writer Edith Wharton (1862–1937), 'Good objects of art give to a room its crowning touch of distinction' (Wharton and Codman 1901: 187). A room so decorated was even deemed artistic, valorized as an expression of personal creativity, as 'composition . . . is the principle part of invention' (Davis 1886: 31). Through artful selection and placing, the desired effect replicated a painting, with spots of colour and novel juxtapositions. But success required accustoming 'the vision to seize on and make mental note of beautiful combinations' (Davis 1886: 37). The homemaker was now cast as a '*décorateur*' or '*metteur en scène*', literally a 'scene-setter' or inventor of interiors, cultivating the myth of expressing flair and originality through décor (de Goncourt 2003: 25–6). As novelist Henry James opined, art was 'all discrimination and selection' (1908: v); true artists declared their genius in the 'arrangement and effect of everything' (James 1908: 249). Originality was achieved through diversity and the display of rarities and curios, which might be anything from anywhere—seventeenth- and eighteenth-century furniture; Chinese, Japanese and Islamic ceramics; Renaissance bronzes; and Persian carpets—a subjective view of the past and other cultures. This ensemble was personalized with family heirlooms, memorabilia and souvenirs selected and placed with an eye for colour and harmony to create a 'pleasing whole' (Goncourt 2003: 25–6). This demonstration of discriminating eclecticism has been defined by Judith Neiswander as the 'cosmopolitan interior' (2008). However, although homemakers were encouraged to materialized personal preferences and superior knowledge by layering the drawing room with tokens of their life, blatant personal revelations were frowned on; photographs and personal 'relics, which are only treasures from association ought to be kept for the private apartments or locked draws of those to whom they belong' (Loftie 1878: 81). 'Personal impress' should not violate 'the laws of harmony' or offend 'good taste' (Humphreys 1896: 105).

The drawing room as a self-conscious enactment of personal taste was by definition a fugitive ensemble rarely able to survive the demise of the homeowner; what appeared to the owner a logical assemblage, linked by personal threads, seemed to the next generation a chaotic jumble of curiosities. Paintings and photographs capture these 'subject-object relations' (Brown 2001: 4); they memorialize a person by recording their possessions. Lord Ronald Gower's sitting room had 'bric-a-brac of all sorts scattered about', many things to occupy any caller 'if at all artistically inclined', notably his collection of Marie Antoinette memorabilia (1888: 6; Figure 3.1) Artists were drawn to capturing an effect that was transitory, a staged mise-en-scène, with objects and their settings equal participants, interwoven in a spontaneous, playful, allegedly artless way connoting individuality. Replicating a portrait, an interior could enshrine for posterity individual identity. Yet the interior is a posed artifice, a contrivance that conceals as well as reveals; it is both

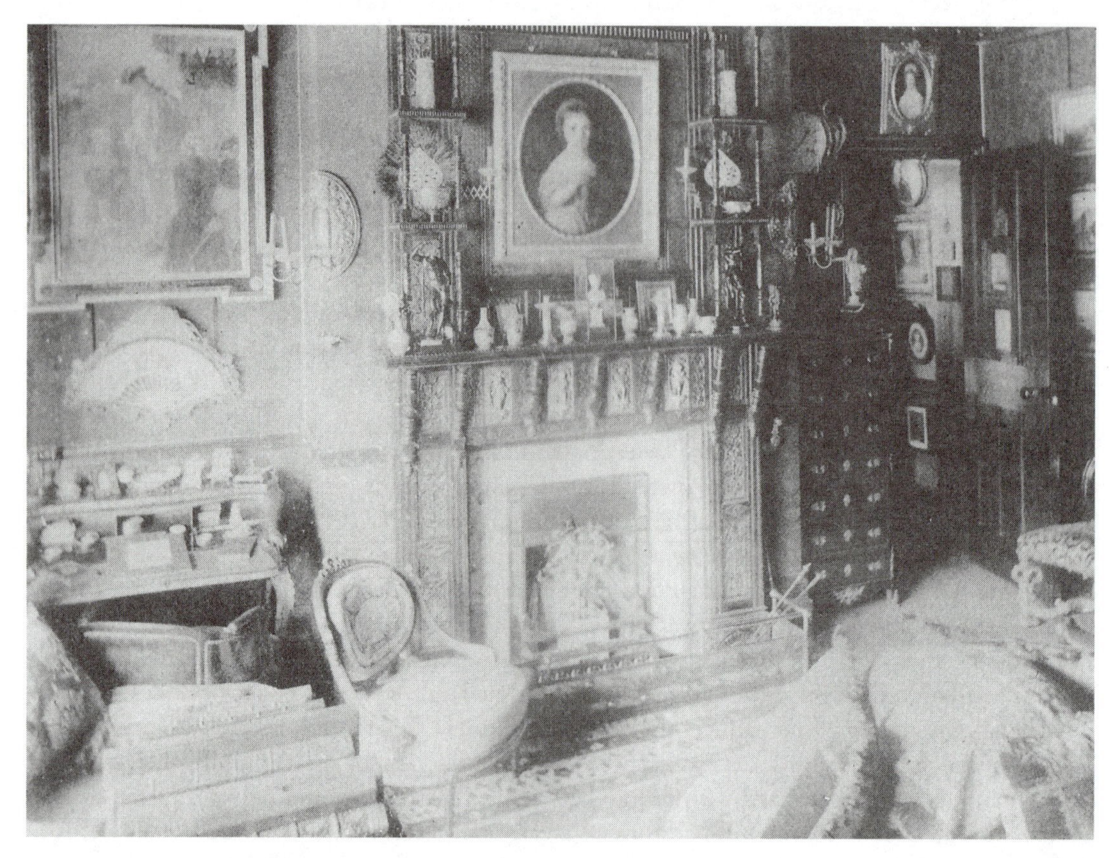

3.1. Lord Ronald Gower, *Sitting Room No. 2*, in *"Bric À Brac", Or, Some Photoprints Illustrating Art Objects At Gower Lodge, Windsor*, London: Kegan Paul, Trench & Co., 1888. Credit: Anne Anderson.

'real and 'ideal'. Thus the interiors of Belgian artist Alfred Stevens (1823–1906) have been defined as 'an art of attitude', combining 'the desire to mark oneself out with the need to declare oneself' (Draguet 2009: 93). The desire to assert 'difference' will be framed here within the debates surrounding taste, beginning with the condemnation of new furniture by the cognoscenti, including Ruskin.

GHASTLY GOOD TASTE

> The very headquarters of the commonplace . . . its pretentious uselessness . . . It is tabooed to the children and avoided except on occasions, by the dwellers, who are deterred by its lack of comfort and the false tone of its general arrangements . . . Such is the withdrawing room to which, because of its showy discomfort, no one withdraws. (Orrinsmith 1878: 2)[4]

The mid-Victorian, Christian, middle-class home expressed 'character' and 'respectability' through a formal, highly regulated, drawing room. A uniform standard of conduct based on fixed principles, character was 'associated with reputation, duty, honour and integrity: its aim was to be respected' (Halttunen 1989: 187). Character focused on moral probity and preached the virtues of self-control; the drawing room was a bastion of these values. Its appointments included heavy curtains, a densely patterned carpet, ornate furniture and a huge range of ornaments. Comfort was secondary to formality: 'The ordering of the Victorian drawing room was governed by the need to impress, a need felt by even the working-class homemaker' (Massey 1990: 8). But as Grant Allen, better known as an 'armchair evolutionist', opined in 'The Philosophy of Drawing Rooms', this 'mystical precinct' or 'solemn shrine' was 'regarded as far too sacred for common and everyday usage': the family lived in the parlour or the breakfast room and only approached the 'higher sanctum on Sunday afternoons' (Allen 1880: 312). The 'serious minded and respectable English drawing-room' offered a 'minimum of repose'; a 'prevailing coldness' and 'strict artificiality' meant no one could be at 'ease' or 'dare to be comfortable' (Allen 1880: 312–13).

Ruskin took umbrage with the 'useless expense', decrying in *The Seven Lamps of Architecture* (1849) such showy 'fineries' as 'cornicing of ceilings and graining of doors, and fringing of curtains, and thousands such' (1903: 38); such 'things' had caused 'half the expense of life', destroying 'more than half its comforts, manliness, respectability, freshness, and facility' (1903: 38–9). The 'meretricious' setting of William Holman Hunt's *The Awakening Conscience* (1853–4) enhanced its authenticity and didactic purpose; Ruskin, who recognized the 'fatal newness of the furniture' in explicating the narrative, defended the endless proliferation of detail (Ruskin in Bronkhurst 1984: 121). Hunt's thoroughness led him to Woodbine Villa, 7 Alpha Place, St John's Wood, a '*maison de convenance*', where he hired a room fitted with commercial furniture characterized by French Rococo styling and French polish, its falseness suggestive of moral impropriety. The Rococo was tainted with the extravagance of the Ancien Régime; in his famous 'House Beautiful' lecture, delivered across North America in 1882, Oscar Wilde condemned French furniture as 'gilt and gaudy . . . very vulgar, monstrous and unserviceable' (1999: 919). New furniture smacked of new money, the 'man of business' who, being devoid of heirlooms, had to buy his own furniture. A lack of lineage, as well as a lack of probity, is expressed through vulgar décor: the gaudily patterned, machine-made carpet that utilizes newly invented synthetic colours,[5] the overly gilt mirror and the French ormolu clock that depicts Chastity binding Cupid. These trappings of financial success, a veneer of respectability, cannot disguise moral failure, as this drawing room frames a 'kept woman'; she has been lured into this den of iniquity by her lust for things and a life of ease. Women were deemed wanton, driven by foolish, even dangerous, desires for the fashionable and luxurious. The female appetite was fuelled by the profusion of goods, all the 'commodities that indulged the body and enhanced physical life' (Kowaleski-Wallace 1997: 5); lacking self-control, such desires could even lead to sexual promiscuity. But Hunt's intent was to portray a victim, a woman realising the error of her ways by hearing the 'still small voice' of spiritual revelation and redemption (Bronkhurst 1984: 121).

Augustus Leopold Egg's *Past and Present No.1* (1858) was far more sensational; in this drawing room, adultery is insinuated through French polish, a sham papier-mâché chair, the gilt neo-rococo mirror and paintings that explicate the story; Clarkson Stanfield's *The Abandoned*, a sinking ship, for him and the *Expulsion from Paradise* for her. A victim of love, the mistress of the house is about to be cast out exposing a hidden truth: a loveless marriage.[6] Family life has been destroyed by carnal desire, the seeds of corruption sown by immoral French literature, a novel by Honoré de Balzac providing no foundation for the tumbling house of cards. This 'marriage of convenience' has foundered; a life of ease and the trappings of respectability have failed to ward off seduction.

Newness also exposed fraudulence; Anthony Trollope's *The Way We Live Now* (1875) was a scathing attack on the pervading dishonesty of the age, commercial, political, moral and intellectual. Wealthy foreign financier Augustus Melmotte, a 'horrid, big, rich scoundrel . . . a bloated swindler . . . and a vile city ruffian' is loathed by an aristocracy who hypocritically gather at his house to 'see and be seen' at his wife's ball: 'Of the certainty of the money in daily use there could be no doubt. There was the house. There was the furniture . . . and all the nice things that money can buy' (Trollope 1991: 220–1, 29). But this money was obtained by deception, shares in the South Central Pacific and Mexican Railway. New furniture, now an expression of society's preoccupation with the frippery denoting class and position, was untrustworthy. The Veneerings, in Charles Dickens's *Our Mutual Friend* (1864–5), are 'bran-new people in a bran-new house in a bran-new quarter of London':

> All their furniture was new . . . they themselves were new . . . For, in the Veneering establishment, from the hall-chairs with the new coat of arms . . . all things were in a state of high varnish and polish. And what was observable in the furniture was observable in the Veneerings—the surface smelt a little too much of the workshop and was a trifle sticky. (2009: 7)

What was needed was a home 'spotlessly free from vulgarity', a rejection of 'grand shows' that spawned rivalry or 'vain effort after possession' (Eliot 1996: 162). In the financially troubled 1870s and 1880s, the era of the Long Depression, money alone would not facilitate the 'impress of our individuality, in order, beauty and grace, on our abiding places' (Orrinsmith 1878: 3); the impersonal new would be replaced by the personalized antique. The drawing room was to express new values; contemporary furniture, 'superficial, showy without worth, elegant without beauty and elaborate without fitness . . . designed by those who lack knowledge and principally executed by machine', would be ousted by 'furniture more than a century old' whose 'excellent condition and fitness for modern needs' proved the desirability of 'clever, earnest, honest handiwork' (Orrinsmith 1878: 83–4). Good taste would now rule the drawing room.

A TASTEFUL ROOM

> We may condemn a lady's politics . . . disparage her favourite author . . . But if we venture to question her taste. . . . we are sure to offend. (Eastlake 1872: 9)

Although operating within the accepted prejudices of society, Nancy Armstrong argues that 'taste became the privilege and obligation of women' and that the 'female subject' was now identified by her 'things': 'She was what she bought, wore and put in her house. Upon her self-restraint rested the well being of British husbands and children, the well being . . . of the nation itself' (1990: 34). Being so heavily invested in her things roused the spectre of 'dangerous appetites', which both male and female cultural critics attempted to curtail. While architect Owen W. Davis accepted that the drawing room was 'the lady's temple', a 'marked effeminacy' was to be avoided 'with all its train of stuffiness, caprice, and uncertainty' (1886: 22). Aymer Vallance, an associate of William Morris, also dared to censure 'the ladies' province': this 'alien man' dared to criticize the superfluous and flimsy knick-knacks that overwhelmed the drawing room (1904: 111). Vallance's readers would be 'painfully familiar' with the 'rubbish' he had in mind: 'In vain does the long-suffering man . . . endure the intrusion into his home of all this contemptible frippery, chafe against its vexatious tyranny' (1904: 111). Husbands inevitably sought refuge in their clubs, where common sense and practical convenience held undisputed sway. Clearly, women were reckless consumers, seduced by the unnecessary and susceptible to the blandishments of the 'shopman'.[7] Women liked clutter, a 'crowd of things' that were 'simply useless', an 'irritating presence' that did 'violence' to the purpose of the drawing room, which was to be a place of repose. What was needed was 'a clearance in the drawing room' (Vallance 1904: 112).

Being what 'she bought and put in' in her drawing room, women were drawn to bric-a-brac and bibelots, which encompassed heirlooms, mementoes and souvenirs that had 'sentimental' value (Stewart 1994: 254–7; Bollas 1992). It became natural to associate objects with events, places and people, while houses became laden with goods saturated with emotional associations. Commodities could now express the 'self', while a room became 'a practical, aesthetic and psychological extension, beyond that provided by dress, of the occupant' (Sparke 2008: 124): 'We are inscribing in our 'every-day art', annals of our life and inmost character; and if we impress our works with true earnestness, our individuality will not fail to favourably assert itself' (Davis 1886: 7). Originality was to be realized through 'taste', 'the *personal equation* of Aesthetics' (Allen 1877: 47) or one's idiosyncratic preferences. Selection was based on a mental, emotional, even physical response to objects; desires were now the 'embodied part of taste' (Psomiades 1997: 137). With the drawing room now cast as a 'portrait of the mind' with an 'explicit statement to make' (Nicholson 2003: 100), a woman was faced with a daunting task, the materialisation of her taste or 'deepest self'. For designer Cecil Beaton, individual taste transcended fashion, as it was based on 'personal choice' (Nicholson 2003: 112). Personal choice fulfilled a spiritual need; it also provoked unbridled desires.

'Good' taste remained highly contested, as it demanded a display informed by careful selection and arrangement, a discrimination that signalled distinction. In *India in Paris, the Exotic Trinket*

(c. 1865–6), Alfred Stevens appears to critique the shameless indulgence of a generation that had acquired wealth too rapidly: 'wealth that drives people to amass without taste, to display without intelligence and to follow blindly the fashion for excess' (Derry-Capon 2009: 150). Enchanted by 'grotesque' Oriental goods and a love of opulence, women's unbridled desires caused consternation; Eastlake saw the 'materfamilias' led astray by novelty and social emulation (1872: 3). Taste was to be based on rational principals and informed knowledge, not the whims of fashion.

It was the intention of writers as diverse as Eastlake, Robert W. Edis, Mrs H. R. Haweis, Rev W. J. Loftie and William Morris to set the crooked straight. Mrs Haweis, one of a bevy of lady advisors, noted, 'Most people are now alive to the importance of beauty as a refining influence. The appetite for artistic instruction is even ravenous' (1881: 3). Following Eastlake's *Hints on Household Taste* (1868), advice proliferated: Loftie's *Art at Home* series was published by Macmillan from 1876 to 1883, while Clarence Cook's *House Beautiful* (1878) became a bestseller on both sides of the Atlantic.[8] The frontispiece by Walter Crane, *My Lady's Chamber*, offered a

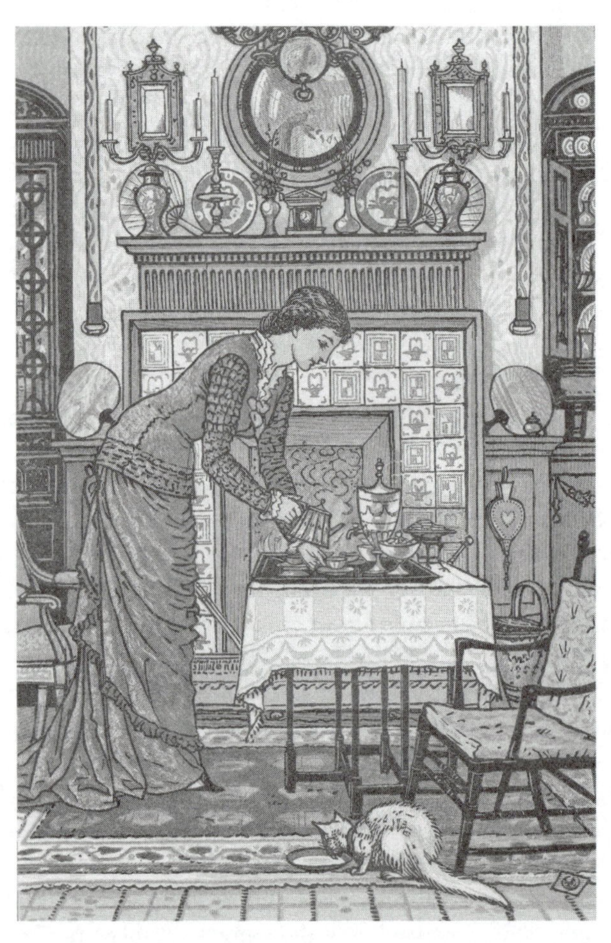

3.2. Walter Crane, *My Lady's Chamber*, in Clarence Cook, *The House Beautiful*, New York: Scribner.

blueprint for the insecure home decorator unsure of correct taste: an array of genuine antiques or reproductions is complimented by a Persian rug, a Morris 'Sussex' chair and Japanese paper fans (Figure 3.2). The fireplace, a 'largely poetic installation' imbued with 'magic' (Muthesius 2009: 257), is beautified with blue tiles, its mantel loaded with Old Blue china. A natural nucleus, Mrs Harriet Spofford declared that the mantelpiece should be the first thing to arrest attention upon entering the room (1878: 233). Here, Eastlake recommended gathering 'really good specimens of art-manufacture' to educate the 'eye': 'An Indian ginger-jar, a Flemish beer-jug, a Japanese fan, may each become in turn a valuable lesson in decorative form and colour . . . A little museum may thus be formed, and remain a source of lasting pleasure to its possessors' (1872: 137–8). Jug or fan was to be 'fingered musingly, to be shifted or replaced in accordance with your mood' (Watson 1897: 34).

The inviting warmth of the hearth, 'the deity of the home' (Spofford 1878: 233) around which 'so many tender memories of early days are centred' (Holly 1878: 57), frames the hostess who is 'at home'; as queen of the tea-table, she takes centre stage in a tea gown designed for public exposure, its closely fitted silhouette, long sleeves, high neckline and fashionable back train in no way challenging feminine respectability. The gate-legged table supports a dainty eighteenth-century Adam-style tea service; understated refinement pervades a scene of domestic tranquillity. As Alice Kellogg observed in1904, serving tea from a tea table was enjoying a popularity not known since the 'days of our great-grandmothers'; the tilt table was deemed an 'artistic acquisition' for the drawing room (1904: 247). Ideally, the tea service should be of old china that spoke of 'bygone history', perhaps enhanced by a set of Apostle spoons gathered on a Continental tour or handed down from 'earlier eras of tea makers' (Kellogg 1904: 248–9). Most precious of all was the 'homespun linen' that adorned the tray, the work of some thrifty, industrious ancestor. *My Lady's Chamber* stands for generations of women who have ruled the tea table, a symbol of order and repose.

As the ritual of taking tea signalled gentility, artists used the motif to picture an ideal 'civilising' femininity that quelled the brutish. Based on Japanese rituals, the Art of Tea required simplification and called for 'harmony', 'reverence', 'purity' and 'tranquillity', all essential constituents of an 'orderly life' (Suzuki 1998: 56). Harmony was also read as 'gentleness of spirit', suggestive of an inner peace. The tea table was a 'feminine locus' where the civilising process took place: 'Here the stream of hot liquid is mastered and ceremoniously controlled signalling discipline' (Kowaleski-Wallace 1997: 21). But it was also a performance through which women could exert cultural dominance, legitimately displaying their bodies and their seductive powers to control masculine behaviour. The ritual of 'taking tea', connoting exemplarily taste, privilege and class distinction, would have appealed to an audience accustomed to viewing a woman as the 'lady of the house'.

Cook saw *My Lady's Chamber* framed not by a formal drawing room or 'disagreeable parlor', a 'ceremonial desert' that alienated the visitor, but by a 'living-room' committed to comfort and leisure: 'the pleasantest and most accessible room in the house' was to be given up to the 'wife and children in the day-time and to the meeting of the whole family when evening comes' (1878: 45–8). Enhanced with the 'ornament of life', casts, pictures, engravings, bronzes, books, the 'chief nourishers in life's feast', this space was transformed into 'an important agent in the education of life'; an enriching environment that even had the power to shape growing children (Cook 1878: 48–9). Above all, this room 'ought to represent the culture of the family—what is their taste, what feeling they have for art; it should represent themselves' (Cook 1878: 48).

A ROOM OF ONE'S OWN

> Like hermit crabs we gather round us a medley of objects, present and recollected, that become almost a part of our personality. (Watson 1897: 152–3)

The physiological change from character to personality can be linked to the ascendance of Aestheticism, with its emphazis on consumption as a means to fulfilment and happiness (Gagnier 1993, 1999). Aestheticism privileged the householder, the educated amateur; according to Mrs Panton, 'Every lady should endeavour to arrange her own drawing room in such a way that it will at once express in some manner her own individuality, and indicate immediately what are her tastes and pursuits' (1887: 344).[9] Mrs Orrinsmith encouraged 'individual fancy, personal arrangement, self-willed ideas' rather than 'adherence to the "correct style"' (1878: 118–19).

Experts refrained from proscriptive directions, preferring to assist 'a more self-helpful Art-knowledge'; homemakers should not be told how to furnish a drawing room, rather they should 'learn to *feel*, that certain harmonies of form and colour are admirable and desirable' (Orrinsmith 1878: 9). The quest for harmony dominated interior decorating manuals; furnishing 'required serious thought, when the end to be attained is one of harmony, simplicity and refinement (Kellogg 1904: vi). *Artistic Homes* stressed, 'The carpet strikes . . . the key-note of the chromatic harmony'; upon its careful selection 'the harmony and propriety of that room depends' (Anon 1881: 17, 30). Carpet and wallpaper were to form 'the background of the picture'; a 'restful and rich-looking mass of neutral colour' would provide a backdrop to colour accents—a piece of china, a Japanese fan or a vase of flowers (Allen 1880: 316). The successful mingling of colours would 'rest the eye and awaken admiration', thus ensuring 'an air of completeness about the room which will render its occupancy pleasing' (Holden 1882: 214).

But, according to Harry Quilter, art critic for the *Spectator* and archenemy of Aestheticism, in order to avoid an 'unendurable discordance' the 'favourite colour for hangings is sage-green, or dusty Indian-red . . . they form harmonious combinations with the blue china, which is also fashionable . . . because it goes with the other decorations' (1880: 911; Anderson 2005). The whole thing was a 'monstrous fallacy, which rests upon the assumption that harmoniousness of effect is the whole of art' (Quilter 1880: 911). Individual thought and action had been replaced by dogma. Despite Mrs Haweis's exhortation, 'In dress, in home-adornment, in every department of art—regardless of derision, censure and "advice"—WE MUST DO AS WE LIKE' (1878: 224), the fashion conscious aesthete followed a code.

Consumer choice expressed aspirations, the wish to gain admittance into a socioeconomic network known as Aestheticism. Walter Hamilton rightly concluded that the 'essence' of the movement was 'the union of persons of cultivated taste to define, and to decide upon, what is to be admired, and their followers must aspire to that standard' (1882: vii). Aesthetes proved their fitness to belong to the clique through the possession of tasteful things and knowing how to artfully arrange them. The drawing room demanded a demonstration of 'good' taste, a commodity that set its possessor apart. A 'life lived in art' meant renouncing the commonplace, the mass-produced and the factory made. Striving for originality meant investing in the unique, the 'arresting object', poet Charles Baudelaire's 'object that blinds you' (1968: 689–90), sumptuous textiles and lavish porcelains that enhance life. Old and new objets deluxe were judiciously blended to shape a mise-en-scène: 'Chippendale furniture, dadoes, old-fashioned brass and wrought-iron work, mediaeval lamps, stained glass in small

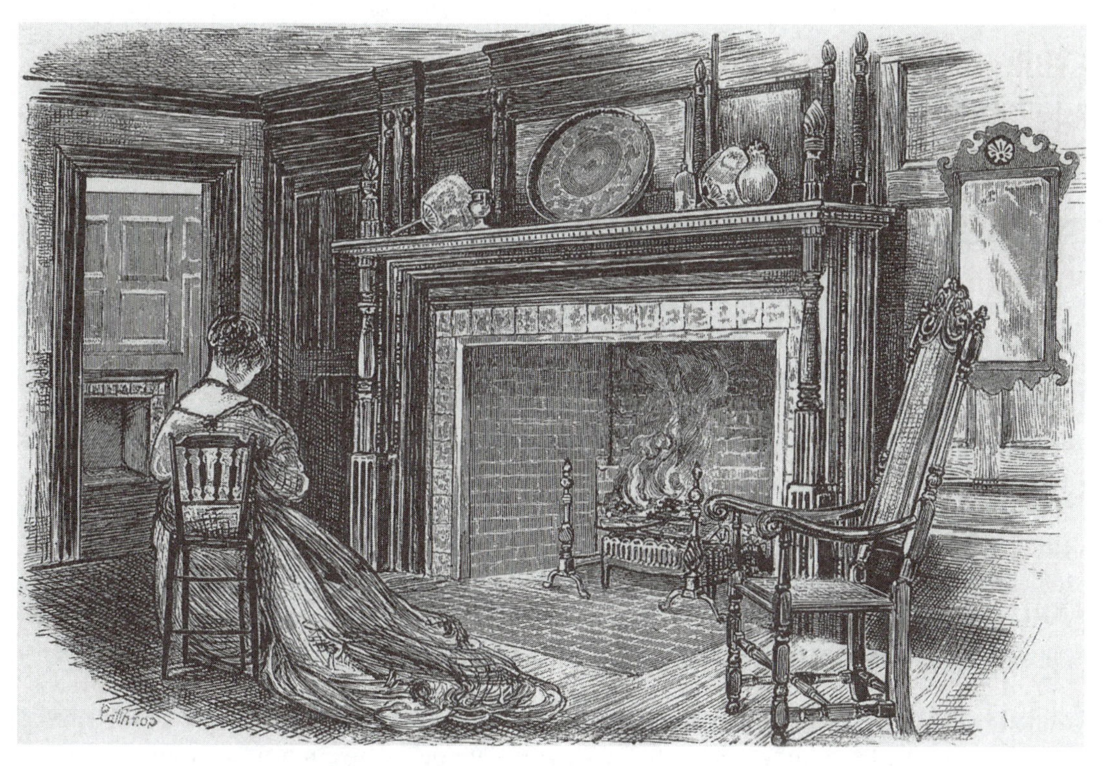

3.3. Francis Lathrop, *Things Old and New*, in Clarence Cook, *The House Beautiful*, New York: Scribner, Armstrong & Co., 1878, No. 64: 189. Credit: Anne Anderson.

squares, and old china are all held to be the outward and visible signs of an inward and spiritual grace and intensity' (Hamilton 1882: 34; Figure 3.3). Peacock feathers, sunflowers and Old Blue china signalled allegiance to the Cult of Beauty and a lifestyle devoted to fashioning a unique home.

For many women, the personal touch meant making it yourself; the sentimental home was lovingly adorned with home-crafted Berlin tapestries, embroidery and even taxidermy. Although offering individualization, the amateur arts were censured for encouraging clutter, with sentiment clouding aesthetic judgment. Vallance scorned feminine ingenuity, which perversely turned 'drain-pipes, set up on ends, into vases for bulrushes and dried grasses; milking stools into flower-stands; cauldrons into coal-scuttles; whereby square pianos, disembowelled of their works, become "silver tables", and sedan chairs, fitted with shelves, become china cabinets' (1904: 111–12). The Cult of Beauty had ladies painting doors, china and glass; the Arts and Crafts ushered in a preference for more robust crafts, metalworking and woodcarving. But Rosamund Marriott Watson, in *The Art of the House* (1897), abhorred second-rate amateur work, chiding the out-of-control female decorator to resist the urge to attack furniture and china:

> Nothing is sacred to the amateur decorator, especially if she be a woman . . . she attacks with fury and at large; never a door panel or an uncovered wall space that is safe from her enthusiastic pencil . . . Once allow an unoccupied woman (and her name is legion) to

suppose she is imbued with artistic ideas, give her her head and some paintings materials, and she will run amuck. (1897: 189)

True housewifely sentiment should rather be expressed in the choice of table linens and menu cards, arranging flowers and caring for the best china, and especially by collecting rather than crafting things; women ought to be connoisseurs valuing 'patina', a mellowing with time or 'pleasing decay' that defies mechanical reproduction. Through patina, 'the fact of oldness and the value of oldness enter complex relationships' (Muthesius 2003: 138); for Watson, oldness 'offered individual charm' and 'sentiment that simulates memory' (1897: 82, 23). Moreover, patina reconciled disparate objects facilitating a harmonious ensemble.

The materiality of age was now perceived as beautiful: 'Set in the deeper places of the heart [is] such affection for the signs of age that the eye is delighted even by the injuries which are the work of time' (Ruskin 1886: 104). Stefan Muthesius contends that liking oldness is relatively new, that antiques can be seen as forming 'part of 20th century Modernism' as they offer an alternative or 'difference' (2003: 138). An important part of being modern was being anti-modern (Berman 1983, 14); being driven by dissatisfaction and the desire to reform and elevate contemporary life, the antique can be read as a form of protest, denoting a counterculture. Yet, although aesthetes used their connoisseurship to oppose the middle-class consumerist ethos, ironically they merely popularized a new range of commodities.

Antiques, as they 'extend the owner's subjectivity' (Schaffer 2000: 91), were perfectly positioned to articulate 'personality'. The antique was a unique possession, redolent with historical associations and enshrining ancestral lineage, untrammelled by industrialisation and mass-production. Embodying the old ways of handcrafting, the unalienated work of the preindustrial era, the antique was rare as few were made in the first place: 'Originality is the great charm of the *antique*. The furniture was not turned out by the thousand . . . the charm of *human* expression hangs about the work' (Holden 1882: 281). Susan Stewart suggests that the antique connects the owner with a preindustrial 'authentic' lifestyle, as opposed to the mass-produced present (1984: 141).

Antiques enshrine personal sentiments and affections; in George Eliot's *Daniel Deronda* (1876), the Meyricks's home 'was filled with objects always in the same places, which, for the mother held memories of her marriage time', while 'the chairs and tables were also old friends preferred to new' (1996: 162). This attachment to old furniture, 'the fashions of our fathers', signals not only refinement but also an understanding of human relations, the notion that the past lives on in the present, an endless conversion of 'ancestors into objects' and 'objects into descendants' (McCracken 1988: 53). Talia Schaffer argues that the collector places himself in a 'respected series of connoisseurs . . . a symbolic genealogy' which 'is the real pleasure of antique buying' (2000: 81). Antiques inscribe a personal history of seeking and finding, as well as recalling distant lives and eras; they allow us to live in the here and then. Read as 'moments', objects are 'congealed actions, passionate acts of seeking, selecting and situating' (Brown 2003: 146).

In the fluid society of the later nineteenth century, the concept of a 'genealogy of owners' would have an obvious appeal to the arriviste. Conversely, the possession of antiques no longer acted as a guarantor of authentic class status. For George du Maurier, in 'The Six-Mark Teapot', the value of an Old Blue teapot no longer resided in its function—its original purpose being to make a good cup of tea—or even its aesthetic appeal, its beauty, uniqueness or antiquity, but in its ability to confer distinction: 'In the old regime possession by nobility conferred cachet upon the work; in the bourgeois world it is the other way around' (Saisselin 1984: xv).

FURNISHING WITH ANTIQUES

> For the present the art of furnishing must be closely connected with the judicious buying of old furniture. (Loftie 1875: 539)

The principle psychological motivation for furnishing with antiques was the promise of an original *habitus* that embodied the unique personality of the owner. Home decorators pounced on bric-a-brac, as it gave 'free scope to individual taste and fancy instead of merely reflecting the stereotyped notions of the professional decorator' (Allen 1880: 321). This was the art of the 'personal touch', using a few smaller, carefully selected items to make a unique statement. Mrs Haweis achieved the 'cachet of individuality' by mingling colours and textures, arrangements suggestively quixotic: 'a bowl of red berries, a little pot with some weed in it . . . some novel use of the fender . . . and

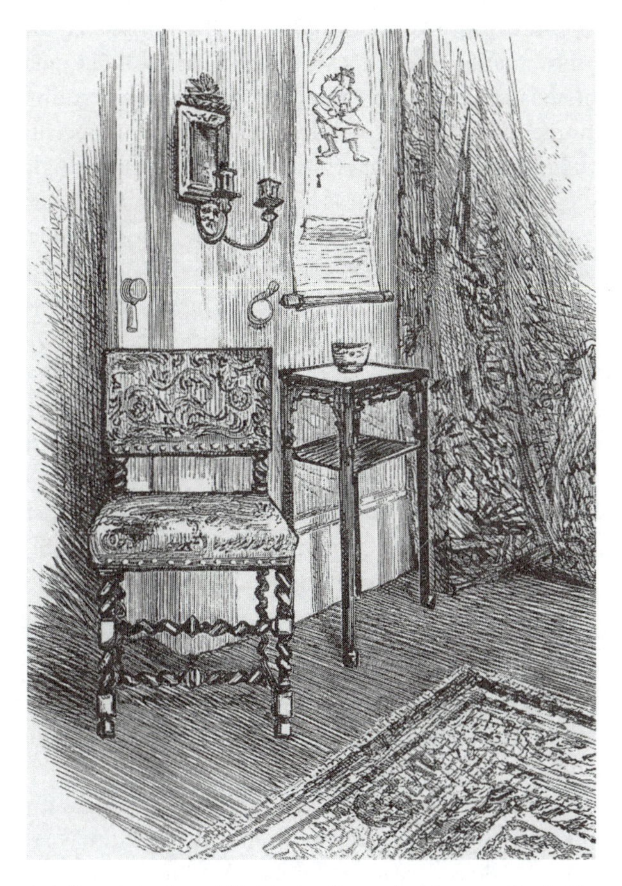

3.4. Francis Lathrop, *We Met by Chance*, in Clarence Cook, *The House Beautiful*, New York: Scribner, Armstrong and Co., 1878, No. 62: 184. Credit: Anne Anderson.

gay dishes . . . the original touch comes unexpectedly . . . like a sparkling dew-drop, gone like a bird's wing' (Haweis 1889: 369). Objects were to occur artlessly, this 'happen chance' an inflexion of the owner's taste. Variety was the means to achieve an expressive and meaningful display: 'A hundred things might be named, not one being costly, yet each, in its own way, beautiful and interesting' (Orrinsmith 1878: 133). Anachronisms that caught the eye were encouraged rather than scorned, provoking comment and inquiry: Lathrop's *We Met by Chance*, in which a Japanese scroll, seventeenth-century-style wall sconce and oak chair jostle for attention, implies artlessness (Figure 3.4).

Muthesius asserts that the fashioning of the 'old home' with 'old curios' constructed identity, with 'home' being a metaphor that telescoped across scales, from a nation to a town, a house or one corner of a room (2009: 212–14). Nationalism synthesized Tudor, Elizabethan, Jacobean, Stuart and Georgian into 'Olde English'. The contradictory Queen Anne style embraced Chippendale, Adam and Hepplewhite furniture, now deemed axiomatic of English workmanship. Queen Anne was 'a warm, comfortable and stately style', the eighteenth century 'so near to us and yet so far' (Muthesius 2009: 249).[10] The goal was not to simulate a period room; rather, this was a personal view of the past, mixing 'times for the sake of their beauty, choosing ornaments by way rather of reminiscence than of reproduction' (Meynell 1885: 3). 'Reminiscence' offered a fantasy of the past; the 'Olden Times' movement projected a vision of 'Merrie Olde England'[11] onto the 'period' country house. Here, conviviality ruled supreme, the drawing room exuding warmth and creature comforts. The 'happy home' privileged those elements deemed 'especially homelike'—the fireplace, the table, the cupboard and the cradle. Those in search of Olde England still hankered after inglenook fireplaces and even minstrel galleries (Figure 3.3). Dear Old English furniture from the hand of the village carpenter was increasingly correlated with good craftsmanship; a love of timber was motivated by antipathy to the flawless perfection of trade finish. The consumer was now urged to be sensitive to subtle variations in texture and colour; oldness had become synonymous with the traditional, rather than simply surrounding oneself with antiques. In this way, the distant old was merged into an acceptable modern interior.

Painters and sculptors, emerging as 'celebrity figures', led the way in this new appreciation of the old 'for its own sake'. Possessing the 'finest sensibilities', Mrs Haweis deemed them tastemakers; with surroundings important for both 'the cultivation of the eye and the enhancement of our inner and outer self', the public naturally turned to the 'great army of artists to tell us what to do' (1878: 207). For those aspiring to be artistic, their preferences and choices offered an informative guide; Harry Marillier claimed Dante Gabriel Rossetti (1828–82) as a pioneer in the use of antiques for decor:

> He was destined to pave the way for the modern craze for old furniture and blue china . . . it was a purely original idea in those days to buy old furniture for use, and to enrich the walls of a house with panelled carvings and treasures from Japan. (1899: 121–2)

'The prince of poets and painters' came to 16 Cheyne Walk, Chelsea, after the death of Lizzie Siddal in 1862. Rossetti had a large period house to fill but no money to engage an architect to transform his home into an abode fit for an artist/poet. Yet 'the house by degrees took on the casual, extravagant personality of its tenant', the early Georgian architecture 'gradually overlaid by

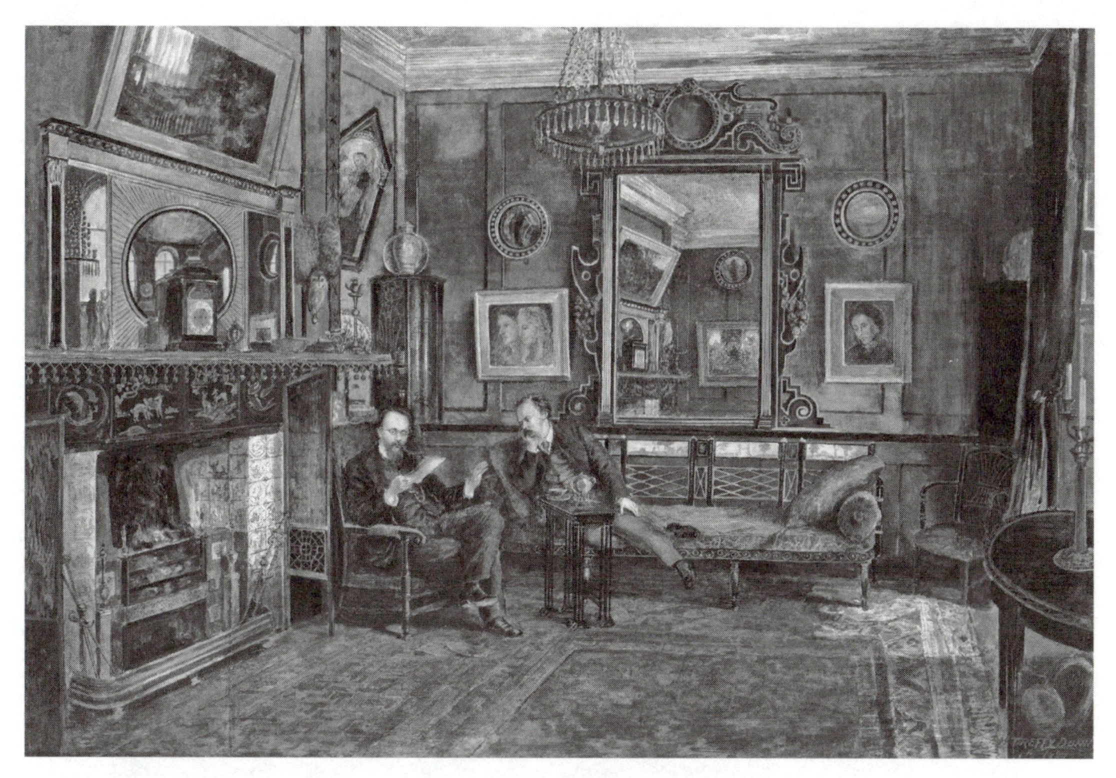

3.5. Henry Treffry Dunn, *Dante Gabriel Rossetti and Theodore Watts-Dunton in the Parlour or Sitting Room at 16 Cheyne Walk* (1882), watercolour. Credit: © National Portrait Gallery, London.

the mystic profusion of objects and ideas' (Gaunt 1954: 120), Rossetti's new interest in collecting being stimulated by Charles Augustus Howell and James McNeill Whistler.[12] Henry Treffry Dunn's *Dante Gabriel Rossetti and Theodore Watts—Dunton in the Sitting Room at 16 Cheyne Walk* (1882; Figure 3.5) enshrines the artist's taste:

> One of the prettiest and most curiously furnished old-fashioned parlours that I had ever seen. Mirrors and looking-glasses of all shapes, sizes and design lined the walls. Whichever way I looked I saw myself gazing at myself. What space there was left was filled up with pictures, chiefly old and of an interesting character. (Dunn 1904: 17–18)

Rossetti, as master of his tea-table, is 'at home' surrounded by works of art that commemorate his family (drawings of his mother and sister) and reveal his interests, the delicate Chinese 'Nankin' blue-and-white teacups and the Blue Willow plate hanging on the wall behind. Endorsement by leading artists and celebrities including Oscar Wilde, who claimed he could not 'live up' to his Old Blue,[13] has ensured that blue-and-white china is still lauded as a mark of good taste (Anderson 2009a and 2009b). Rossetti's circle popularized 'Persian' carpets and ceramics, German copper and brass, seventeenth- and eighteenth-century English furniture, notably 'old oak' and all manner of antique textiles, especially tapestries.

Leicester Square and Hammersmith became favourite haunts for finding oddities: 'It was Rossetti's utmost delight to drive round in a cab, loading it with china and brass and carved oak picked out from the litter of second-hand furniture shops and pawnbrokers' (Waugh 1928: 118). Evidently, he was looking for the old, rare and unique to enhance his works and enrich his environment; he also had a good eye for a bargain.

Atkinson Grimshaw (1836–93), best known as a 'painter of moonlight', commemorated his own taste for the antique in a remarkable series of interiors (*Dulce Domum*, 1885; *Spring*, 1875; *Summer*, 1875; *The Chorale*, 1878; *The Cradle Song*, 1878; *In the Artist's House*, 1878; *Daydreams*, 1877). He clearly aspired to the rank of connoisseur, joining the Leeds Fine Arts Club, an important forum for the sharing of enthusiasms and expertise. *Summer* (Figure 3.6) shows the morning room of Knosthrop Old Hall, Leeds, a seventeenth-century manor house which he rented in 1870; this provided a perfect setting for his 'hard-won possessions', his Delft pottery and Chinese porcelains, seventeenth-century marquetry and ebony chairs and Japanese textiles and fans. Yet these beautiful works of art surround the mistress of the house rather than the master, now cast as another ornament in the House Beautiful; the image invites you to see, as the title of a song suggests, 'A Bird in a Gilded Cage' (1900). Alexander Robertson, Grimshaw's biographer, concludes,

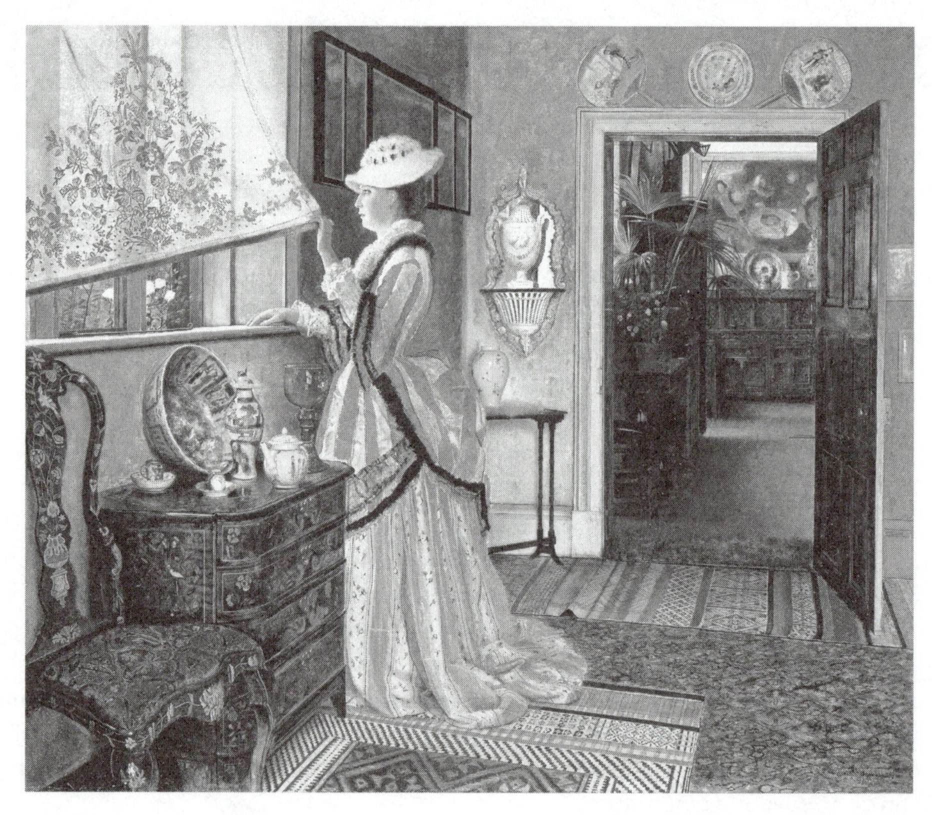

3.6. *Summer* by John Atkinson Grimshaw (1836–93). Roy Miles Fine Paintings, The Bridgeman Art Library.

'There is no apparent meaning in the painting, other than the display of the artist's powers, unless the model herself is to be seen as an "object", a highly desirable acquisition to be shown alongside the other possessions in the room' (1988: 39).[14] In her beautifully patterned dress, the model certainly resembles the works of art around her. Like a jewel in a casket she is encircled by Dutch marquetry, old English oak, Oriental and European ceramics and Japanese paper fans, although her dress is ironically fashionable rather than artistic; her afternoon dress, dating to 1872–3, resembles an eighteenth-century *polonaise,* its pink stripes denoting a synthetic dye such as mauveine or magenta. Lifting a muslin blind, to peek outside, this correctly attired young lady may be expecting a visitor for tea; she is about to be 'at home'. This tour de force in capturing materiality resembles a still life painting; the green glass *roemer*, which complements the Old Blue, commonly features in seventeenth-century Dutch still life paintings as it enhanced the colour of white wine, seen golden-yellow through the green glass. Grimshaw may have paid six pounds for his specimen (Ehrman 2011: 91). For such displays, Allen recommended a 'unpretentious ebonised *etagere* mirror' for 'small vases and other knick-knacks', showing to advantage a 'few pieces of Venetian glass . . . a bit of hawthorn-pattern porcelain . . . with a bright flower or two . . . to liven up the whole' (1880: 321). Mrs Panton still clung to her dado as the place to 'hang our favourite nicknacks [*sic*]' and prized 'pet possessions' (1889: 75).

EPILOGUE

Good taste, based on the principle of restraint, would save the drawing room from clutter and commercial debasement. Edith Wharton, Ogden Codman Jr, Elsie de Wolfe, Nancy Lancaster, Stanford White and Duveen & Co., did their utmost to curtail the idiosyncrasies of the homeowner. With the professionalization of the art of furnishing, interior decorators were entrusted with the task of creating a 'tout ensemble'; the untutored homeowner did not possess the educated eye, the discrimination, necessary to fashion the drawing room of good taste:

> The man who wishes to possess objects of art must not only have the means to acquire them but the skill to choose them—a skill made up of cultivation and judgment, combined with a feeling for beauty that no amount of study can give. (Wharton and Codman 1901: 187)

Yet the mission of the professional decorator was still to help the owner 'express his individuality'; antiques, 'the key to the taste and personality of the owner', were not to be 'cast out for the modish pieces associated with the decorator's art' (Hart 1926: 25). The decorator may be likened to the couturier, fashioning individualized 'custom-made' spaces 'the main function of which was to both express and form the identities of their [female] inhabitants' (Sparke 2008: 124). Sparke concludes that Elsie de Wolf's self-publicity utilized individualism to establish 'product identification', to sell her 'brand' as a 'signature-designer' (2008: 128). American Nancy Lancaster (1897–1994), who perfected the English country house style, would employ the same strategy, purchasing Colefax and Fowler in 1944. Like de Wolf, Lancaster also traded a 'conservative feminine modernity' that spoke of gentility and refinement through antiques and reproductions, a 'humble elegance' that was a 'rich amalgam of the understated and romantic' (Wood 2005: 110). Consumers could still achieve individualization through product choice, while the affirmation of 'good taste' also bestowed social status. Even the purchase of an advice book or magazine was a key decision, offering the reader access to a world of fantasy and desire.

The priority shifted to fashioning a retreat from the hustle and bustle of the outside world, a luxurious oasis of calm, a place for the rich to relax and dream in. Here a 'backward glance' recalled more genteel times: the court of Louis XV or the era of Robert Adam. Americans wanted beautiful homes, claimed Virginia Packard Hart, not period detail; antiques should blend in and be subservient to a new scheme. If these pieces were 'strong in beauty' they could provide the 'keynote for the whole house' (Hart 1926: 22). The 'most liveable results in interior decoration' combined 'modern comfort with the charm and subtlety of the antique' (Hart 1926: 25); the unique antique, the aptly named 'signature piece', could still be injected into the professionally crafted interior in order to assert individuality. Impersonal new furnishings 'say nothing'; a love of old things signifies a common heritage and communal memory. Valuing the 'material old' developed from revivalist styles, via collecting, into 'an individualised and a completely personalised sphere' (Muthesius 2009: 314); seeing the old as individual went hand-in-hand with decor as an expression of personal tastes.

Antiques are still used to fashion a distinctive and distinguished home; through such agency, antiquing has become a popular hobby rather than an elitist pursuit. As Clive Wainwright notes, the number of interiors furnished exclusively with contemporary manufactures is smaller than one may think (1989: 272). Muthesius claims that the gulf between 'individual old' and 'impersonal new' may be the 'nineteenth century's most influential legacy for domestic design' (2009: 314). The hand-made inevitably usurps the machine-made in the quest for originality, freedom, spontaneity and human warmth. Antiques have stood the test of time; only the 'fittest' have survived. They stand as a guarantor of good taste.

NOTES

This research was made possible with a Henry Francis Du Pont Winterthur Museum and Library Fellowship.

1. The phrase, originally Bunyan's, was taken by Clarence Cook as the title of his book (1878) and purloined by Oscar Wilde for his American lecture (see Freedman 1990:106).
2. For the cult of individuality, see Judith A. Neiswander (2008), *The Cosmopolitan Interior Liberalism and the British Home 1870–1914*, New Haven and London: Yale University Press, and Deborah Cohen (2006), *Household Gods, The British and their Possessions*, New Haven and London: Yale University Press.
3. For a feminine version of modernity, see Alison Light (1991), *Forever England: Femininity, Literature and Conservatism between the Wars*, London: Routledge.
4. Mrs Lucy Orrinsmith (1839–1910) was the sister of Charles Faulkner, one of William Morris's 'Oxford Gang' and the first manager of Morris, Marshall, Faulkner & Co.
5. Inexpensive aniline dyes made brightly tinted fabrics affordable across a wide social spectrum; it was the German chemist Otto Unverdorben (1806–73) who created the first aniline dye from indigo in 1826. By the end of the 1860s, most natural colours could be produced synthetically.
6. Egg was inspired by Tom Taylor's play *Victims* (1857), a tale of 'ill-assorted marriages'.
7. Eastlake's term. For the 'retail tastemaker' see Clive Edwards (2005), *Turning Houses into Homes, A History of the Retailing and Consumption of Domestic Furnishings*, Aldershot: Ashgate.

8. Four volumes dealt specifically with aspects of interior decoration; the editor Rev William J Loftie (1839–1911), a learned author, antiquarian and editor of the *People's Magazine*, began the series with a volume advocating collecting and furnishing with antique furniture: *A Plea for Art in the House with Special Reference to the Economy of Collecting Works of Art and the Importance of Taste in Education and Morals* (1877), London: Macmillan (see Ferry 2003).
9. Mrs Jane Ellen Panton, the daughter of painter William Powell Frith, was a professional journalist and writer.
10. For a discussion of the Victorian rediscovery of the eighteenth century, see Linda Dowling (1977), 'The Aesthetes and the 18th Century', *Victorian Studies*, 20/4: 357–77.
11. See Peter Mandler (2006), *The English National Character: The History of an Idea from Edmund Burke to Tony Blair*, New Haven and London: Yale University Press.
12. Whistler moved to 101 Lindsey Row with his Old Blue china, Japanese fans and prints in 1863 (for Howell, see Anne Anderson (2010), 'The Pre-Raphaelite Lovejoy: Dante Gabriel Rossetti and Charles Augustus Howell, the Eponymous 'Dodgy Dealer', *The Review of the PRS*, 18/1: 21–9.
13. Encompassing Chinese K'ang Hsi porcelain (1662–1722), European Delft and early-nineteenth-century Staffordshire earthenware.
14. The model is thought to be his wife, Frances (Fanny) Theodosia Hubbarde, though most of her time was committed to raising their ever-growing family.

REFERENCES

Allen, G. (1877), *Physiological Aesthetics*, New York: D. Appleton.

Allen, G. (1880), 'The Philosophy of Drawing-Rooms', *Cornhill Magazine*, 41: 312–26.

Anderson, A. (2005), 'Doing As We Like: Grant Allen, Harry Quilter and Aesthetic Dogma', *Journal of Design History*, 18/4: 335–55.

Anderson, A. (2009a), '*Chinamania:* Collecting Old Blue for the House Beautiful c. 1860–1900', in J. Potvin and A. Myzelev, eds., *Material Cultures, 174–1920: The Meanings and Pleasures of Collection*, Aldershot: Ashgate: 109–28.

Anderson, A. (2009b), 'Rossetti's China: the Origins of 'Blue Mania' in the 1860s', *The Review of the Pre-Raphaelite Society*, XVII/2: 10–38.

Anderson A. (2010a), 'She Weaves by Night and Day, a Magic Web with Colours Gay: Trapped in the Gesamtkunstwerk or the Dangers of Unifying Dress and Interiors', in A. Myzelev and J. Potvin, eds., *Material Identities: Fashion and Interior Design*, Aldershot: Ashgate: 43–66.

Anderson, A. (2010b), 'The Pre-Raphaelite Lovejoy: Dante Gabriel Rossetti and Charles Augustus Howell, the Eponymous "Dodgy Dealer"', *The Review of the PRS,* 18/1: 21–9.

Anon (1881), *Artistic Homes or How to Furnish with Taste a Handbook for All Housekeepers*, London: Ward, Lock & Co.

Armstrong, N. (1990), 'The Occidental Alice', *differences: A Journal of Feminist Cultural Studies*, 2/2: 3–40.

Baudelaire, C. (1968), *Oeuvres complètes*, Paris: Éditions du Seuil.

Berman, M. (1983), *All That Is Solid Melts Into Air: The Experience of Modernity*, London: Verso.

Bollas, C. (1992), *Being a Character: Psychoanalysis and Self Experience,* New York: Hill and Wang.

Bronkhurst, J. (1984), 'The Awakening Conscience', *The Pre-Raphaelites*, exhibition catalogue, London: Tate Gallery, Cat.58.

Brown, B. (2001), 'Thing Theory', *Critical Inquiry Special Issue on Things*, 28/1: 1–22.

Brown, B. (2003), *A Sense of Things The Object Matter of American Literature*, Chicago: University of Chicago Press.

Calloway, S., and Orr, L. F. (2011), *The Cult of Beauty: The Aesthetic Movement 1860–1900*, exhibition catalogue, London: V&A.

Colomina, B. (1996), *Privacy and Publicity: Modern Architecture as Mass Media*, Cambridge, MA: MIT Press.

Cook, C. (1878), *The House Beautiful, Essays on Beds and Tables, Stools and Candlestick*, New York: Scribner, Armstrong & Co.

Cooper, H. J. (1876), *The Art of Furnishing on Rational and Aesthetic Principles*, London: Harry S. King.

Davis, O.W. (1886), *Instructions of the Adornment and Embellishment of Dwelling Houses Entitled Interior Decorating*, London: Windsor & Newton.

de Goncourt, E. (2003), *La Maison d'un artiste*, Dijon: L'Echelle, de Jacob.

Derry-Capon, D. (2009), 'Bourgeois Exoticism: The Woman Staged', in *Alfred Stevens, 1828–1906, Brussels-Paris*, exhibition catalogue, Brussels: Mercatorfonds: 149–75.

Dickens, C. (1964–65), *Our Mutual Friend*, Google Books: Digireads, 2009.

Draguet, M. (2009), 'Capitalism and Decoration: Alfred Stevens the Modern Poet', in *Alfred Stevens, 1828–1906, Brussels-Paris*, exhibition catalogue, Brussels: Mercatorfonds: 83–105.

Dunn, H. T. (1904), *Recollections of Dante Gabriel Rossetti and His Circle*, London: Elkin Mathews.

Eastlake, C. L. (1872), *Hints on Household Taste in Furniture, Upholstery and Other Details*, London: Longmans, Green & Co.

Ehrman, E. (2011), 'Artistic Interiors', in J. Sellars, ed., *Atkinson Grimshaw Painter of Moonlight*, exhibition catalogue, Harrogate and London: Mercer Art Gallery and the Guildhall Art Gallery: 87–111.

Eliot, G. (1876), *Daniel Deronda*, London: Wordsworth Editions, 1996.

Ferry, E. (2003), 'Decorators May be Compared to Doctors: An Analysis of Rhoda and Agnes Garrett's *Suggestions for House Decoration in Painting, Woodwork and Furniture*', *Journal of Design History Special Issue: Domestic Design Advice*, 16/1: 15–33.

Freedman, J. (1990), *Professions of Taste: Henry James, British Aestheticism and Commodity Culture*, Stanford, CA: Stanford University Press.

Gagnier, R. (1993), 'On the Insatiability of Human Wants: Economic and Aesthetic Man', *Victorian Studies*, 36/2: 125–53.

Gagnier, R. (1999), 'Productive Bodies, Pleasured Bodies: On Victorian Aesthetics', in T. Schaffer and K. A. Psomiades, eds., *Women and British Aestheticism*, Charlottesville: University Press of Virginia: 270–89.

Gaunt, W. (1954), *Chelsea*, London: B. T. Batsford.

Gower, Lord R. (1888), *Bric-A-Brac, Or, Some Photoprints Illustrating Art Objects At Gower Lodge, Windsor*, London: Kegan Paul, Trench & Co.

Halttunen, K. (1989), 'From Parlor to Living Room: Domestic Space, Interior Decoration and the Culture of Personality', in S. J. Bronner, ed., *Consuming Visions: Accumulation and Display of Goods in America, 1880–1920*, New York: W. W. Norton & Company: 157–90.

Hamilton, W. (1882), *The Aesthetic Movement in England*, London: Reeves & Turner.

Hamlett, J. (2010a), 'The Dining Room Should be the Man's Paradise, as the Drawing Room is the Woman's: Gender and Middle-class Domestic Space in England 1850–1910', in K. H. Adler and C. Hamilton, eds., *Homes and Home Comings: Gendered Histories of Domesticity and Return, Gender and History*, 21/3: 576–91.

Hamlett, J. (2010b), *Material Relations: Domestic Interiors and Middle-class families in England 1850–1910*, Manchester: Manchester University Press.

Haweis, Mrs H. R. (1878), *The Art of Beauty*, New York: Harper.

Haweis, Mrs H. R. (1881), *The Art of Decoration*, London: Chatto and Windus.

Haweis, Mrs H. R. (1889), *The Art of Housekeeping*, London: Sampson Low, Marston, Dearle and Rivington.

Hart, V. P. (1926), 'Antiques in Interior Decorating; Working with a Few Antique Pieces They May be Fitted in without Detracting from Their Charm', *The Antiquarian*, 5/6: 22–5.

Holden, Mrs J.M.S. (1882), 'Part Three Interior Decoration or How to Make Homes Beautiful', in A. C. Varney, ed., *Our Homes and Their Adornment or How to Build, Finish, Furnish and Adorn a Home*, Detroit: J. C. Chilton & Co: 214–300.

Holly, H. H. (1878), *Modern Dwellings in Town and Country Adapted to American Wants and Climate with a Treatise on Furniture and Decoration*, New York: Harper & Bros.

Humphreys, M. G. (1896), 'House Decoration and Furnishing', in *The House and Home a Practical Guide*, II, New York: Charles Scribner's Sons: 103–80.

James, H. (1908), *The Spoils of Poynton, The Novels and Tales of Henry James*, vol. 10, New York: Scribner's.

Kellogg, A. M. (1904), *Home Furnishing Practical and Artistic*, New York: Frederick A. Stokes Company.

Kerr, R. (1865), *The Gentleman's House, or, How to Plan English Residences, from the Parsonage to the Palace*, London: John Murray.

Kowaleski-Wallace, E. (1997), *Consuming Subjects: Women, Shopping and Business in the 18th Century*, New York: Columbia University.

Loftie, Mrs M. J. (1878), *The Dining Room*, Art at Home series, London: Macmillan & Co.

Loftie, Rev W. J. (1875), 'The Art of Furnishing', *Cornhill Magazine*, 31: 532–47.

Logan, T. (2000), *The Victorian Parlour*, Cambridge: Cambridge University Press.

Mariller, H. C. (1899), *Dante Gabriel Rossetti: an Illustrated Memorial of his Art and Life*, London: Bell.

Massey, A. (1990), *Interior Design of the 20th Century*, London: Thames and Hudson.

McCracken, G. (1988), *Culture and Consumption New Approaches to the Symbolic Character of Consumer Goods and Activities*, Bloomingdale: Indiana University Press.

Meynell, W. (1885), 'Laurens Alma-Tadema RA', in W. Meynell, ed., *The Modern School of Art*, vol. II, London: Cassell & Co: 1–22.

Muthesius, S. (2003), '*Patina:* Aspects of the History of the Look of Age in the Decorative Arts in the Late 19th Century', *Zeitschrift fur Kunsttechnologie un Konservierung*, 1: 138–42.

Muthesius, S. (2009), *The Poetic Home: Designing the 19th Century Domestic Interior*, London: Thames & Hudson.

Neiswander, J. A. (2008), *The Cosmopolitan Interior: Liberalism and the British Home 1870–1914*, New Haven: Yale University Press.

Nicholson, V. (2003), *Among the Bohemians Experiments in Living 1900–1939*, London: Penguin.

Oliphant, M. (1866), *Miss Marjoribanks*, London: Zodiac Press, 1969.

Orrinsmith, Mrs L. (1878), *The Drawing Room*, London: Macmillan & Co.

Panton, Mrs J. E. (1887), 'Artistic Homes and How to Make Them: The Drawing Room', *The Lady's World*, August: 344–7.

Panton, Mrs J. E. (1889), *Nooks and Corners*, London: Ward & Downey.

Psomiades, K. A. (1997), *Beauty's Body: Femininity and Representation in British Aestheticism*, Stanford, CA: Stanford University Press.

Quilter, H. (1880), '*The Cornhill* on Coal-scuttles', *The Spectator*, 17 July: 911–12.

Robertson, A. (1988), *Atkinson Grimshaw*, Oxford: Phaidon Press.

Ruskin, J. (1886), *Modern Painters*, vol. 4, New York: John Wiley & Sons.

Ruskin, J. (1903), *The Seven Lamps of Architecture*, London: George Allen.

Ruskin, J. (1910), 'Of Queen's Gardens', *Sesame and Lilies*, London: Collins.

Saisselin, R. G. (1984), *The Bourgeois and the Bibelot*, New Brunswick, NJ: Rutgers University Press.

Schaffer, T. (2000), *Forgotten Female Aesthetes: Literary Culture in Late Victorian Britain*, Charlottesville: University Press of Virginia.

Seale, W. (1975), *The Tasteful Interlude American Interiors through the Camera's Eye, 1860–1917*, New York: Praeger Publishers.

Sparke, P. (2008), 'The Crafted Interior: Else de Wolfe and the Construction of Gendered Identity', in S. Alfoldy and J. Helland, eds., *Craft, Space and Interior Design*, Aldershot: Ashgate: 123–38.

Spofford, H. P. (1878), *Art Decoration Applied to Furniture*, New York: Harper's.

Stewart, S. (1984), *On Longing: Narratives of the Miniature, the Gigantic, the Souvenir, the Collection*, Baltimore: Johns Hopkins University Press.

Stewart, S. (1994), 'Objects of Desire', in S. M. Pearce, ed., *Interpreting Objects and Collections*, London: Routledge: 254–57.

Suzuki, D.T. (1998), 'Zen and the Art of Tea', in C. Korsmeyer, ed., *Aesthetics: The Big Questions*, Oxford: Blackwell, 1998: 55–8.
Tange, A.K. (2008) 'Redesigning Femininity: 'Miss Marjoribank's Drawing-room of Opportunity', *Victorian Literature and Culture*, 36/1: 163–86.
Tange, A.K. (2010), *Architectural Identities: Domesticity, Literature and the Victorian Middle Class*, Toronto: Toronto University Press.
Trollope, A. (1991), *The Way We Live Now*, Oxford: Oxford University Press.
Vallance, A. (1904), 'Good Furnishing and Decoration of the House: The Drawing Room', *The Magazine of Art*, 2: 111–18.
Von Falke, J. (1878), *Art in the House Historical, Critical, and Aesthetical Studies on the Decoration and Furnishing of the Dwelling*, tr. C. C. Perkins, Boston: L. Prang & Co.
Wainwright, C. (1989), *The Romantic Interior The British Collector At Home, 1750–1850*, New Haven: Yale University Press.
Watson, R. M. (1897), *The Art of the House*, London: George Bell and Sons.
Waugh, E. (1928), *Rossetti: His Life and Works*, London: Duckworth.
Wharton, E., and Codman, O., Jr (1901), *The Decoration of Houses*, New York: Scribner's.
Wilde, O. (1999), 'House Beautiful', in *Collins Complete Works of Oscar Wilde*, centenary edn, Glasgow: Harper Collins: 913–25.
Wood, M. (2005) *Nancy Lancaster English Country House Style*, London: Frances Lincoln.

4.

DINING ROOMS: MEASURING THE GAP BETWEEN THE EDWARDIANS AND THE MODERNS

john c. turpin

The Western ritual of dining developed around the fire pit. In search of light and warmth, humans gravitated continuously toward the glowing embers to eat, gather and converse. As civilizations developed, manners and etiquette dictated socially accepted behaviours for all human interaction, but the act of consuming food proved to be the most challenging. The mouth's location on the face, a point of eye contact when communicating, drew unwanted attention when eating. The process was raw as teeth grinded, the tongue bulldozed, and saliva softened flesh before being dumped into the stomach. Of all the bodily functions, eating exposed part of its process to other humans and yet occurred most frequently in public situations or, at least, in the presence of others. An additional complication involved the mouth's role in communication, which quickly became an expected activity when consuming food with others.

With the institution of more civilized social rules and regulation, talking became the emphazis when dining in public. According to Boisse (1858):

It must not be imagined that the dinner to which you are invited, is simply given for the purpose of giving a gross and material pleasure; no, it is to put you in company with persons of consideration, and to give an opportunity to display your intelligence, or cause your good qualities to be appreciated in the species of demi-intimacy which may result from it. (quoted in Leland 1864: 128)

From Boisse's perspective, the act of eating—relegated to a 'gross' act—needed to be suppressed in favour of other more civilized activities. From a twentieth-century perspective, the art of conversation at the dinner table was a way for humans to 'rise above food' (Visser 1991: 262). Consequently, the quality of conversation experienced close scrutiny. In ancient Greece, passionate conversations ruled the day, but as time progressed Western societies began to control and temper the talking until English Victorian etiquette refined social intercourse in the dining room to a level of harmless, meaningless chatter that was prized more for its delivery than its content. In order to support, if not enhance, the art of conversation and dining, the space in which these activities collided had to be considered carefully.

Once the feeding of the family for survival was not the sole function of meal times, the dining room evolved into a physical manifestation of social expectations. The overall styling of the room reflected the fashion of the day, whether it was a progressive statement of modernism or a reaffirmation of historicism. The furniture and accessories, however, revealed a complicated set of rules and regulations for the ritual itself. Countless pieces of silverware, glassware, plate ware, serving dishes and utensils suggested that each guest had a working knowledge of how and when to use

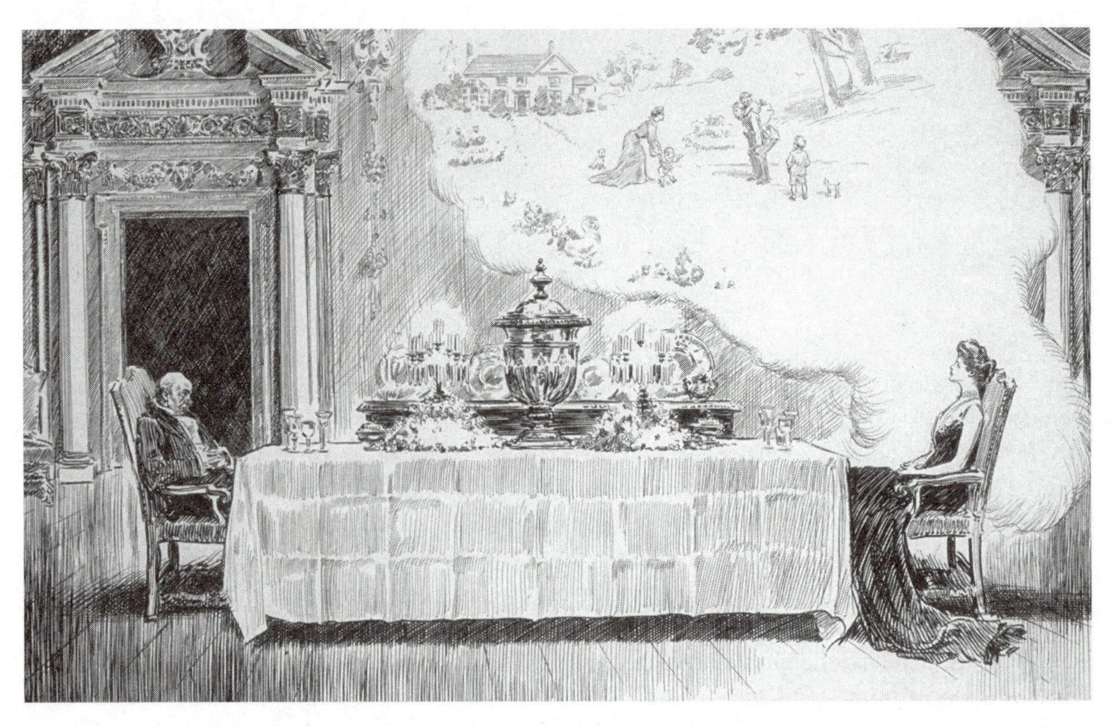

4.1. *A Castle in the Air* by Charles Dana Gibson from *Time & Life* (1903), 1 January. Photo: Charles Dana Gibson/Time & Life Pictures/Getty Images.

each artefact. The decorations on the table indicated the social significance of the ritual as beauty was an intended goal. In fact, Longstreet (1890) suggested that one should dress in his or her best clothes as an acknowledgement of the beauty of the decorated table and an attractive dinner. Everyone played a part in the beauty of the event, even the guests.

Nowhere else in the home did a single ritual define so much. Eating, which started out as a physical need for survival, transcended to Maslow's definition of self-actualization. The expression of identity through décor, social validation through etiquette, and social acceptance through conversation merged in the dining room to create an atmosphere—both physical and conceptual—that revealed the human desire to be more than a biological beast just trying to survive.

Two pieces of American art offer stark contrasts of the environment of the dining room—both physically and behaviourally—that occurred between 1900 and 1940 in the United States. Charles Dana Gibson's *A Castle in the Air* (1903; Figure 4.1) reveals a poignant moment in American history: the eventual decay of the Edwardian Age as experienced by America's leisure class. The formality and impersonality stand in opposition to Norman Rockwell's *Freedom from Want* (1943; Figure 4.2), which reveals a significant relaxing of the rules of décor and decorum. The physical

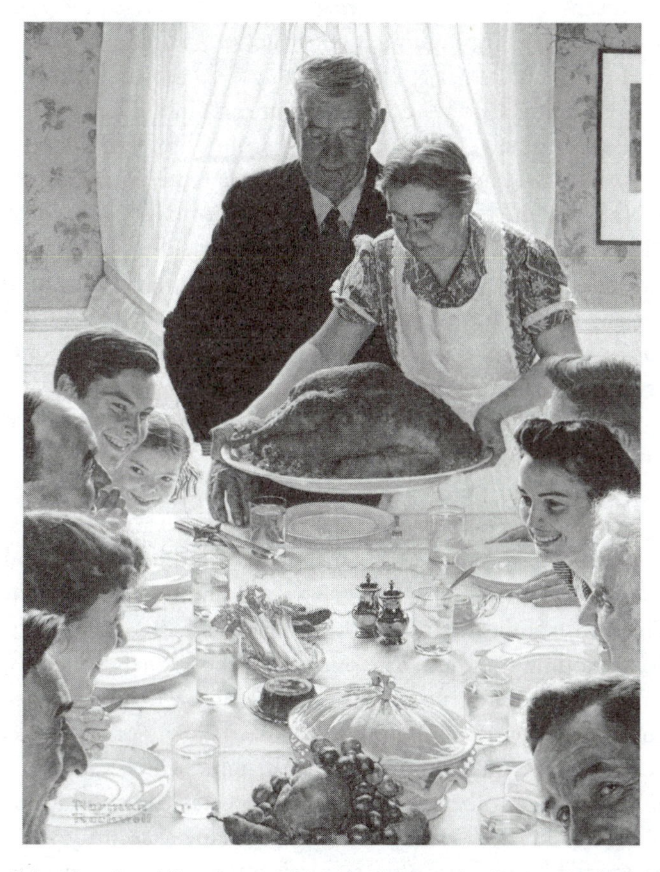

4.2. Norman's Rockwell *Freedom from Want* first published in the *Saturday Evening Post* (1943), 6 March: 10. Printed by permission of the Norman Rockwell Family Agency. Book Rights Copyright 1943 © The Norman Rockwell Family Entities.

and behavioural copies of upper-class European refinement that occurred in the United States lack cultural depth and are abandoned quickly as Americans experience modernity in the twentieth century in which a general simplification of décor and manners occur due to a new set of values driven primarily by the maturation of the middle class. No longer focused on desires of emulation, the middle class embarks on a life defined on what they have, not what they could have (Baritz 1989).

Social expressions can be both physical and abstract. Within the realm of the domestic environment, cultures utilize decoration and speech as core methods for communicating class values. The following discussion of changes in the dining room environment elucidate a shift away from the traditional values of the nineteenth century, which were based on European models, to a uniquely American experience that embraced freedom, self-expression and informality.

THEORETICAL FRAMEWORK

The domestic interior is a human construct (literally and conceptually) defined by objects. Architectural planes provide boundaries, furnishings articulate function, and decorative accessories and art stimulate the visual senses. In the realm of material culture, these objects convey meaning and express the identity of the owner through their construction, materiality and styling. Symbolic interactionists, such as Erving Goffman (1922–82), analyse the object from the standpoint of each user, believing that its meaning changes depending on each individual's interaction with the object. According to Csikszentmihalyi and Rochberg-Halton, objects in the domestic interior 'serve to socialize a person to a certain habit or way of life and are representative signs of that way of life' (1981: 21). The object transcends its base function and informs socially constructed, often class-defined, rituals and ceremonies. The study of objects has yielded important information about those who have used them, but what about the space around them? Can the absence of an object or the void reveal equally significant information?

A void in isolation is, in fact, a void—emptiness. However, when we redefine the void by specifying the 'space between', a relationship surfaces. Time and distance, measurements of temporal and physical space, become critical points of discussion in understanding the meaning of the objects, users and rituals embedded in the 'space between'.

The formal dining room is an excellent case study for such an endeavour because of the role it plays in Western society. Descendant of a ritual that dates back to the earliest civilizations, the formal dinner—in which a host demonstrates his or her social, economic and/or political power by selecting guests and providing food for them—is not about eating. Etiquette and decorating books during the nineteenth and early twentieth century make this clear to the reader; this literary genre continues a longstanding tradition. The purpose of the formal dinner is to socialize and gain a recognized place in society (e.g. Learned 1923; Stevens 1934). Being fed by someone else falls far below the importance of the invitation, which recognized the guest as an acceptable addition to the host's social circle, and the conversation around the table which validates the host's judgment that his or her guests are indeed to be his or her worthy peers. The decoration of the dining room communicates the host's good taste, social position and financial security.

The dining room 'space' houses many objects, receives the presence of people regularly and stimulates verbal communication, all while supporting one of the most basic human needs: the consumption of food. It is a decorated stage for a series of actors to perform a virtually predetermined script; that was how it was at least up until the early part of the twentieth century. Each of these components—the stage, the actors and the script—is very much defined by the space between. The interior is a careful orchestration of objects placed in relation to each other. Actors move to their designated spots where they intently await the delivery of their lines as defined by their necessary silence to allow others to speak. An examination of the space between is crucial for each and offers insight into the meaning embedded in these voids as measured by their separation.

TRADITIONAL SPACE: THE EXPANSION

The United States experienced a particular social challenge during the nineteenth century. The absence of a native hereditary aristocracy prevented the infusion of etiquette into a society whose masses were mainly middle class. Yet, the need for direction was becoming increasingly important during the eighteenth and nineteenth centuries as the young country moved onto a global political stage. Women quickly took charge of the issue of etiquette and were viewed as the principle guardians of decorum in the middle and upper classes. The dining room became the most significant domestic space in which one's manners were on display. One author during the early twentieth century summarized the relationship with great clarity. Richardson Wright, editor of *House & Garden*, believed the hall should be hospitable and the living room should be liveable, but that the dining room should be elegant. Elegance, he continued, 'is the concomitant of gentility and culture; a fundamental quality always active in certain strata of society and quiescent at least in others' (Wright 1920: 41). The upper class defined the active strata, while those in the middle class looked on with great interest, but little authority.

A Castle in the Air depicts a wealthy couple in the formal dining room. The accoutrements of wealth surround them, and the apparent and disproportionate amount of negative space around the table begs for guests to fill it. The backstory of this painting focuses on the unhappy bride who has married for money, not for love. Charles Dana Gibson, an American illustrator known for his mocking of the overly formulaic and prescribed life of the upper class, presents the unhappiness of the wife by revealing her dreams of life in a far less formal environment in the country—away from the unyielding rules of decorum of the nineteenth century. The dining room reflects a moment of transition in American society: the pomp and circumstance of the Gilded Age (c. 1860–1896) in the immediate past and the desire for a less restricted life in the future. The implied 'space between' sets up the temporal parameters of this discussion. An examination of this space in its final days of glory at the beginning of the twentieth century marks the experiences in the dining room that will linger in an ever-shrinking portion of American society.

The values of the upper class in virtually every society have remained unsurprisingly conservative, and thus static. Bank accounts, land holdings and successful businesses have provided them the means to acquire positions of social authority. Any change has suggested an unacceptable risk that their influence would be affected adversely. During the late nineteenth and early twentieth centuries, middle-class Americans attempted to emulate their social superiors because in the United States financial success—and thus social climbing—was possible. Examples abound and eventually the creation of a new class, the leisure class, also known as the *nouveaux riches*, occurred. With matching (if not surpassing) bank accounts, the *nouveaux riches* offered a challenge to the old guard's social superiority. The old guard shielded its position by tightening the rules of decorum. In order to master all of them, one had to have been born into a family that required them. Heritage or 'good breeding' became the barrier between the battling classes of the wealthy.

For the leisure class, etiquette was 'a code of unwritten laws for the protection and comfort of society' (Logan 1889) and a term applied to correct behaviour in social life (Morton 1908). Perhaps more importantly, and implied, etiquette supplanted the bank account as a means of defining someone from the 'superior' social class. Members of the old guard wielded etiquette to manufacturer a distance or 'space between' themselves and the rest of society—particularly the *nouveaux riches*. Numerous social rules adopted by the old guard created discrete physical and abstract voids.

Temporal manifestations of the void initiated the process of a formal dinner. Invitations, highly valued for their implications of social acceptance, had to be returned within small windows of time. 'No social obligation is more binding than that of returning a very prompt and very courteous answer to a dinner invitation' (Roberts 1913: 165). A day too early suggested unwanted eagerness—the calling card of the social climber; a day too late suggested an individual who could not manage time or was simply less than excited to attend. The latter implied that the invitee deemed the event a social obligation instead of a social privilege. The night of the formal dinner, guests had an even smaller time frame in which to arrive. 'Do not arrive even a minute late . . . nor 10 minutes early' (Longstreet 1890: 27).

Upon arrival, the guests became part of a masterfully orchestrated social mechanism. They were cogs in a machine that had to behave precisely in order for the event to have been considered a success and the individual to have been considered an appropriate member of the social elite. With the exception of having been escorted in as pairs, guests were not to touch each other at the table. One was not to lean across the table or too far toward their neighbours. Hands remained in the lap unless engaging the implements on the table. The chairs occupied by the guests implied powerful barriers, especially when considering they were often armless. The temptation was to move into the 'space between', but the mind had to persevere and etiquette had to prevail. Consider Charles Dana Gibson's *Studies in Expression: Showing a Newly Engaged Couple at Dinner* (Figure 4.3). The guests to the right and left of the new couple occupy the space between. The image is uncomfortable—even today—as viewers recognize a breach of propriety. Freud would certainly comment on the fact that the men move behind the young woman, and the older ladies intrude in front of the young man.

All of these rules suggest a clear social hierarchy between those who attended and those who did not, and even between the host or hostess and his or her guests, and the guests themselves. Even the requirement to address each other by using only proper names is an example of a social void (e.g. Thorpe 1896). Addressing someone by a prefix and his or her last name emphasizes temporal space (the time it takes to address someone) and enhances existing social structures. As the twentieth century progressed, middle-class couples begin to emulate the upper class by hosting formal dinners. Etiquette books abruptly warn the reader not to create an event beyond his or her means—to imply a social station that he or she does not occupy (e.g. Thorpe 1896; Morton 1908). Imitating the behaviour is acceptable, but imitating the social position is not.

Conversation was equally overburdened with rules and regulations, but it was perhaps even more terrifying since a guest automatically drew attention to himself or herself when speaking. The pace and tempo of conversation revealed the significance of audial voids. First and foremost, conversation played an important role in the event. It 'prevents the mind from dwelling on the grinding of the digestive mill' (Thorpe 1896). One had to know when to speak and when to listen. One

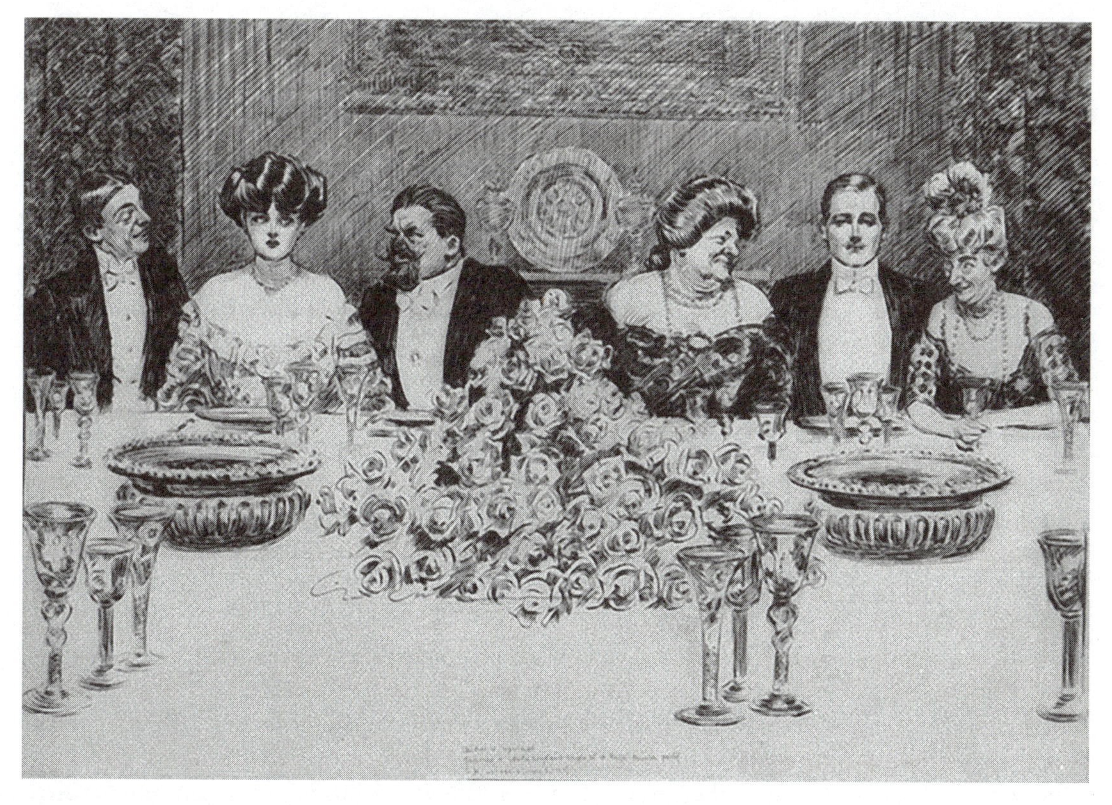

4.3. Charles Dana Gibson's *Studies in Expression: Showing a Newly Engaged Couple at Dinner.* First published in *Life* (1904), 43/5 May: 434–5. Located in the Cabinet of American Illustration, Library of Congress, United States.

never interrupted; the effect was similar to the guests entering the physical space of another. When speaking, the content revolved around topics everyone could appreciate and engage in. One could think of this as a way of actually creating a void or space that someone could enter. If a guest spoke about topics unfamiliar to others, then a barrier was created with no space for others to enter and participate. Authors also cautioned readers to avoid 'social deceptions' (Thorpe 1896; Morton 1908). Insincerity closed a space because no one wanted to enter it. Those who mastered the art of conversation were 'highly prized' and rewarded by their peers with honour and esteem (Bradley 1889: 339) because of the value Americans placed on this skill. In fact, supporting conversation was and is part of the function of the design and decoration of the dining room.

The layout of the dining room table was a complex orchestration of decorative objects, each with a very specific role in the ritual. However, voids or the space between were particularly significant in order to lubricate conversation. Logan stated, 'Decorations should not interfere with the guests' view of one another' (1889: 5). Floral decorations and the once-towering castor, a revolving stand for condiments that was the central glory of the dinner table, were not to be so bold as to fill the voids that offered visual access to other guests. At very large events, less concern was given to views across the full length of the table. The guests had to be able to see their neighbours and hosts. The accessible visual paths provided cues as toward whom one should focus their conversation and who was in control of the evening's events—the hostess, as a result of her social lineage with the famous French *salonnieres* of the eighteenth century (Sandra and Spayde 2001). However, the hostess was tested for her position in society by the accuracy of the table setting.

One place setting could easily require four forks, four knives, four spoons, two plates, four glasses and a napkin; each with a particular location as defined by its distance from other objects, as well as its temporal distance in the meal. The assembly depended on the number of courses. The Victorians sometimes had up to twelve. The meticulous layout of the objects reflected the hostess's knowledge of etiquette relative to orchestrating, planning and supervising a formal event. Servants received strict instructions as to the layout of each setting. Many carried measuring devices to assist in the proper placement of each item.

During the meal, when eating and conversation shared temporal space, diners faced a growing degree of complex situations. The consumption of food could easily affect the tempo of conversation. Too much space—or silence—was just as undesirable as not enough. Guests took small bites that could be chewed quickly and easily so that if a response was necessary, they could sustain the seemingly musical rhythm of the conversation. In this instance, décor, etiquette and conversation converged, and only the most well-bred individuals could manipulate all three simultaneously—at least according to the old guard. With little room for error, the socio-spatial problem begot the formality of the ritual.

Another instance in which the void had to be managed came near the end of the meal. As sparkling china, polished silver and cut glasses dwindled, the often white damask table cloth expanded undesirably. Morton's solution relied on the ever-present floral arrangements in the middle of the table. Without some element to fill the space between, 'the desert stretch of linen looked like the white ghost of famine mocking the feast' (Morton 1908: 74). Morton's statement emphasized the general importance of objects and their relationship to space.

Stepping away from the table itself, the dining room played an important role in the overall experience. Wright believed that the quality of the décor affected the perceived quality of the food and was crucial in establishing an atmosphere of elegance. 'Delight of eye is twin to delight of palate; difference between good hash and bad hash is how it is served and the room it is served in' (Wright 1915: 41). Interiors were to represent calm and order, which implied a formal approach. Consequently, historicism remained a dominant theme at the turn of the century, but it was tempered by a desire to create 'cheerful' or 'gay' spaces (e.g. Bradley 1889; Thorpe 1896; de Wolfe 1920; Wright 1915; Post 1930). This represents an aesthetic shift as the dull colours of the Victorian era gave way to proto-modern tendencies that valued light, colour and empty space. The Victorians feared space and consumed it through the display of countless machine-made objects. By the turn of the century, restraint had entered the American design lexicon thanks to decorators such as Elsie de Wolfe.

Authors encouraged viewers with greater frequency to allow the home to be a reflection of the inhabitant. Full agreement in how this was manifested does not exist. Wright believed the home should reflect the inhabitants' heritage. They were to avoid a composite of styles or the 'unorthodox nouveau art'. Rosiere agreed, but emphasized that the home was not be a museum; thus there was an attempt to reduce the temporal space between the inhabitant's past and present. It is perhaps not a surprise that Emily Post, a child of the Gilded Age, spoke passionately about the importance of heritage: 'Without it . . . what are we? Nameless, family-less—born in the foundling asylum' (1930: 495). She too opposed the modern style, and, in her case, the void was a social necessity to preserve the existence—customs, rituals and therefore relevance—of her social group.

Gibson's *A Castle in the Air* is a poignant critique of the upper class's ritual of dining, as well as an indication that the twentieth century values differed from those of the previous century. Gibson presents the viewer with a couple: an elderly, albeit rich, husband looking sternly across the table and the young wife who has slipped into a daydream of a 'better' life. The young woman marries the older gentleman for money—plain and simple. She and/or her family are social climbers or members of the old guard whose fortunes are waning with the passage of time. In stark contrast to her immediate surroundings, the wife imagines a life free of the rigid rules and restrictions that determine life in this social class. The value of a carefree life, one of informality, increases throughout the century as individuals seek greater personal expression and freedom.

Gibson's decision to depict the couple during a private, family dinner is powerful. The table sits ready for guests—a constant reminder of the woman's duty to entertain as part of her and her husband's social obligation. The desert stretch of linen dropping from the table surface exposes the absence of guests brutally and reinforces the loneliness in the image. The two armchairs express the couple's social entrapment. The large floral arrangements, candelabras and silver urn create physical barriers and absorb the space that would entice conversation between the couple. Gibson chose the backdrop with careful intention. Highly ornate, classical detailing—a favoured method of communicating wealth—stands stoically behind the husband, yet is somehow dwarfed by the much smaller country home and gracious fields seen in the wife's vision of happiness. Here, the shift between the nineteenth and twentieth centuries and formality and informality are clearly articulated.

Under the nineteenth-century social criteria of formal dinners, the image is depressing. The space overwhelms due to the absence of guests, which indicates their significance in defining the lives of the couple. The image depicts emptiness. The wife's dream of a better life, however, expresses a very different perception of void. On the one hand, space abounds, even more so than in the dining room. The absence of objects to define the 'space between', however, prevents the viewer from perceiving emptiness. The close relationship of the family in the dream, as evident by the physical contact, suggests that the space is for their pleasure, and their freedom—desire and ability to play or be informal—thus, allowing them to fill this space and preventing the viewer from seeing it as empty. With the progression of time, space collapses as twentieth-century values shift toward informality.

MODERN SPACE: THE COLLAPSE

In many ways, space began to collapse in conjunction with modern life in the twentieth century. Various advancements in transportation shrank time and distance: radio informed at lightning speed, the telephone permitted (and demanded) more immediate responses, and countless other new technologies, especially in the kitchen, began to reduce social distances at least in that fewer families maintained servants in the home. Sociopolitical distances shrank as government regulations attempted to protect the public, women gained the right to vote and America experienced the humbling Great Depression. Finally, World War II united a nation, and as a result, the middle class began to redefine its values. They chose to live well as opposed to living the good life as defined by the upper class. Perhaps more aptly stated by Carilyn Stevens, the middle class no longer chased the 'grand manner' (1934: 34).

By the turn of the twentieth century, basic etiquette regressed as the bustling American city interfered with ceremonious intercourse. The increased tempo of daily life encouraged a greater desire to relax during free time as opposed to perform (Webster and Hopkins 1930). An added obstruction was the exodus to the suburbs, which physically limited social interaction (Schlesinger 1946). The Roaring Twenties dealt a hard blow to decorum. America shared in its first major victory in a world war, the economy was strong, and prohibition spawned the speakeasy. According to Helen Sprackling, 'Good manners became a sign of social weakness' (1953: 3). Doris Webster and Mary Alden Hopkins, editors of *Mrs. Grundy is Dead*, surveyed college students on their views of etiquette. The respondents interpreted their parents' habits as 'stiff and ridiculous' (1930: 58). Being less punctilious, less laboured and obvious, more flexible and more informal were more acceptable traits.

As a consequence, dining became a lost art and entertaining diminished to a free-for-all (Sprackling 1953: 3). Advice books told the tale. Ellin Learned (1923) informed her readers that short dinners with fewer courses were the new fashion in the early 1920s. The event did not require long periods of 'chatting' in the drawing room. Less time eating and speaking at a formal dinner alleviated guests from performing within the strict boundaries of Edwardian etiquette. Strictly formal dinners became even more rare—not surprisingly—through the 1930s. Lillian Reid (1940) recognized such events were beyond the average purse and too ceremonious for the enjoyment of most. The reference to 'most' marks the gradual shift of the middle class toward a more informal lifestyle. Cocktail parties made their debut in the twentieth century and become an instant hit. They took much less time and allowed someone to meet their social obligations all at once by inviting a much larger number of people than would have been possible for a formal dinner (Moats 1933).

Norman Rockwell's iconic *Freedom from Want* articulates with great power the shift in American values. The painting is similar to *A Castle in the Air* in many ways. Many Americans, no matter what their social status, celebrate Thanksgiving as a formal dinner. Guests are invited to share in a ritual of eating and conversation. The table is set with great care using the finest plates and silverware. The ceremony of presenting the food exceeds normal expectations for a family gathering. However, in relation to Gibson's piece, Rockwell's is more informal and thus space, according to the author's hypothesis, should be treated differently.

Etiquette has not lost its influence over human behaviour—and likely never will. Certain general rules still apply. For example, guests are not supposed to nudge or slap each other at the table. Personal space is still respected, but that spatial bubble has shrunk significantly. The guests in *Freedom from Want* lean far over the table in order to make deeper personal connections with whomever they are speaking. The barrier directly above the table that was previously an important space between guests and the objects on the table is now being shared. The furniture lacks the perceived restrictions it had at the turn of the century. Space in an informal setting ignores the same edges or barriers as space in a formal setting.

The space between social classes has also collapsed. Families and their guests may range in economic status, but that is of no importance. The event itself denies the recognition of financial bias. Rockwell makes this point clear with the gentlemen in the bottom right hand corner who peers out of the frame and at the viewer. The viewer, no matter who they are, has been invited to participate in the feast because middle-class American's value family and having food on their table—not social pretence, economic status and rigid rules of etiquette.

The table is still set with military precision, according to Lillian Reid (1940), but it can be done with a set of individual knives, forks and spoons, and a few serving pieces, in recognition of the general move toward more informal dining. The guests at the Thanksgiving feast are sitting at just such a table. However, although the place settings are accurate, the centre of the table lacks the order of the Edwardian Age. The space between the salt-and-pepper shakers, celery dish, aspic and large silver serving dish is carefree and random. The placement of the objects does not suggest regulation, but convenience and practicality. The objects are within easy reach and may be passed when required by another guest—a necessity now that servants are not part of the home and each guest does not have his or her own salt cellar. Most noticeably, the table offers no visual obstructions. Objects are not on display. People are here to interact.

The rules for conversation changed as the strict formality of the Edwardian Age fell out of favour. Etiquette books may have continued to suggest certain guidelines. One should have still been able to listen and then respond in a pleasing voice (Reid 1940); conversation remained a 'duet, not a duel' (Priestley 1926: 43). However, multiple conversations existed in one space. Speaking mainly to one's neighbour was less of a requirement. Individuals with unique life experiences came to the table to share. The space filled with pairs and small groups of guests engaged in expressing their lively opinions or recanting stories of humour, intrigue or even daily life. The sacredness of formal space and its control yielded to freedom of expression. Reid went so far as to suggest that guests should 'draw people into . . . [the] story' (or draw them into your space) by reflecting on feelings of inadequacy or embarrassment during a certain situation (Reid 1940: 221). The admittance of human inadequacy created a safe space for others to share similar experiences without being judged.

The Great Depression's effect on every aspect of human life likely played a significant role in the relaxing of rules. It would have seemed impractical to be so concerned with formal etiquette at a time when many had so little to eat. These types of experiences became the hallmark of daily conversation and reflected Reid's suggestion above that allowed people to find solace in those who have shared difficult times as well. The tension felt by so many even required etiquette to bend in a way that would have seemed incomprehensible to the nineteenth-century formal dinner guest. At the close of the 1930s, Goodrich noted that 'pleasant disagreement' became acceptable as long as it was delivered in a pleasant manner (1939: 42).

Norman Rockwell's *Freedom from Want* captured the spirit of middle-class America in the 1940s. Modernity brought forth many changes in American values. Two world wars and the Great Depression sobered the American dream. The goal of living happily with friends and family supplanted the desire for extreme wealth. The middle class would continue to desire progress, just not at the pace experienced during the Reconstruction Era. Spatial distances decreased significantly as families yearned to be closer together. With the acute awareness of human mortality, Americans embraced space as something to be shared, something that allows intimacy, something that assures the family is safe. Along with the technological advancements in transportation and communication, temporal spaces offer fewer hindrances and permit conversations to conceptually eradicate any distance. Informality abhors space.

CONCLUSION

According to Peter Quennell, 'Between conversation and civilization, the art of talking and the art of living, there has always been a vital link' (1980: 9). The relationship between the stage, the actor and the performance is inextricably linked in the social orchestration of human interaction.

Both etiquette and decoration 'express the progress of civilization . . . both [are] a way of choosing language that reflects the presence of some cultural framework for organizing many kinds of human experiences' (Grier 1988: 1). Clearly, frameworks change. In this case, the dining room as a private residential space was witness to significant shifts in values as Americans experienced the tumultuous first half of the twentieth century. While the modern era offered the potential of hope and prosperity through social (e.g. Progressive Era) and technological advancements, the actual events of the early twentieth century forced a re-examination of values. The meteoric rise of many American families into the upper echelons of society, because of fortunes made in any number of industrial endeavours during the Reconstruction Era, invigorated the American dream and the desire of the middle class to attain it. However, World War I, the Great Depression and World War II forced a reordering of values in which economic advancement fell below freedom, self-expression and individuality.

The formality that defined the Edwardian Age—and much of the last half of the nineteenth century—relied on the creation and adoption of social systems that intentionally created a space between humans and objects, both literally and metaphorically. The goal was the preservation of an aristocratic society that wielded much of the social and political power in the United States. In an attempt to mimic social superiors, the middle class adopted the behaviours of those superiors in preparation of a potential ascent on the social ladder. The American Civil War, now in the past, was certainly not going to happen again. However, the American spirit was tested with the events that followed.

Civil liberties and technological advancements may have begun the social levelling process, but the horrors of war and the humbling Great Depression made 'space' a cruel void that housed fear, hunger and utter sadness. Americans at every social level attempted to obliterate that void by filling it with loved ones and opportunities for personal expression and self-actualization. The informality that washed over the American social landscape brought the void into the light and made it much more of a shared space. The idea is certainly not to suggest that formal dinners or occasions were not desirable—*Freedom from Want* proves otherwise—but that formality as a means of culturally defining a social system lost its grip and the American middle class found bliss in the simple pleasures of cocktail parties, picnics in the backyard and family dinners.

Looking at the absence of objects offers a different perspective for understanding social behaviour. By examining the space between, stylistic trappings or physical manifestations of wealth become irrelevant. The object no longer distracts us. The intent of creating space and the rules for its use provide equally revealing information. For example, a formal dinner could use plastic knives and plates. Does the materiality of the object make it less formal if it is set in the grand manner of the Edwardians and behaviour responds similarly? Does a picnic with fine silver and china become a formal dinner? Another way to validate the significance of understanding the void or space between is to reconsider *A Castle in the Air* and *Freedom from Want*. The latter literally has fewer material objects, but arguably actually has 'more' in that familial relationships are treasured far above the objects on the table.

An analysis of the physical and temporal space between objects in the dining room removes the gossamer intentions of the Edwardians whose way of life was slowly fading into oblivion—the ultimate space of fear. The room can be read from the view of the negative in order to understand mechanisms in which humans attempt to exert control shrouded by rules of formality. As the century progresses, space becomes the unintended battleground between the classes in the United

States. Some wish to expand space, while others desire its continued collapse. The core issue has not changed. The determination of space is a reflection of class values.

REFERENCES

Baritz, L. (1989), *The Good Life: The Meaning of Success for the American Middle Class*, New York: Alfred A. Knopf.

Boisse, Baron de Mortemart (1858), *La Vie Elegante a Paris*, Paris: Hachette.

Bradley, J. (1889), *Modern Manners and Social Forms*, Chicago: James B. Smiley.

Csikszentmihalyi, M., and Rochberg-Halton, E. (1981), *The Meaning of Things: Domestic Symbols and the Self*, London: Cambridge University Press.

de Wolfe, E. (1920), *The House in Good Taste*, New York: Century Company.

Goodrich, L. (1939), *Living with Others: A Book on Social Conduct*, New York: American Book Company.

Grier, K. (1988), *Culture and Comfort: Parlor Making and Middle-class Identity, 1850–1930*, Washington, DC: Smithsonian Institution Press.

Learned, E. (1923), *Everybody's Complete Etiquette*, New York: Frederick A. Stokes.

Leland, C. (1864), *The Art of Conversation with Directions for Self Education*, New York: Carleton.

Logan, M. (1889), *The Home Manual: Everybody's Guide in Social, Domestic, and Business Life*, Philadelphia: Thompson Publishing.

Longstreet, A. (1890), *Dinners: Ceremonious and Unceremonious and the Modern Methods of Serving Them*, New York: Frederick A. Stokes.

Moats, A. (1933), *No Nice Girl Swears*, New York: Alfred A. Knopf.

Morton, A. (1908), *Etiquette*, Philadelphia: Penn Publishing.

Post, E. (1930), *The Personality of a House: The Blue Book of Home Design and Decoration*, New York: Funk & Wagnalls.

Priestley, J. B. (1926), *Talking: An Essay*, New York: Harper & Brothers.

Quennell, P. (1980), *Affairs of the Mind: The Salon in Europe and America from the18th to the 20th Century*, Washington, DC: New Republic Books.

Reid, L. (1940), *Personality and Etiquette*, Boston, MA: Little, Brown and Company.

Roberts, H. (1913), *The Cyclopedia of Social Usage: Manners and Customs of the Twentieth Century*, New York: G. P. Putnam's Sons.

Sandra, J., and Spayde, J. (2001), *Salons: The Joy of Conversation*, Gabriola Island, BC: New Society Publishers.

Schlesinger, A. (1946), *Learning How to Behave: A Historical Study of American Etiquette Books*, New York: Macmillan.

Sprackling, H. (1953), *Setting Your Table: A Complete Guide to China, Glass, Silver, Linens, Flower Arrangements, and Etiquette*, New York: M. Barrows.

Stevens, C. (1934), *Etiquette in Daily Living*, Chicago: Associated Authors Service.

Thorpe, R. (1896), *As Others See Us or the Rules and Customs of Refined Homes and Polite Society*, Detroit: F. B. Dickerson.

Visser, M. (1991), *The Rituals of Dinner: The Origins, Evolution, Eccentricities and Meaning of Table Manners*, New York: Grove Weidenfeld.

Webster, D., and Hopkins, M., eds., (1930), *Mrs. Grundy is Dead*, New York: Century Company.

Wright, R., ed., (1915), *Inside the House of Good Taste*, New York: McBride, Nast & Company.

Wright, R., ed., (1920), *House & Garden's Book of Interiors*, New York: Conde Nast.

5. STUDIOS: LIVE (RED) MATTER; MATISSE'S *L'ATELIER ROUGE*

julieanna preston

METHOD MATTERS

Since its creation in 1911, Henri Matisse's *l'Atelier Rouge* (*The Red Studio*) has been the subject of criticism amongst art historians, most of whom attempt to contextualize its meaning and mastery (or lack thereof) within a specific social and cultural milieu. That this painting appears to represent a furnished room, perhaps even Matisse's own home studio, lends to its value as a reflection of modern domestic interiors. Hence, this painting conjures the confluence of two established lines of inquiry: fine art criticism and interior design theory. Together they employ a dominant method of 'reading' a text or a work of art from a semiotic perspective, an approach that seeks to find meaning from the study of signs, processes, designation, likeness, analogy, metaphor, signification and communication. Examination of this painting has historically concentrated on the symbolic inferences produced in the painting's use of colour, its stylistic relation to Fauvism, its alignment with the artist's biography and its composition. And yet I sense that there is something more to this picture.

My search for an expanded view gravitates towards Mieke Bal and Norman Bryson's position on the prevailing use of semiotics to contextualize a work in a positivistic manner. 'When a particular work of art is placed "in context," it is usually the case that a body of material is assembled and juxtaposed with the work in question in the hope that such contextual material will reveal the determinants that make the work of art what it is' (Bal and Bryson 1991: 176–7). All of the contextualizing factors are assumed to merge and terminate at the work of art itself. This presumes that works are singular in time and place, instead of, as Bal and Bryson argue, repeatable and iterative and part of a plurality that

> is subject to all of the vicissitudes of reception; as a work involving the sign, it encounters from the beginning the ineradicable fact of semiotic play. The idea of convergence, of causal chains moving toward the work of art, should, in the perspective of semiotics, be supplemented by another shape: that of lines of signification opening out from the work of art, in the permanent diffraction of reception. (Bal and Bryson 1991: 179)

To summarize, the context for a work is never given, simple, natural, limited nor the product of truth-seeking and historical accuracy; it is an open and interpretive construction inclusive of the author's and the receiver's interaction in that practice (Bal and Bryson 1991: 175). This said, such antirealist semiotic practice is human-centred.

How might a material-centric semiotic practice work? What if *The Red Studio*, Matisse, his home studio, its furniture, its decorations and many other 'vicissitudes of reception', including those prompted by material objects, were part of an elaborate network of relational, live, spatial and politically charged things? What might occur if Jane Bennett's special strain of actor-network theory (ANT) called 'vibrant matter' embraced *The Red Studio* such that the lines of flight (Latour and Yeneva 2008: 82), not signification, opened out from the work of art? This method would highlight ANT's propensity to serve as a travel guide where it does not map what lies between here or there or highlight the known landmarks; these are signs of what has already been charted. Instead, practitioners are lent how-to advice to what is possible or, in other words, what has yet to be mapped. ANT is the mapping process itself (Latour 2005: 23). A brief summary of ANT's basic principles will assist to navigate within a realm of knowledge that has not, until recently, been a part of design's discourse.[1]

Actor-network theory was first developed in the early 1980s by Michael Callon, Bruno Latour and John Law at the Centre de Sociologie de l' Innovation (CSI) of the École nationale supérieure des mines de Paris. Geared towards understanding processes of innovation and knowledge-creation in science and technology, their research collectively articulates an affirmative, productive and affective mode of what it is to be social. Their efforts, along with many others, imagine the benefits of employing ANT not as a theory but. instead, as a 'material semiotics' method constantly circulating between materials and concepts. The name 'actor-network theory' demonstrates this point: as a constellation of assembled relations, a network emerges as a result of ongoing responsive interaction between actors (or actants as Latour calls them). This is ANT's performative attribute. An actant is anything that has efficacy; the ability to alter the course of events, produce effects, or make a difference, and a network is the relational conduit between actants (quite distinct from computer networks) (Law and Hassard 1999: 3–9).

ANT has three distinguishing attributes: first, an ANT project will avoid stabilizing what it is to be social; it will not restrict connective associations. Second, ANT seeks to overcome dispersion, destruction and deconstruction. It is solely concerned with future thinking with a view towards 'new institutions, procedures and concepts able to collect and reconnect the social' (Law and Hassard 1999: 11). (This characteristic distinguishes ANT from postmodern critique.) And third, ANT asserts that humans (subjects) and nonhumans (objects) are actants. Agency, the power, authority or force to incite action, is attributed to neither. Instead, agency proliferates in heterogeneous associations developing in the assemblage of things. 'Nonhumans have to be actors and not simply the hapless bearers of symbolic projection' (Latour 2005: 10). All things are relational; sociability is a relational condition not exclusive to humans.

ANT resists the use of binaries that reinforce essentialist concepts. It upsets the anthropological and heterogeneous traditions of thinking (and acting) in nature/culture and subject/object paradigms, and, in doing so, ANT reconsiders the hierarchical nature of power relationships; rather than seek unity across a spectrum of actants or networks, it welcomes the realities (and possibilities) that dissonance or non-coherence offers to keep matters mobile and open.

In the past two decades, ANT has been adopted as a methodological tool in a range of fields including anthropology, economics, feminist studies, geography, health studies, informatics, organizational analysis and sociology, and, in the case of this chapter, art and interior design. One of the most lucid ANT variants is Jane Bennett's notion of vibrant matter. In her advocacy of material's power to invoke a difference, she attempts to overturn the artificial divide between that which is deemed to be passive, raw and inert substance (material things) and that which has had privilege as animate, cultured and alive (human things). Here we find her challenging modernity's definition of nature as mechanistic and lifeless; this acts to demystify the messiness and unruliness of bodies and the world as well as perpetuate a seemingly insatiable state of consumption. Geared towards realizing new modes of freedom and sustainability in the pursuit of human survival and happiness, her project imagines a new ecologically based economy guided by this question: 'How would political responses to public problems change were we to take serious the vitality of (nonhuman) bodies?' (Bennett 2010: viii) Bennett's mappings offer assemblage-forming narratives that engage materials, objects and systems common to everyday life. In an interview with Peter Gratton, a professor of philosophy, Bennett states, 'My political strategy is indirect because its target is not the macro-level politics of laws, policy, institutional change but the micro-politics of sensibility-formation' (Gratton 2010).

Led by Matisse's search to create a logic of sensation (Labrusse 2005: 298) and Jane Bennett's philosophy of vibrant matter, this chapter assembles a sensibility-forming narrative catalyzed by *The Red Studio*. It is a practice of material semiotics that operates through descriptive narrative rather than foundational theory. It respects John Law's insistence that ANT emphasizes how things happen over explaining why. Rather than theorize,

> it tells stories about 'how' relations assemble or don't . . . It is better understood as a toolkit for telling interesting stories about, and interfering in, those relations. More profoundly, it is a sensibility to the messy practices of relationality and materiality of the world. Along with this sensibility comes a wariness of the large-scale claims common in social theory: these usually seem too simple. (Law 2007: 2)

AT FIRST SIGHT

I am standing in gallery six, floor five of the Museum of Modern Art (MoMA) in New York, a room of white surfaces propping up a handful of paintings pivotal to the emergence of modern art. There it hangs—the painting I have been seeking—Henri Matisse's 1911 painting *L'atelier rouge* (*The Red Studio*; see Figure 5.1). Larger in both directions than I am tall, the painting dominates my view. From across the room, it conveys a flatness made familiar by all the web sites and art books I have accessed the past three decades. I am stunned by how it commands the space but fails

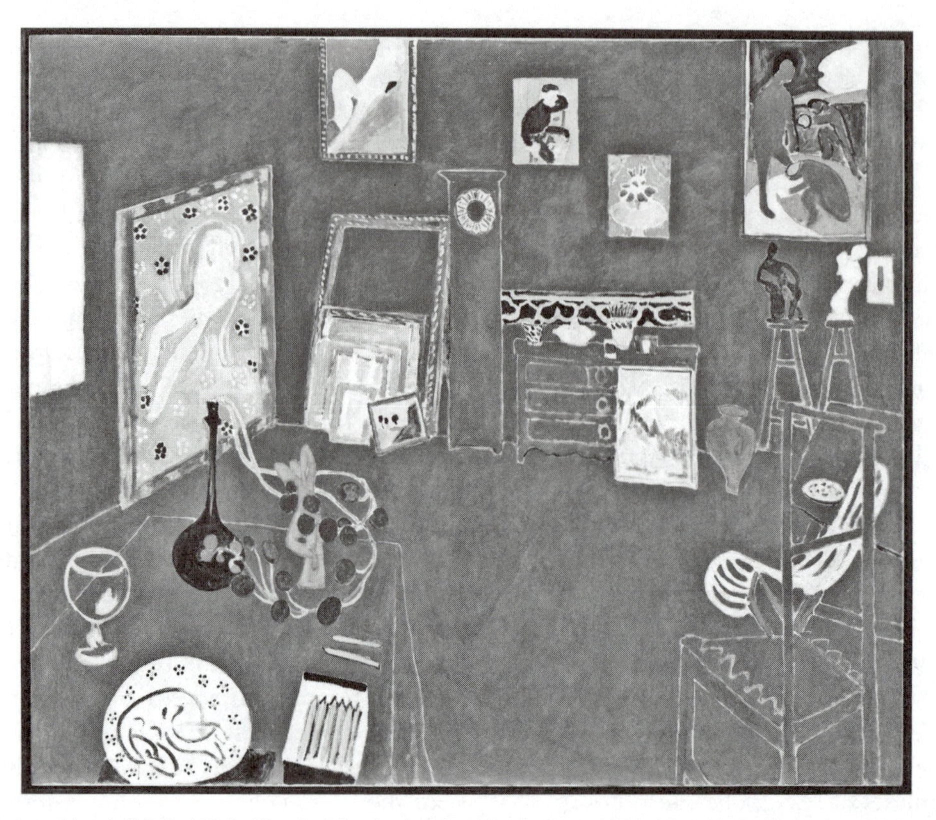

5.1. Matisse, Henri (1869–1954): *The Red Studio*. Issy-les Moulineaux, 1911. New York, Museum of Modern Art (MoMA). Oil on canvas, 7' ¼" x 7' 2¼" (181 x 219.1 cm). Mrs. Simon Guggenheim Fund. Acc. n.: 8.1949. © 2011. Digital image, The Museum of Modern Art, New York/Scala, Florence and Photo: Archives Henri Matisse.

to have an atmospheric effect. Is this the fault of the museum's stark neutrality or my expectations that this painting would compel an environmental impact?

Matisse painted *The Red Studio* at the commission of his long-time and primary patron, Russian art collector and textile merchant Sergei Shchukin (Labrusse 2005: 296). If not for the public scandal over its unmodulated colour, its eupeptic brush strokes and its disregard for pictorial conventions, it would have been one of numerous works by Matisse decorating a small domestic parlour in Shchukin's home, the Trubetskoy Palace in Moscow. How ill at ease it might have been in a culture still endeared to landscape realism, and yet how at home it might have been amongst the deep reds and gilds of Russian icons. Too foreign, not familiar enough, Shchukin rejected *The Red Studio* (Kostenevich n.d.).

The Red Studio hangs subdued by MoMA's the gallery dedicated to the early moderns, where 'its masterpieces, beyond their individual merits, serve a higher purpose: to spread the gospel of modern art' (Lubow 2004). This masterpiece offers no visible resistance to the décor of hardwood floors and smooth gypsum walls of a 'stark museological pantheon' (Lubow 2004). The room is conceptually vibrant but audibly silent. Was this what American art historian and MoMA founding director, Alfred Barr, saw and heard when he coined Matisse's *The Pink Studio*, *Painter's Family*, *Interior with Aubergines* and *The Red Studio* as the symphonic interiors? If so, this is a far cry from the scene of people laughing in fits and scratching at the canvases, and a critic exclaiming, 'A pot of paint has been flung in the face of the public' at the first Fauvist exhibition at Salon d'Automne, Paris, 1905.[2] Matisse was the Fauvist leader. How unlikely that heckles of 'barbaric', 'uncivilized', 'pictorial aberrations' and 'unspeakable fantasies' would even be whispered here today (Matisse: Life and Painting n.d.; Elliot n.d.). How tame this room of modernist paintings is! Where are those invertebrates, those incoherents, those wild beasts?[3] Are they trapped behind the plaster that covered over the beige burlap called 'monk's cloth' that Barr used to clad the museum walls along with his free-flowing charts mapping the evolution of modern art as it happened (Lubow 2004)? The smell of woven jute and linseed oil–based paint must have paid tribute to the Fauves 'spontaneity and roughness of execution as well as their use of raw color straight from the palette to the canvas,' yet more importantly, how they promoted 'a way less of seeing the world than of feeling it with one's eyes' (Matisse: Life and Painting n.d.).

As I venture within arm's reach of the canvas, the immensity of red generates a liminal threshold.[4] I can feel it vibrating my retina. Mesmerized by animal or vegetal magnetism, I struggle to identify its materiality. Its substance does not appear singular or uniform but, instead, embodies some kind of concoction smeared across the canvas, perhaps a mixture of autumn light, curry, seared peppers and iron-rich clay, ground up ground, blood and bone meal, a slow-releasing, organic, nitrogen-rich fertilizer transforms curvaceous decorative motifs from simple visual stimulation to sensorial delight.

The gallery is void of any physical signs of creature comfort; the only chairs available are a representational pair of stools in the painting serving as pedestals to small figurines and a straight ladder-backed dining seat. They are caught up in the painting as mere outlines, suggestive of their immersion into material abstraction. Matisse acknowledged that he dreamt of an art that had 'a soothing, calming influence on the mind, something like a good armchair which provides relaxation from physical fatigue' (Matisse 1908: 38), a statement that likely drew criticism of *The Red Studio* as 'a perfected expression of bourgeois affluence and decoration' (Müller-Tamm 2005: 18). It confounds me how a simulacrum could be a satisfactory substitute for a cushion as it hardly offers the same kind of comfort that oscillates between material fit to a physical body and emotional, spiritual or moral contentment (Crowley 1999: 751). I weigh the pros and cons of succumbing to the floor's beckoning surface, an impropriety in public space but a frequent luxury at home and certainly, the site of where all good things happen in my home-studio practice. Instead, the canvas lures me into its perspective.

IN A (FLAT) ROOM

The conventions of pictorial representation portray *The Red Studio* as the space of an inhabitable room. Perspectival construction lines prevent one from getting lost in the monotone colour (Matisse: Life and Painting n.d.). As such, the lines manage the objects within the picture plane, ensuring that they adhere to laws of gravity—that is, a vase rests on a table, a chair stands upright in opposition to the floor and paintings lean upon or hang against a wall. The flat surface of paint persuades my eyes to see volumetric mass just shy of donning material substance. Like a detective, if I consider the value of each object, its adjacency and posture to other objects, I should be able to extracted meaning from this intimate and domestic scene, an approach cited as a one of the closed aesthetic systems of modernist art (O'Doherty 2007: 6). Given that the centrally located clock has no hands, the interior looks to be stable and fixed (MoMA PS1 n.d.), an appearance also blamed on the power and beauty of perspective drawing (Latour and Yeneva 2008: 81). But appearances can be deceiving.

Matisse was well-known for the manner in which he drew on walls from a distance using a very long stick. Recalling the numerous images of this act, I step back from the painting and the wall approximately the same distance and reach out as if to redraw the chair in view. My clumsy gesture follows the chair's profile and extends the notion of instrumentality to a phenomenal experience that might have 'played with paint' (Alpers 2010: 134). Before my own eyes and by my own hand, the chair as a thing is made new in itself. My body, my arm, the imaginary stick and the canvas are conduits to the experience of making things sensible, making things present.

Shadowed by the museum docent, I scrutinize how brushstrokes might expose technical and conceptual conflation. To my surprise, the lines hinting of distorted perspective are not inscribed into the cadmium membrane but, instead, they are a space of absence that sections the overall field. A fragile radiance of white canvas segregates figure from ground and prevents edges of paint feigning as 'an artificial Oriental paradise' from mingling (Spurling 2005: 80). The brushstrokes lap up in unison against the reserve line demarcating an illusory fiction of room. Wild, raw, red figures[5] leap out as a result of these domesticating contours. Figure and ground are inverted. Together they consume the room's architecture. No longer governed by 'allegory', figures approximating chairs, a clock, a vase, a bureau, a plate, pencils, an easel and paintings drift loosely, tethered and semi-submerged in a viscous pool of 'primordial' and 'profane' scarlet fluid (Spurling 2005: 80).

The swelling relief of paint on the canvas returns the moist force of my breath just as the docent signals for me to step away. I relocate myself to the far side of the gallery and bolster my jetlagged body against the sharp edge of a door frame. Like the painting, everything is both far and near, condensed to a surface. Her glaring sneers guard the painting. I see red. Perhaps she will be swallowed up in the fictive depth of the churning surface where she would be trapped in the formidably flat room/plane as the classic female figure,[6] missing from view and disrupting the unity and sanctity of this still life scene[7] (Müller-Tamm 2005: 19).

A chime sounding the end of open hours breaks my fantasy, and in haste I snap a few illicit photos of the painting in situ before making a quick exit. A closed circuit television security camera perched in the corner eyes me up as prey. From behind inoperable windows, the late afternoon sun herds gaggles of museum visitors to the congested street below which is steadily filling with noxious fumes and impatient horns bound for the suburbs, a mass retreat away from the urban chaos to the comfortable chairs of home.

THE INTERIOR OF MATISSE'S HOME STUDIO

That *The Red Studio* describes not just any room, but the interior of Matisse's own studio is plausible. In the summer of 1911, Henri Matisse shifted his residence and studio practice to Issy-les-Moulineaux, a suburb fifteen minutes by train from the centre of Paris. Records describe it as a medium-sized, solid, unpretentious, unremarkable, mansard-roofed three-story house occupying a double-corner plot 'on the summit of a hill in an area already parcelled out into speculative building lots' and 'surrounded on three sides by high walls and at the front with a metal grill' (Spurling

2005: 36). A prefabricated studio building was constructed against the far boundary wall of the property, separated from the main house by an alley of cypress trees. It possessed all the attributes typical of late-nineteenth-century artists' studios—glass doors, huge windows and northern-oriented skylights for plentiful and consistent daylight (Kelly 1974: 114)—and was furnished with practical items instrumental to the painting process such as easels, mirrors, paints, vases and still life objects. It also contained Matisse's 'working library', an abundant collection of tapestries, curtains, costumes and other textile goods gathered in his travels to Algeria, Tahiti and Morocco (Matisse: Life and Painting n.d.). The studio was a private retreat set apart from the chaos of the city, his community of contemporary artists and the sharp-tongued critics. This studio interior served as 'a world within a world: a place of equilibrium that . . . produced images of comfort, refuge, and balanced satisfaction' (Hughes 1991: 134).

Photographs of the Issy studio survive (Figures 5.2 and 5.3). The correspondence between the interior depicted in *The Red Studio* and the photographs of the Issy studio interior is striking. These photographic images confirm that objects familiar to Matisse's home studio were susceptible to assimilation into his art works (Hughes 1991: 139) as much as they were subjects accommodating the comforts of living (Neilsen Blum 2010: 15). Contemplating 'a benevolent world from a position of utter security', Matisse stated, 'My purpose is to render my emotion. This state of soul is created by the objects which surround me and which react in me: from the horizon to myself,

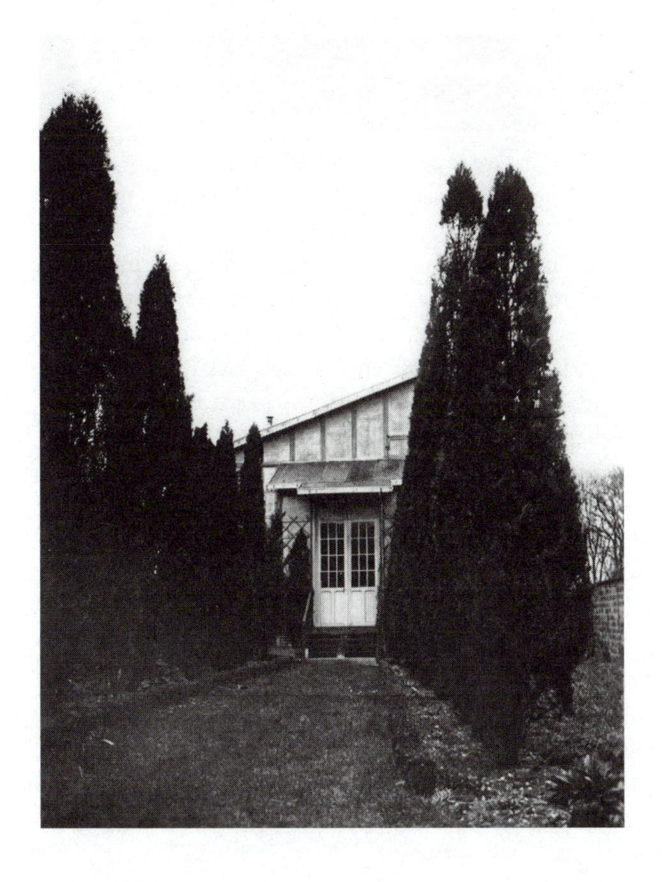

5.2. An exterior view of Matisse's home studio at Issy-les-Moulineaux, France 1910. Photo: Archives Henri Matisse.

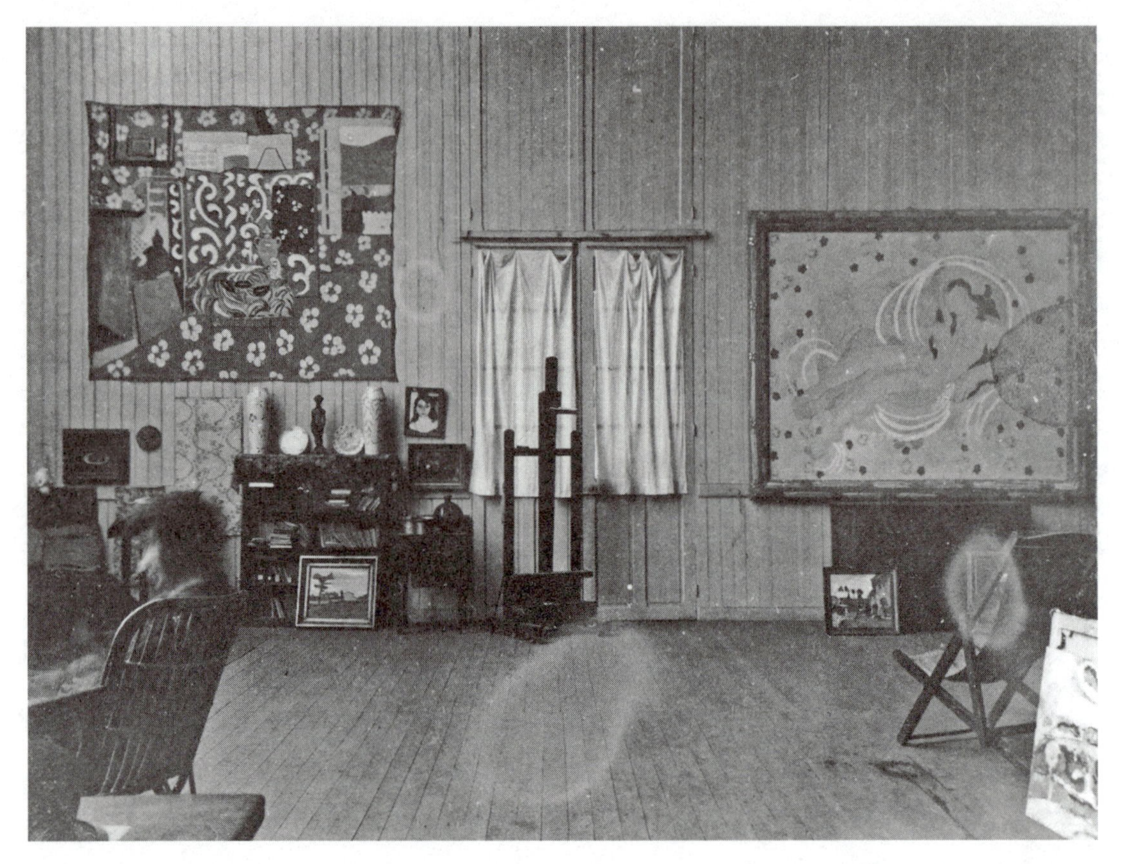

5.3. An interior view of Matisse's home studio at Issy-les-Moulineaux, France 1911. Photo: Archives Henri Matisse.

myself included' (Hughes 1991: 141). 'The idea of the room was inseparable from its use as his studio' (Christie's n.d.). This self-referential and reciprocal relationship between the artist and his studio, his belongings and his artworks, reinforces the studio as a space of creation, an imagination chamber supported by the artist's tools and materials.[8] As a double enclosure, a social construct and fetish, lingering in modern art, 'the studio stands for the art, the artist for the process, the product for the artist, the artists for the studio' (O'Doherty 2007: 6, 14). Home and studio, perhaps even the artist, were one and the same (modern) interior.

The two photographs also enunciate how to enter (and depart) this chamber. I note that the studio's only set of doors is dead centre to the artificial vanishing point in each picture, the exterior relentlessly framed by tress and the interior cloaked by a privacy curtain. 'Why do we always fall back on Euclidean space as the only way to "capture" what a building is' (Latour and Yeneva 2008: 82)? A modest awning and short set of steps protect and welcome while a mobile easel impinges the free-flowing circulation between inside and outside, and, conceptually speaking, interior and exterior.

The Red Studio reinvests in this dualism with possible derision for the binary condition. I am led to consider this as a matter of profound philosophical speculation. That which is solid and vivid (such as paintings, ceramics and vases) inventories an external world, a place where

> the outside of things—a body next to and among other bodies always in orbit around them or on some trajectory with regard to them. These other bodies are things whose interiors are inaccessible or that reveal, when broken open, yet more outsides, smaller bodies inside with unbreachable shells, 'components', jostling, poised, or circulating in empty space . . . [effectively] reducing space to an ensemble of things that 'see' each other's outward surfaces only, it denies the cognitive or emotional validity of interiority as an equally universal perspective. (Benedikt 2002: 21)

From an exterior point of view, matter is hard, space is soft and bodies are distant. That which is made present by a faint outline (furniture) is provisional and ethereal, offering an alternative mode of being in the world that promotes interiority as a sense of enclosure and immersion capable of generating a feeling of looking out and around. Inanimate objects are 'charged' by the proximity of both physical and immaterial presences (Benedikt 2002: 2–4).

Examples of objects charged with the function specific to sitting are housed in the Issy home studio and the interior of *The Red Studio*. A lounge chair made of a canvas sling supported by a folding stick frame pauses in Matisse's studio suggesting that the wall of paintings is best contemplated with one's buttock clutched lower than one's knees and hovering above the ground in a posture based on relaxation unique to the nineteenth century, neither sitting or lying, more akin to a garden or beach setting (Giedion 1948: 396). This chair asks one to surrender slightly to gravity and trust the rudimentary frame's dynamic response to ambling mass. Across the open floor/lawn of the interior, the camera has caught a spindle-back chair equally cloaked by the anonymous condition of everyday late-nineteenth-century domestic life hugging the body of a hat-adorned figure. The palisade of spindles holds the nearly 300 muscles directly or indirectly connected to the motion of a sitting body (Giedion 1948: 400) attentively engaged with the edge of the table that prompts a conversation out of view. In a performance united with function, the top rail of the chair reeks of the screams of bent wood fibres and an Arts and Craft ethos in an era that split thinking and feeling (Giedion 1948: 480). Whereas once propped by the easel at the far end of the room, *The Red Studio* hints at a chair that wavers indecisively between material and conceptual presence. Its outline acts as a ghostly membrane with enough definition to render its timber-joined knees. Its ladder-back commands one's ears to align with one's shoulders in military style, and yet its profile looks too thin to be strong unless it is made of tubular steel. These qualities are all clear signs of modernism's hold on furniture design. The speculative turn that this semiformal and semi-abstract figure presents is perhaps less for passive relaxation than for stimulating the idea of a chair and its relation to comfort. Certainly, these objects are far from inanimate.

MODERN (HOME) INTERIORS

The creation of *The Red Studio* occurred at a critical point in modernism's impact on everyday life. Though domesticity may seem to be the antithesis of modernism, modernism's far-reaching, multilayered project redefined the forms and meanings of middle-class private life expressed through interior design (Rosner 2005: 12). Of particular interest is the role interior furnishings played in this cultural shift towards the modern.

Mimi Hellman's exploration of furniture and interiors suggests a highly animated form of social interplay between objects and bodies in eighteenth-century French parlours. She suggests that decorative objects conveyed meaning not simply through possession but also through usage, through a spatial and temporal complicity with the cultivated body that produced the appearance of leisured, sociable ease. 'The practice of consumption . . . was visual and kinetic; objects were not simply owned, but indeed performed' (Hellman 1999: 417). The domestic parlour supported upholstered armchairs; gilded frames; figurines; lacquered panels; tables for writing, dressing and game playing; chairs for reading, reclining or conversing—a landscape for every enticing and uneasy posture and social interaction:

> The sofa is sumptuous and convenient, perpetually available to receive the body and to display it to advantage. At the same time, however, it is an agent of surveillance, as ready to discern the flaws of its users as it is able to enhance their charms. Its apparent innocent presence as 'mere decoration' disguises its role as author, its capacity to witness and verbally represent human interactions. (Hellman 1999: 416)

She speculates that 'perceptual and cognitive faculties might lurk beneath the inanimate surfaces of domestic adornments' and questions whether or not a piece of furniture could be 'a social actor, an observant entity that participates in human encounters, object-as-narrator' (Hellman 1999: 415). As furniture became lighter in structure and weight, and it assumed more curvilinear form, stylistic surface decoration and kinetic elements such as hidden drawers and tilting panels, it took on animate and interactive characteristics (Gideon 1948: 390–1). The idea of chairs with attitude, fireplaces that sulked and objects that were clever enough to prescribe behaviour scripted new codes of intimacy, privacy and display in domestic life (Pringle 2010: 342). As an aesthetic instrument of delight, pleasure and politeness, furniture was the wild, undisciplined element capable of governing, upsetting and interfering in environments and events. Far from mere decoration, furniture had social power (Hellman 1999: 423–7).

By the end of the nineteenth century, the domestic interior had changed from a domain where artful selection and arrangement of artefacts and objects within ornamental and décor-conscious rooms supported a myriad of social liaisons and events (Praz 1964: 14) to a 'possible antidote or counterbalance to the dangers of the street . . . a sheltering retreat from the shock and dissonance of urban life . . . the home restores individuality' (Rosner 2005:147). While George Simmel's 1903 essay 'The Metropolis and Mental Life' saw the interior as a psychological respite from the mayhem of urban sensation (Rosner 2005: 147), Walter Benjamin wrote of the late-nineteenth-century bourgeois interior as a secure space fortified by soulless furniture arranged to ward off a harsh exterior (Rice on Benjamin 2007: 15). One narrative prompts an image of pushing the furniture up against a bolted door while the other insinuates that the culprit has already entered the house pretending to be an antidote. Surrounded by lavish collections of furnishings, the interior became private, isolated, uniquely individuated and, as Benjamin points out, a site of mortification. That which prompted an exotic, intoxicating illusory and dream-like state and left traces of inhabitation, was, in fact itself, commodified and dead (Rice 2007: 33–5). Here we find signs of the interplay between the domestic interior as a fixed room or the inside of architecture and that of interiority, or, as Charles Rice expresses, a mutual emergence that assumed a state of doubleness (Rice 2007: 2) that brings 'interior' and 'interiority' into a ambiguous state of mutual interdependence. In this insistence, I am borrowing Victoria Rosner's definition of interiority, which refers

> to a cluster of interdependent concepts that extend from the representation of consciousness to the reorganization of home life; revised definitions of persona; privacy, intimacy and space; and new assessments of the sexualized and gendered body. These categories not only influence each other but also construe each other, holding modernist interiority in tension between abstraction and materiality, between metaphor and literality. This definition is far broader and more permeable than the generally accepted critical view of modernist interiority, which emphasizes the mind's ability to craft an individual reality, to live in a world exclusively populated by personal associations and memories. (2005: 11)

Just as *The Red Studio* evokes, interiority and interior fluctuate between abstract and material, imaginary and real, animate and inanimate, humans and objects.

Back in New Zealand, in my suburban, unfinished, basement home studio, I consider the stolen moments of my encounter with *The Red Studio*. Scattered on a hollow-core door masquerading as a workbench, the snapshot images retell the event with fitting justice and serendipity. Bathed in the museum's artificial lumens and the consuming pulse of cool recycled air, *The Red Studio* secretes no shadows; it leaves no traces other than blurred patches of synthetic colour vibrating in a light-sensitive emulsion. Definition eludes the (furnishing) frames (Figure 5.4).

A modest black timber frame retains *The Red Studio* from leaking onto the sacred surface of the gallery. It could be mistaken for a minimalist gesture but the dents, poorly filled nail heads and

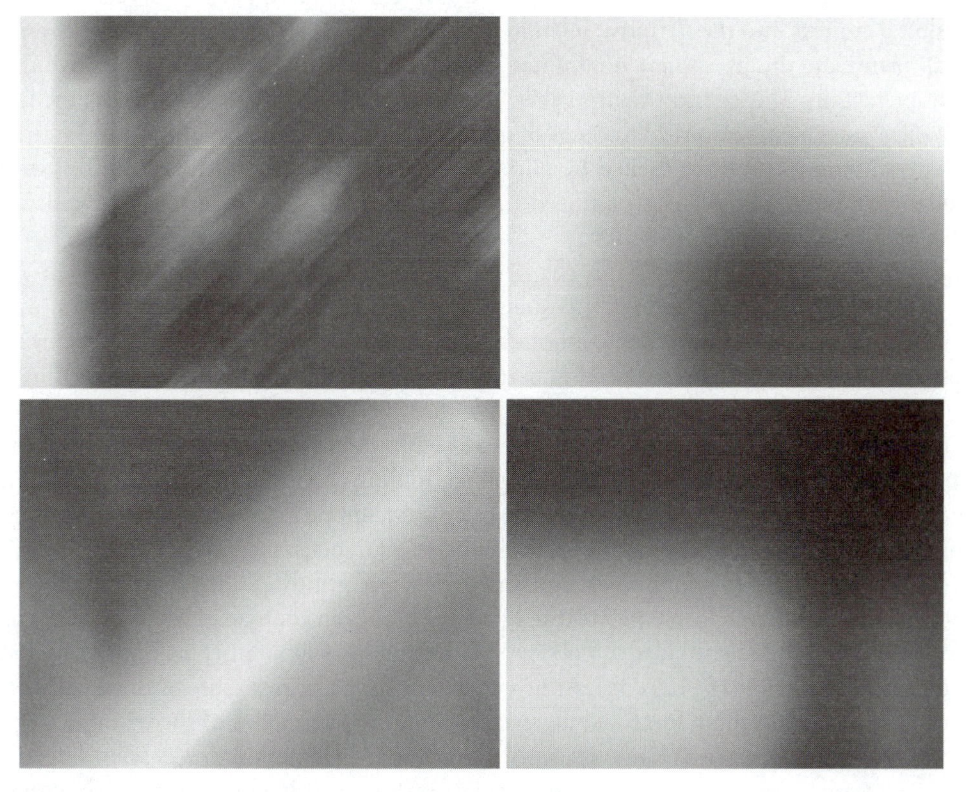

5.4. Four frames taken upon exiting Gallery Six. Julieanna Preston © 2007.

chamfered edges belie handcrafted joining instead of machine extrusion. Unlike the lavish frames depicted in the painting, this frame pulls the painting more squarely into a modernism notorious for efficient and economical means and its association with clean lines. A gap nearly the same size as the thickness of the frame separates the wall from the floor, a recess for all dust and debris to collect as well as a modern Euclidean detail severing the sky from the earth.

The inhabiting body formerly not present in the painting comes into view as a dark-legged profile, an interloper to a non–still life scene:

> The experience of ambiguity is part of the process of perceiving. By pictorial ambiguity I refer to the possibility of the painter representing the perception of a thing, and representing it for viewers, in such a way as to encourage the mind to dwell on perceiving as a process; the painter's experience of an object coming into its own, distinguishing itself from other things, taking shape. (Alpers 2010: 135)

LIVE MATTER ACTING OUT

This chapter assembles an array of historical data, personal experience, theoretical analysis and subjective speculation associated with *The Red Studio* as a work of art; as a representation of a room; as a description of an actual room—Matisse's studio at Issy; and, in relation to early twentieth-century (modern) domestic interiors. Throughout, I have intentionally woven aspects of the social and cultural context into the narrative including those approaches that regard symbolic, representational, inanimate things as inert nonhuman objects, things only tangentially affective through human interaction. This commitment to keep things open and in circulation thwarts the temptation to offer judgement, empirical findings or critical proclamations in keeping with the attributes of a material semiotic practice fuelled by notions of vibrant matter and the ANT. This does not preclude that residue or salvage is produced from this assembling process; it merely resists being conclusive.

In the process of researching for this chapter, I sought to create the colour red used in *The Red Studio*, from scratch. I came upon a web site that catalogued more than thirty recipes, many of which induced salivation due to their connotations to cooking—walnuts, poppy seeds, cloves, rock salt, eggs and lavender; there were also connotations to sculpting because of the high tactility factor of many of the ingredients in the recipes—marble dust, beeswax, amber and chalk (Myer 2010). The surface of my home-studio workbench bears the brunt and beauty of my experiments to reconstitute that famous red. My seat, a small, wooden folding chair that has followed me across the equator three times and to uncountable construction sites, appears as wounded as my dust coat. A canvas lying prone on the table organizes small daubs in a forgotten sequence noted by indecipherable handwritten notes. The methodical and repetitive act of grinding, stirring and folding minerals into oil and turpentine formed a volatile olfactory bloom in the space. My system of trialling was foiled by play, the science lost to poetics and the studio as laboratory rearranged as a retreat into interiority (Alpers 2010: 127–34). At no other time have I been so sure of the vitality of matter: furniture as a co-dwelling force and material encounter as a practice of theorizing.

More impressive is the web site's listing of historic red pigments indexed according to code name, common name, Latin name and properties, including colour description, the long-term effects of light, opacity, light fastness, oil absorption and toxic rating, as well as miscellaneous notes. The names for red pigment sound exotic: Sophoretin, Kermes, Cochineal, Madder Lake, Rheumine, Santalin, Alizarin Purple, Vermillion, Tin Violet, Quinacridone Red and so on. The chemical compositions bestow a form of empirical assurance which is soured by notes about pigments that fade, a triumph of the subjective and temporal over the absolute. It is not simply that the colour red symbolizes blood, communism, fertility, danger, passion, courage, sin, anger or good luck, or that it stimulates the heart to beat faster, is worn by outgoing people, or consists of the longest wavelengths visible to the human eye. It is the crisscrossed network of associations red taps into that gathers a depth masquerading as a monotone surface, what might be called in oil-painting terms 'fat over lean' (Pyle and Pearce 2001: 75). The charts of pigments and recipes bear the currency and complexity of the assemblage obviously fuelled by a globalized mineral market and hampered by the invention of tube paint in the late 1800s. This is a political agency of colour, of *The Red Studio*'s colour in particular—a micro-political sensibility-forming force of affect and difference.

NOTES

1. Please note: the size and breadth of written material about actor-network theory is immense and often complex. Therefore, any overview runs the risk of being reductive or disrespectful to the intricacies that are critical to its practice and intent.
2. The critic's name was Camille Mauclair, which was a pseudonym Séverin Faust (1872–1945) used. Faust was a French poet, novelist, biographer, travel writer and art critic (Emmons and Lewis 2006: 303).
3. The Fauves were a short-lived experimental early modern art group credited with the advent of modernism in art. At the time of their first exhibition, they were known as 'The Invertebrates', which was quickly changed to 'The Incoherents'; finally a name given by critic Louis Vauxcelles stuck: 'The Fauves' (French for *wild beasts*) (Burgess 1910).
4. Svetlana Alpers (2010: 137–8) attends to the proximity between an artist (a painter) and the object he and she is painting and/or modelling. I perceive in her text a sense that the paint, the brush, the oil, the roughness or smoothness of the canvas, and the hand are instrumental in acting as conductive forces that not only overcome the distance of space but also that rendered by representation. This is a one-to-one, full-scale sensual interaction.
5. Here, I am using 'figure' in the contemporary sense: 'Recent perspectives on figure place emphasis on the figure as performative, transformative and configurative qualities, not a fixed shape but rather a pattern turned in on itself that unfolds procedurally and dynamically. Figura means the ability to move, modelled and transformed (note the active nature of this agency), in contrast to forma, rigid' (Müller-Tamm 2005: 19).
6. 'The concept of modernism is famously difficult to define. Unquestionably, though, one of the basic tenets of modernist art is a subordination of the putative subject matter (the person in a portrait or the mountain in a landscape) to the peculiarities of the medium (the application of paint to a flat canvas or the relationship between a sculpture and its pedestal)' (Lubow 2004).
7. 'The still-life assemblage has been understood as a bourgeois phenomenon. This is to consider its objects as subordinate to man, for our use, manipulation, and enjoyment, conveying our sense of power over things [still life as a portable possession]. But by taking the empty room as the baseline, there is a prior sense in which the objects on the table—one can expand this to any objects or people in the studio—put pressure on or exact something from the painter who has retired there . . . The painter represents the perception of the thing and encourages the mind to dwell on perceiving as a process. The difference that the studio makes is that it frames the ambiguity as originating under particular circumstances . . . as if it was a matter of discovery, not just a demonstration' (Alpers 2010: 134–6).

8. 'Every studio has its stock of special devices, the secret essences and recipes that account for so much of an image's power. They might include an ancient treatise on anatomy or a couple of spray guns, finely ground lapis lazuli or a bottled mayonnaise that has proved useful as a binder; but they always constitute an amalgam of what the artist has learned from tradition and what he himself has found while pursuing a particular vision or deliberately searching for a new technique. An understanding of the enormously varied substances and methods that artists have used over the centuries may take one closer to the heart of visual creativity than volumes of fine aesthetic appreciation alone' (Peppiatt and Bellony-Rewald 1982: V).

REFERENCES

Alpers, S. (2010), 'The View from the Studio', in M. J. Jacob and M Grabner, eds., *The Studio Reader: On the Space of Artists*, Chicago: School of the Art Institute Chicago.

Bal, M., and Bryson, N. (1991), 'Semiotics and Art History,' *The Art Bulletin*, 73: 174–208.

Benedikt, M. (2002), 'Environmental Stoicism and Place Machismo,' *Harvard Design Magazine*, 16: 21–7.

Bennett, J. (2010), *Vibrant Matter: A Political Ecology of Things*, Durham, NC: Duke University Press.

Burgess, G. (1910), 'The Wild Men of Paris: Matisse, Picasso and Les Fauves', *The Architectural Record*, 1–3, reproduced by K. Lerner at *In The Cause of Architecture: An Online Journal of Ideas from Architectural Record*, <http://archrecord.construction.com/inTheCause/0702MenOfParis/MenOfParis1.asp> accessed 2 Jan. 2012.

Christie's, 'Sale 2437/ Lot 29: HENRI MATISSE (1869–1954), *La fenêtre ouverte*', <http://m.christies.com/sale/lot/sale/23045/object/5433464> accessed 11 Oct. 2011.

Crowley, J. E. (1999), 'The Sensibility of Comfort', *The American Historical Review*, 104/3: 749–82.

Elliott, R. 'Henri Matisse', *World's Greatest Artists*, Art School Online, <http://www.fortunecity.com/victorian/parkwood/249/five.html> accessed 16 Oct. 2011.

Emmons, S., and Lewis, W. W. (2006), *'Mauclair, Camille'. Researching the Song: A Lexicon*. Oxford: Oxford University Press.

Giedion, S. (1948), *Mechanization Takes Command*, New York: Oxford University Press.

Gratton, P. (2010), 'Vibrant Matters: An Interview with Jane Bennett', *Philosophy in a Time of Errors*, <http://philosophyinatimeoferror.wordpress.com/2010/04/22/vibrant-matters-an-interview-with-jane-bennett/>.

Hellman, M. (1999), 'Furniture, Sociability, and the Work of Leisure in Eighteenth-Century France', *Eighteenth-century Studies*, 32/4: 415–45.

Hughes, R. (1991), *The Shock of the New*, New York: McGraw-Hill.

Kelly, F. (1974), *The Studio and the Artist*, New York: St. Martin's Press.

Kostenevich, A. 'Sergey Shchukin and Others', <http://www.hermitage.nl/en/tentoonstellingen/matisse_tot_malevich/achtergrond-sjtsjoekin.htm> accessed 20 Dec. 2011.

Labrusse, R. (2005), 'The End of the Image Cult: Some Remarks on the Symphonic Interiors', in P. Müller-Tamm, ed., *Henri Matisse: Figure Colour Space*, Germany: Hatje Cantz Verlag.

Latour, B. (2005), *Reassembling the Social: An Introduction to Actor-network Theory*, Oxford: Clarendon.

Latour, B., and Yeneva, A. (2008), '"Give Me a Gun and I will Make Buildings Move": An ANT's View of Architecture', *Explorations in Architecture: Teaching Design Research*, Berlin: Birkhäuser.

Law, J. (2007), 'Actor Network Theory and Material Semiotics,' 25 Apr., <http://www. heterogeneities.net/publications/Law2007ANTandMaterialSemiotics.pdf> accessed 20 Dec. 2011.

Law, J., and Hassard, J., eds, (1999), *Actor Network Theory and After*, Boston and Oxford: Blackwell Publishers.

Lubow, A. (2004), 'Re-Moderning', <nytimes.com, http://www9.georgetown.edu/faculty/irvinem/vi . . . zine-Reopening-MOMA-Re-Moderning-10–3-04.html> accessed 15 Oct. 2011.

Matisse: Life and Painting, <http://www.henri-matisse.net/biography.html> accessed 18 Sept. 2011.

Matisse, M. (1908), 'Notes of a Painter', in J. D. Flam, ed., *Matisse on Art*, Oxford: Phaidon Press.

MoMA PS1, <http://www.moma.org/collection/object.php?object_id=78389> accessed 27 Dec. 2011.

Müller-Tamm, P. (2005), 'Foreword', in P. Müller-Tamm, ed., *Henri Matisse: Figure Colour Space*, Germany: Hatje Cantz Verlag.

Myers, D. (2010), The Colour of Art—Pigments, Paints and Formulas, <http://www.artiscreation.com/red.html#pigment1> accessed 23 Dec. 2011.

Neilson Blum, S. (2010), *Henri Matisse: Rooms with a View*, New York: Monacelli Press.

O'Doherty, B. (2007), *Studio and Cube: On the Relationship Between Where Art is Made and Where Art is Displayed*, New York: Columbia University.

Peppiatt, M., and Bellony-Rewald, A. (1982), *Imagination's Chamber: Artists and their Studios*, London: Gordon Fraser.

Praz, M. (1964), *An Illustrated History of Interior Decoration from Pompeii to Art Nouveau*, London: Thames & Hudson.

Pringle, P. (2010), 'Performing Interiors: A Situation Comedy', in *Imagining . . . 27th Annual SAHANZ Conference*, Newcastle, Australia, 341–7.

Pyle, D., and Pearce, E. (2001), *The Oil Colour Book: A Comprehensive Resource for Painters*, Middlesex: Windsor & Newton.

Rice, C. (2007), *The Emergence of the Interior: Architecture, Modernity, Domesticity*, London: Routledge Press.

Rosner, V. (2005), *Modernism and the Architecture of Private Life*, New York: Columbia University.

Spurling, H. (2005), *Matisse the Master: A Life of Henri Matisse, The Conquest of Colour, 1909–1954*, London: Alfred A. Knopf.

6. KITCHENS: FROM WARM WORKSHOP TO KITCHENSCAPE

imma forino
Politecnico di Milano

In the history of interior design, the kitchen is the most traditional room in the house, for it has evolved more slowly over the centuries than other spaces that are more on show. In peasant homes, it was the heart of everyday family life: this was where meals were cooked, domestic chores were done, children were tended and even where sleeping pallets were spread on the floor. In nobles' dwellings, the kitchen was occupied by servants and later by other staff: until the nineteenth century, it is far removed from the living and entertaining areas since its smells and noises were not welcome in polite society. As the middle classes became established, it became the scene of the housewife's activities.

This chapter relates the idea of intimacy to the space, furnishing and equipment of the kitchen from 1880 to 1940. The subject is handled chronologically, but with a narrative emphazis based on the visual sequence of the kitchen interiorscape—in other words, by interpolating historical notes and critical commentary among the images: selected highlights orchestrate the kitchen's various interpretations accordingly.

After a brief outline of the kitchen's evolution from antiquity to the seventeenth century, the chapter proper begins with the concept of intimacy as the Dutch of that century gave it modern expression: kitchens in Flemish painting portray a vivid scene of interiority. Later, the 'warm workshop' of chefs and housekeepers in the early nineteenth century turns into the woman's realm of the Victorian era. From 1860 to 1890, a series of inventions simplified the life of the housewife.

A serene interiority links the kitchen of the painting *The Kitchen* (1895), by the painter Carl Larsson, with that of the Gamble House (1907–8) by Greene & Greene: a diluted Art Nouveau informs a tranquil domestic world. In the first decade of the twentieth century, on the other hand, Christine Frederick's scientific kitchen (1913), with its standardized labour and the 'mechanical bride' idea derived from Taylorism, anticipated the fragmentation of the soul in Ludwig Kirchner's *Alpine Kitchen* (1918). In Europe, the experimental designs of the 1920s and 1930s prefigured a minimal and wholly functional kitchen. In America, on the other hand, the next decade saw designs for 'the kitchen of tomorrow'—to paraphrase the title of a book on the home, *Tomorrow's House: A Complete Guide for the Home-Builder*, by George Nelson and Henry Wright (1945). Before 'easier living' arrives, the Streamline interlude (1920–40) represents the idea of the Future with the aerodynamic looks of its utensils. Lastly, Nelson's essays, articles and designs bring the practicality of the American kitchen into the modern era: the 'continuous kitchen' is an idea that has lasted—though with many transformations—until the present day.

KITCHEN FLÂNERIE

> And, indeed, is there not something holy about a great kitchen? . . . The scoured gleam of row upon row of metal vessels dangling from hooks or reposing on their shelves till needed with the air of so many chalices waiting for the celebration of the sacrament of food. And the range like an altar, yes, before which my mother bowed in perpetual homage, a fringe of sweat upon her upper lip and the fire glowing in her cheeks. (Carter 1985: 94–95)

In the history of interior design, the kitchen represents the most traditional environment of the house. Compared to other rooms that are more on show (such as the living room or bedroom), the design of the kitchen has evolved slowly over the centuries. The fact that it is the 'heart' of the house might partially explain its stable nature over time, not so much in terms of form but rather its more profound meaning: if food keeps us alive, cooking food represents the victory of thought over natural impulse. Since the discovery of fire in the primitive age, cooking—even in its most elementary form—has been what differentiates the hungry human from animals. The human being transforms food from simple nourishment, which comes from nature, into an *artefatto* (a product of human art) thanks to their work. The material is first modified and then harmonized by varying its preparation: the kitchen space represents the predominance of reason over instinct, of art over nature.

The kitchen is here investigated through the spatial and empathic relationship which, over the various ages, has existed between people and this specialized environment within the home: the kitchen is therefore seen as a true *interiorscape*, or space of interiority, of men, women and children. While organized chronologically, in examining the topic I have favoured a narrative construction that interpolates images, books and critical reflections: I move then within the *kitchenscape* like a *flâneuse*,[1] who turns her gaze to selected highlights in order to orchestrate the interpretative reading.

It is acknowledged that the modification of the kitchen is connected to the evolution of social customs and the gradual emancipation of the woman within the family and society. Until the Ancien Régime, the staff that handled the cooking and table service in the houses of the wealthy social classes was male: the protection of the master of the house from poisoning was delegated to educated and competent men (Sarti 2006: 199). Furthermore, the honour of the house, represented by sumptuous banquets, also depended on the reliability and expertise of the domestic staff.[2] In more modest households, on the other hand, the woman was assigned the task of caring for the house and kitchen since the Middle Ages, as she was responsible for the family home economics: in the kitchen, she performed many of the daily duties including the preparation of meals and caring for offspring. Indeed, in the peasant culture, the kitchen was the only room in which women were permitted to eat, out of sight of other people who feared the elusive psyche or lunar character of the female being.[3]

During the Victorian age, the middle class concretized the separation of existence into two different spheres, public and private, which were assigned respectively to men and women. A division of labour between the sexes was implemented according to an ideology that emphasized the difference in duties and responsibilities (Hall 1994: 55, 62). The woman was entrusted with the care of the house, from managing the finances to decorating the rooms: the female figure was 'cleansed' of every dark power, transformed in the eyes of others into the exemplary model of mother and 'fireside angel' (Faré 1990: 11).

In addition to being connected to social custom, the sexual division of tasks in the kitchen depended on geographic context and family rank. In the nineteenth century, for example, at the heights of French and Italian aristocracy, it was the men who did the cooking, while in England they took turns with the women, in both middle-class and wealthy families. The English kitchen, therefore, had more pronounced domestic and feminine characteristics than elsewhere, particularly due to the reduced need to be on show in comparison with the very different court life (Sarti 2006: 202).

The history of the woman, the issue of feminism and its implications in the history of the home are reflected therefore in the kitchen environment, long considered the favoured feminine realm.[4] My reflections concern the kitchen as heart of the dwelling, or rather as centre of the family: in fact, the kitchen might be considered a 'beloved' or *topophilic* space within the house, to draw on the thoughts of the philosopher Gaston Bachelard.[5] It represents, therefore, a 'living value' (Bachelard 1984: 83), within which people of both sexes are present. The very terminology used in the past to identify the kitchen demonstrates its interior qualities as well as its domestic ones: '*Firehouse, bodystead, hearth room, house place*—these variant regional names given to such space are terms both functionally descriptive and yet sensually evocative of the hearth and its fire as the structural and psychological centre of the household' (Pennell 1998: 202).

The symbol of the kitchen is the fire in the hearth or stove: this heats and cooks the food (at least it did until the advent of electric energy), representing the dominion of intellect over matter, but its profound meaning is that of the 'lived fire, . . . which gives us energy and life' in the present (Bachelard 1990: 45). Thanks to the slight hypnotism it induces in the human being ('the pensive man'), fire is in fact 'the axis of subjectivity' (Bachelard 1973: 127), around which *rêveries* develop. On the other hand, wrote Bachelard, fire is also a symbol of rest, or invitation to rest (Bachelard 1973: 138), precisely because it warms and comforts us. The very cooking of food then has more profound implications than just a mere material gesture:

> [Fire] is not limited to cooking, it turns the biscuit golden brown. It materializes the joy of men. For as far back as it is possible to go, gastronomic value has suppressed dietary value,

> and it is in joy and not in pain that man found his spirit. The conquest of the superfluous generates a spiritual excitement that is greater than the conquest of the necessary. Man is a creation of desire, not a creation of need. (Bachelard 1973: 139–40)

The 'joy of men' is revealed therefore in gathering around the 'hearth', a term that has always defined the kitchen. And it is from this perspective—the hearth as the centre of the house—that my chapter interprets the kitchen environment over the various ages. The theme of feminine interiority is consequently one of the crucial elements in describing the interior kitchen, but even more important is the theme of family or the people who, with their interiority, become part of the kitchen space.

A TRADITIONAL ENVIRONMENT: FROM MONUMENTAL FORMS TO ORGANIZED SPACE

There are no reliable accounts of the position of the kitchen in the house in ancient times. In the *Odyssey*, Homer designated it as the hearth for cooking food, which the men gathered around (Homer 2008: XIV, 40–50, 420–5) and where the guest might rest (Homer 2008: 520).[6] In the Roman atrium house, exemplified in the city of Pompeii, the *culina* was the hearth where the family would come together. It was protected by the Lari (the images of ancestors), while the jealous care of the larder (*cella penaria*) was entrusted to the *mater familias*. Subsequently a severe family hierarchy would separate the masters of the house and the servants. The hearth became an environment in itself, raised upon a podium, where the *coquus* (the cook) would stand to cook the food (Maiuri 2000: 67). Nearby was the bread oven and, in other spaces, the sink and drain.[7]

In the Middle Ages, the kitchen was a monumental stark and smoke-filled room,[8] of monastic origin.[9] It was, however, the heart of the residence—a 'home within a home'—as it identified, even physically, the family that lived there. Possessing a hearth and a home (*feu et lieu*) was in fact the equivalent of being the head of the household: this was demonstrated by the French census in the late Middle Ages which recorded the population not by individuals but 'by fires', or rather by the number of hearths (Contaime 1993: 360). And one of the duties of the woman of the household (*focaria*) was to keep the fire in the kitchen (*foganha*) alight at all times during the day and cover it at night for fear of a fire breaking out in the house (Contaime 1993: 386).[10]

In the *Ultima cena* (1340–50)[11] by the Bottega di Pietro Lorenzetti, two servants are working in the kitchen: with its lit fire and broad hood that sucked in the smoke, the wooden shelf with a vase on it and a utensil hung alongside, the high coffered ceiling and the bare walls, the room represents a 'prototype' that was destined to be replicated in all of Europe (Praz 1964: 79). In general, the cooking centre also acted as the heating system for the cold houses of the time, although normally people did not sleep in the kitchen. The hearth was open and the lack of cupboards might lead us to hypothesize that the various furnishings and fittings were hung on the walls. Iron grills and pans substituted the bronze crockery of Roman times; spoons and ladles were made of metal or wood. The pans were hung over the fire with chains or rested on tripods; the roasting spit was among the most important cooking instruments. In *Il miracolo delle nozze di Cana* (approximately 1460)[12] by Andrea De Litio, the kitchen is only partially visible: the broad hood of the lit hearth, the floor in rough bricks and the roasting spit, which a servant kept in sight in front of him with a rather perplexed air.

The kitchen would subsequently be transformed into a more organized space, separated from the other rooms: in the Renaissance palazzo, *comodità* (comfort) became an aspiration in all types of homes and united service rooms such as the lavatory and kitchen (Pagliara 2001: 39). In both of these spaces, improvement to the water system and connection to the civic sewage system were essential, so much so that their position within the house was designed a priori. The authors of treatises, such as Leon Battista Alberti or Francesco di Giorgio Martini, insisted on the kitchen being kept apart from the dining room so as to avoid the din of crockery and unsavoury odours. Especially due to the frequent problems of draught chimneys and flues, the kitchen was confined to the cellar or ground floor, removed from the main part of the residence, while in modest homes the family continued to eat in the kitchen (Thornton 1992: 290). They were poorly lit environments, connected to the *sala* (dining room) by secondary staircases and, later, with a type of lift.

The resolution of the smoke problem eventually brought the kitchen to the *piano nobile* (first floor), illuminated by windows that looked over the courtyard. The greatest advantage consisted in the meals not getting cold during table service while the servants ate in the room reserved for them (*tinello*).[13] Equipment included the tub hollowed out in the stone of the sink to rinse the crockery, the 'kitchen hearth' for cooking food, and *armari* or spaces hollowed out in the walls (only rarely closed by wooden doors) for storing the dishware. The larder was the room for foodstuffs, which the master of the house had direct control over (La Ronciére 1993: 150).

BOURGEOIS RESIDENCES: ETHICAL OVERTONES AND SUFFUSED INTIMACY

The idea of intimacy was born in the seventeenth century in the middle-class civilization of the Netherlands (Rybczynski 1989: 65). In a way of life that was as conservative as it was simple in terms of cultural expression, the houses were modest in size and built solidly in brick. Despite the cosmopolitanism of the merchants and businessmen, the residence was perceived as a pleasant refuge to return to. Within their dwellings Dutch families led a cohesive and tranquil life. The rooms were generally 'on a human scale', or, in other words, comfortable and never excessive in decoration nor refined in furnishings. The most thoroughly descriptive and, at the same time, profoundly intimate depictions of the houses of the time are owed to the Flemish artists. The paintings often portray scenes of domestic life and are an interesting documentary source, from which we can begin to understand the relationship between the interior and interiority in traditional kitchens.[14]

The painter Nicolaes Maes set the *Idle Servant* (1655)[15] in a kitchen: a bulky sideboard stands out on a black-and-white chequered floor, serving as the backdrop to the scene; it accommodates on its surface a cat with a game bird between its greedy jaws. The 'idle' servant has her head sadly bent over the terracotta crockery set down on the floor, which she still has to wash, while another woman, perhaps the cook, scorns her sloppiness. In the background, a door opens onto a family scene: two women dressed in the traditional dark clothing with white bonnets are spinning, while even further back, a window of opalescent glass closes in this complex world, without letting us see what is happening outside. Here Maes adopts a visual stratagem that is typical of Dutch painting, the *doorkijkje*, or rather the depiction of interiors through rooms that open on to other rooms,[16] which corresponds to the emphazis on the distribution of spaces *en enfilade*.

The piece might be considered from other points of view: the scene does in fact have a clearly symbolic value. *Acedia* (sloth), one of the seven deadly sins,[17] is personified by the young woman, whose moral counterpart is represented by the elder figure, while in the background the other women silently spin the rhythm of life. The *doorkijkje* consists therefore in the confrontation of different feminine interiorities, placing them as details of a single scene that must be recomposed through the multifaceted vision of the person observing the painting. Maes's depiction consolidates, however, the traditional idea of feminine indolence that is connected above all to youth and does not apparently concern old age. On the other hand, the painting has a typically realistic interpretation thanks to the description of the kitchen in which the scene is set: the depiction is so precise in displaying the entirety of the space and the details of objects and finishes (see for instance the brass hinges of the sideboard) that it might be considered a true account of a historic period (mid-seventeenth century), of a country (the Netherlands), of the living culture of a middle-class family and, finally, of the interior of the time.

Christian Wolfgang Heimbach (*A Kitchen*, 1648)[18] depicted a German kitchen with equal precision. Despite it being a more modest environment, with the hearth on the floor, it is completely equipped with pans, pewter plates and earthenware neatly laid out on the plate rack, from which hang ladles and other utensils. However, this scene also has a precise symbolic meaning since it represents the value of parsimony or 'healthy management', which the head of the household (a spice, tea and coffee merchant) oversees while the women of the house complete their duties. The kitchen is no longer an untidy profusion of food and objects but represents the new bourgeois order, organized by the monetisation of relationships (Senise and Buscagliene 1980: 108).

It is the interiors of Johannes Vermeer that transmit a profound sense of interiority in their depiction of everyday life. The visual stratagem of rooms that open on to other rooms is present in many works: intimacies that reveal other intimacies in the introvert and protective space of the residence. Whereas in others, such as *The Kitchen Maid* (1658–60),[19] the protagonist is isolated in relation to the task she is performing. The kitchen, in which the scene is set, acts only as a backdrop. We identify it as such by means of the objects within it; in particular, the terracotta jug the woman is using to pour the milk. Then we see also the low vessel that the milk is being poured into, the coarse loaves on the table that is laid with a green cloth and the bread in the basket, the ceramics embellished with the Delft blue to hold water and the carelessly folded blue tea towel. The room is austerely simple, with no decoration conceded to walls or floor. The perimeter can only be deduced from the skirting board which is a darker colour than the wall. The typical Dutch window floods the figure with light. The milk-woman is dressed in the traditional style of the time. The light bonnet hides her hair, placing the light oval of her face in the foreground; the tension of the gesture (pouring the milk) reveals her gaze, frozen forever on the painter's canvas. Here too is an underlying symbolic value: the seriousness and innocence of the woman's face and her concentration on the gesture communicate the value of industriousness, quite the opposite of what is expressed in Maes's painting. In Vermeer's work, the kitchen environment is the pure interiority of the human being who inhabits it: the woman, depicted while performing a task, is imbued with the gentleness of a habitual gesture.

FROM THE WARM WORKSHOP TO THE MORAL ASPIRATION FOR ORDER

During the seventeenth century, the trunks and chests that used to be untidy storage places disappeared from the kitchen, replaced by sideboards and other furniture. In addition to this sense of order, which reigned in the kitchen and the rest of the house, tastes for food were also refined: the coarse medieval banquets were replaced with a more refined choice of foodstuffs and methods of preparing them (Flandin 1993: 215). In France, the culinary treaties published between the seventeenth and eighteenth century exalted the gastronomic value of dishes, and cooking became a delicate art, which advanced in step with civilization (Aron 1978a: 124).[20] This change in taste was accompanied by the presentation of food and improvement in tableware with crockery, dishes, tablecloths and cutlery: more refined objects replaced those in common use.

Until 1700, food was cooked on a wood fire, but the use of coal, which began in England in the second half of the century, offered a new opportunity: chimney fireplaces were replaced with cast-iron or brick stoves. The adoption of the *potager* (a large brick oven with twelve or twenty grates) modernized both the kitchen and the preparation of meals. However, the environment was no longer the centre of the house; among the wealthy classes, the greater the distance between the social status of the masters of the house and that of the servants, the further the kitchen was from the dining room.[21]

The kitchen did not undergo any particular transformation until the late nineteenth century. Rather, wrote Mario Praz, it was 'one of the more conservative environments: here function prevailed over ornament, which one might say did not exist at all' (Praz 1964: 232). Praz's collection includes *La cucina di Palazzo Mozzi a Firenze* (1825)[22] by Antonio Digerini (Figure 6.1); it is a painting that is particularly dear to the Anglicist and that, in his autobiography, *La casa della vita*

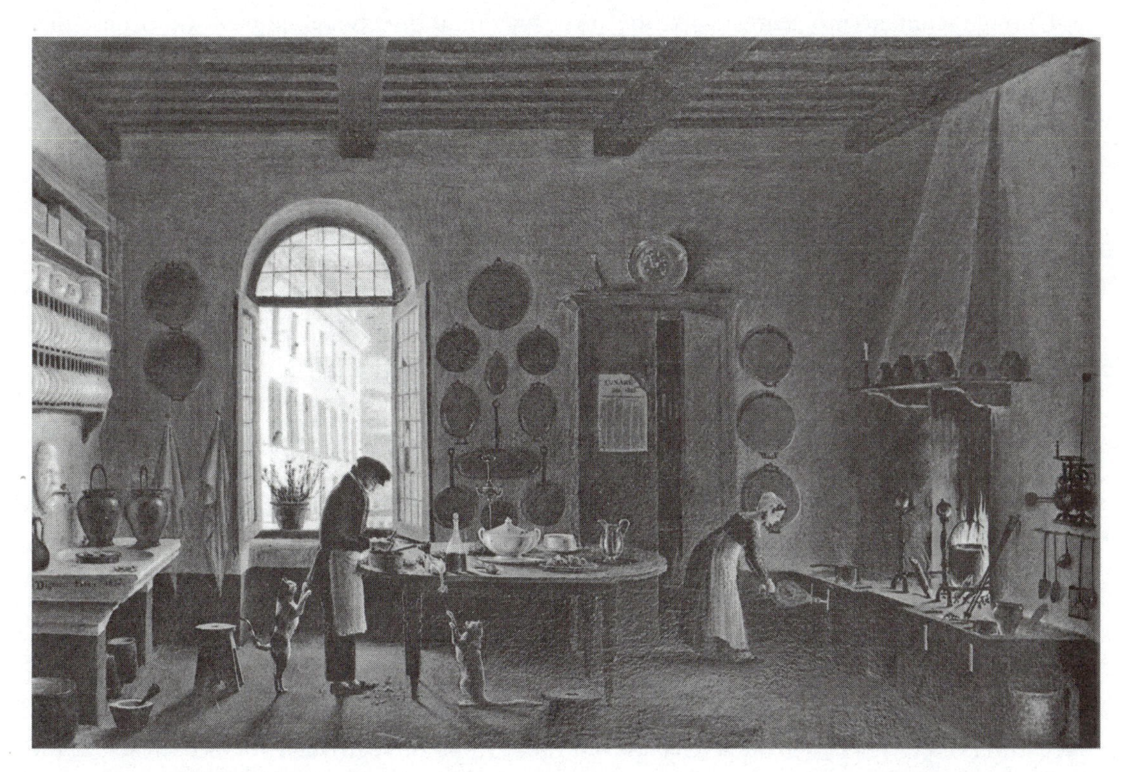

6.1. Antonio Digerini, *La cucina di Palazzo Mozzi a Firenze*, 1825, oil on paper, Museo Mario Praz, Roma. Galleria Nazionale d'Arte Moderna e Contemporanea. Courtesy Ministero per i Beni e le Attività Culturali.

(1958), provides the inspiration for a long poetic digression on his life in Rome during World War II and the perpetual food shortages (Praz 2003: 217).

The precision with which Digerini depicted the interior highlighted every detail of the room. The window overlooks the Lungarno: behind a vase of carnations rise the façade of Palazzo Torregiani[23] and the blue sky of a spring day in Florence. The hearth on a side wall illuminates the room in places and a red light reflects off the utensils, furnishings and figures that animate the scene: a man prepares the herbs in a copper pan, a maid fans the fire with a small pair of bellows and two cats rear up on their hind legs begging for a titbit. It is a large room with a high wooden-beamed ceiling. Every tool (the china and the glass and pewter containers) is destined for a precise purpose as is all the furniture (the plate rack, the work surface, the large central table for preparing food, the half-open sideboard and the chimney hood). It is a 'dark odorous kitchen' (Praz 1964: 232); one can almost smell the soup cooking in the pot on the stove. Here the man and woman, in the service of the Mozzi family, work in silent harmony: the kitchen is the domestic scene of an interiority that feeds on a relaxed and familiar atmosphere.

The depictions by the Risorgimento painter Gerolamo Induno introduce other Italian kitchens in lower middle-class (*La lettera dal campo*, 1862)[24] or working-class (*Donne romane, scena contemporanea*, 1864)[25] settings, yet the two kitchens are not that different. Both sketch the nucleus of family life: sparse environments enlivened by the clutter of utensils and kitchenware, in which the hearth is preponderant. The spice shelves are identical in both kitchens (clearly an item of furniture in common use), as are the red terracotta floor and roughly plastered walls.

During the nineteenth century, 'a subtle amalgamation of functional rationality, of still rather limited comfort and aristocratic nostalgia was noticeable' (Perrot 1994b: 247) in the middle-class house model. Particular emphazis was placed on family life: the residence was a safe refuge from the chaotic industrialized world, the only place in which to cultivate introspection. There was, however, a stark contrast between the houses of the poor and those of the wealthy. The English farmhouses were 'miserable hovels with damp and half-rotten walls, with sagging roofs, infected rooms and little space for sleeping' (Lasdun 1981: 134). Although there was much discussion within the ruling institutions about what the cottage model should be,[26] its improvement depended above all on the issue of morality. In farmhouses of limited space, the family slept together in the kitchen as the hearth was the only source of heat. Victorian morals, however, dictated the separation of the sexes, and this led to the construction of small rooms for sleeping, adjacent to the kitchen in order to take advantage of the heat. The hearth then was even more the centre of life than the kitchen: it probably remained lit all year long in the 'Atlantic' custom, as on the continent the dining-table was the real fulcrum of family life.

The Victorian age promoted a new ideal of life that reached the poorer classes thanks to housing philanthropy. The first phase of industrialization caused increasing migration to urban centres, where workers lived in unhealthy interiors (Mumford 1999: 157–61): the dominating class responded to this dramatic situation (epidemics, high infant mortality rates and an increase in crime) with some containment strategies, such as the laws on the length of the working day, hygiene and safety in the workplace, and a variety of aid institutions. Furthermore, they sought to transfer the model of middle-class life to the lesser-off classes, which interwove the ideology of comfort and privacy with that of hygiene and order (Maldonado 1987: 102). This partially atrophied the role of the kitchen as the vital centre of the family. It became a place for merely preparing food, separated from the rooms where meals were consumed: a new 'food topography' was born (Aron 1978b: 221).[27]

The distribution of space was accurately planned: 'A kitchen should be light, lofty, and airy', states *The London Cookery and Complete Domestic Guide* (1827) (quoted in Wedd 2002: 176). Middle-class houses had a separation between the kitchen, scullery (which in smaller houses was also used as a laundry), larder[28] and coal store. A swinging door separated the kitchen from the scullery, where the crockery and pans were washed, dried and stored.[29] There was therefore a clear functional division between the activities that took place in the kitchen, which corresponded to specific dedicated spaces. In larger kitchens, for example, the area for kneading was separate from the cooking centre, but the real indicator of the wealth of the family was the size of its larder and, above all, the different sections for storing food: wine cellar, dry goods store, vegetable store (near the garden door) and fish larder (with marble slabs cooled by running water).

In 1865, Robert Kerr insisted in particular on the importance of ventilation and illumination in the 'kitchen office' (Kerr 1972: 204–5). According to the architect, the ideal 'cooking-*apparatus*' was made by Fredk. Edwards and Sons,[30] whose model included a lot of instruments and an ordered layout of furnishings for the kitchen and scullery. In addition to the worktable, the most important piece of furniture was the dresser which would rest against the wall; it might have doors on the lower part while a series of open shelves would be located above. The equipment included a cast-iron (initially open, then closed with doors), wood or coal range and the ice house for the refrigeration system, where the winter ice was kept for use in the summer. The first gas-fired range was presented at the Great Exhibition of London (1851): it was commercialized in 1863 (Shrewsbury's Portable Gas Oven) but only really adopted from 1880 onwards, as people feared explosions.[31]

THE PIONEERING KITCHEN AND THE SCIENTIFIC KITCHEN

La table de cuisine (1888–90)[32] by Paul Cézanne represented the last decade of the nineteenth century and visually alluded to the idea of the synthetic modernity that characterized the twentieth-century kitchen. In this representation of reality shaped by the painter's intellect,[33] the kitchen environment is exemplified by objects for the table and food. The room space can only be guessed at: a hint of a chair in the top right, to the left a fragment of another surface, a simple light-coloured floor. The table, laid with snow-white linen, dominates: 'The tablecloth, a breath of innocence', wrote Bachelard, 'is sufficient to anchor the house at its centre' (Bachelard 1984: 78).

A basket full of fruit, a jug, a sugar bowl, a water pitcher and peaches and pears of different quality and size are arranged on the table. The objects, especially in their form and colours, tower over the environment in the painter's pre-cubist interpretation. There are no human figures: their presence is hinted at only by the chair that will receive them. This latter is an item of farming craftsmanship, made of wood and woven straw, which—along with the rough floor—indicates a room in everyday use, probably within a modest residence. Although attributable to the artist's personal maturation, this still life establishes an ideal that is extracted from the kitchen environment, concentrated on the utensils, on things.

It was in the late nineteenth century that the profound transformation of the kitchen began. It is to Catharine Beecher (1870) that we owe the idea of the functional and specialized environment, a concept that would influence design for almost all of the next century. In the text *The American Woman's Home* (published in 1869),[34] she proposed the sharing out of domestic duties among the members of the family and examined the reorganization of the kitchen. Taking the ship's-galley-inspired kitchens as a model, she abolished the sideboard and central table, replacing them with smaller work surfaces lined up along the walls and under the window. All the elements were connected: the width of the sink, provided with water by a pump system linked to the water in the well and rainwater, was equal to the width of the food preparation service area. In a nutshell, it was the first conception of an assembled kitchen. The cast-iron stoves were located in a separate, connected space. It was the first introduction of the idea of a 'single central service nucleus, around which the plan of the house is no longer the result of an assembly of rooms, but a free space, not tied to distribution and at the same time functionally differentiated by means of built-in and specialised furniture and equipment' (Frampton 1978: 93–5).

The discipline of home economics was developed towards the end of the nineteenth century thanks to supporters of the rational approach to household management: Ellen Swallow Richards for example (the first woman to be accepted at the Massachusetts Institute of Technology and founder of the *Journal of Home Economics*, 1910). The articles on home economics published in 1912 by Christine Frederick in the *Ladies' Home Journal*[35] promoted an idea of the kitchen that was influenced by contemporary research into the scientific organization of factory work, developed thanks to the experiments of Frederick W. Taylor and Frank B. and Lillian Moller Gilbreth on the measurement and timing of movements. In their studies, understanding of the degree of readiness and capacity of the individual contributed to the determination of the best task to assign them, so as to further develop efficiency.

In reality, Christine Frederick observed 'ancient procedures with new eyes' (Giedion 1967: 484), completely turning around the work of a cook, arranging the movements needed for different operations and analysing the overall plan of the kitchen. Aimed at freeing the mistress of the house from the burden of domestic duties, her theories ended by anticipating the disturbing vision of a highly mechanized woman who, rather than being freed from the chore of work, just organized her time better. The kitchen was now a workshop, positioned at the back of the house, where the woman mostly worked seated upon a stool, measuring her movements. The twentieth century therefore heralded a genuine 'infatuation with efficiency' (Sparke 2008: 131): in fact, it anticipated the inventions that had already been developed in America during the nineteenth century. The many American patents for machines for washing and ironing, for refrigerating or cooking food or for washing the dishes, were the first sign of an inventiveness that regarded domestic chores as a task to be simplified and made as functional as possible.

THE FAMILY ROOM: A QUIET AND BRIGHT INTERIORITY

Compared to the mechanization of the soul predicted by Scientific Management (originated by Taylor's theories), Art Nouveau reflected another type of interiority, although the light and bright colours of the interiors were also related to the new enthusiasm for hygiene.

In his work *The Kitchen* (approximately 1895), which appeared in his book of drawings *Ett Hem* (1899), the Swedish artist Carl Larsson depicted the kitchen of his house in Sundborn as a quiet room for the whole family (Figure 6.2).[36] In comparison to the Scandinavian taste for dark and gloomy decoration, Larsson's cottage imposed a model of the house with a bright and personal style: there was a renewed interest for the eighteenth-century and ancient Swedish peasant culture,

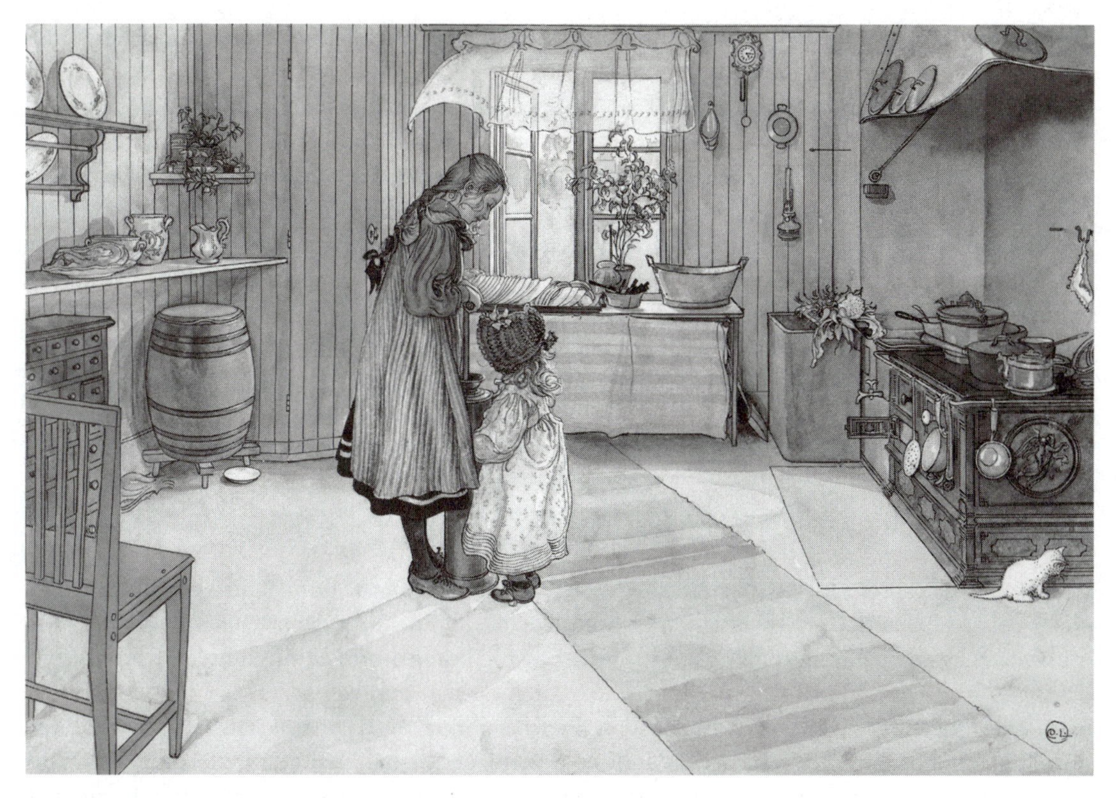

6.2. Carl Larsson, *The Kitchen*, 1895, watercolour on paper (from *Ett Hem* series, 1899). ©Nationalmuseum, Stockholm, Sweden/ The Bridgeman Art Library.

as well as influences from the Arts and Crafts movement and Japonisme (Benton 2006: 227). But the central theme of Larsson's visual poetics was 'living together' in harmony. In fact, the comfortable kitchen environment was the ideal place for children, too. While simply furnished, the room is partly faced with light wooden staves, while the fire area is protected by plaster painted green. A window, which opens onto the countryside, is ajar to allow the smoke to disperse. Every utensil and object (plates, pots and jugs) has its orderly place as soon as it is no longer in use: on the floor, a dish full of milk awaits the white cat whose gaze is caught elsewhere, perhaps by the other members of the family. The kitchen is a domesticated place serenely inhabited by adults, children and animals.

Arts and Crafts, Art Nouveau and Japan Style are, moreover, the influences felt in the Gamble House (Pasadena, 1907–8) designed by brothers Charles Summer Greene and Henry Mather Greene:[37] much more than a simple cottage, it is a residence that is equally elegant and comfortable, in which a profound relationship with the surrounding nature is cultivated, not only through the different views from the glass windows delicately decorated with flowering vines but, above all, also through the outdoor rooms, which allow the family to sleep outside in summer and even when it's raining. In comparison to the main rooms in the house, opulent in terms of materials and decorative details, the kitchen is a more simple space but, perhaps precisely because of this, even more welcoming.

It is separated from the dining room by the butler's pantry, which functions as a larder and a secondary area for serving meals: the route of the serving staff is laid out diagonally, thanks to the position of the two doors, the second of which opens on to the kitchen. It is a genuine workstation, functionally organized, with containers of various heights on the walls and, in the centre of the room, a table with sliding drawers that open on both sides so as not to obstruct anyone working there. The cold room is accessed by a secondary door. The furnishings, doors and trim are made of a certain kind of maple wood (bird's eye maple), which conveys a particular, slightly vibrant light to the whole room. However, the most interesting element in the kitchen is the screened porch, which is intimate and bright, furnished with a circular table: it is the space where the family has breakfast, in visual contact with the garden which its windows overlook. Although this kitchen is on the other side of the Atlantic, just like Larsson's family portrait, it is possible to imagine a calm interiority, which concurs with the warmth of the family reunited around the table.

SOUL FRAGMENTATION: THE PRAGMATIC KITCHEN

In Europe, the expressionism of Fauves disclosed the interiority of the human being through incendiary colours in particular. The kitchen of Maurice de Vlaminck (*La cuisine, Intérieur*, 1904)[38]—influenced by the paintings of Vincent van Gogh, which the painter admired in an exhibition in Paris—is still a gently intimate space, in which a female figure moves silently. A simply set table dominates the scene, while the woman is in a corner intent on drying a plate with a white tea towel. Here, too, distantly preceded by Johannes Vermeer, the habitual gesture ties the person to her everyday reality, reflecting her interiority, while her gaze is indiscernible, obscured by the red stain that depicts her cheek.

Just a few years later, the expressionist kitchen of Ernst Ludwig Kirchner revealed something quite different. The fiery colours, the simplification of forms and the strong central perspective represent an atmosphere of distress and emotional claustrophobia (Acton 2008: 36). Kirchner was considered unfit for active military service and voluntarily withdrew to Switzerland (in the mountains by the village of Frauenkirch, near Davos), where the painter lived through a dramatic period that is depicted in his work *Alpine Kitchen* (1918; Figure 6.3).[39] In the painting, he sits at the table of a rustic kitchen, intent on a lithograph; his soul is reflected in, and almost seems to shatter against, the walls of the room. It is not by chance that in the image a cast-iron stove stands at counterpoint to the figure of the man: Bachelard referred explicitly to the 'fire confined to the stove' as the stimulation for psychoanalytical abstraction or the most sublime and free dreams (Bachelard 1973: 176). The distortion of the space corresponds to the dissolution of a soul that suffers for the fate of mankind. Fauvist tones echo with flashes and explosions from the artillery that blazed in Europe's skies. Kirchner's painting also depicts a profound social and cultural change: it was the end of traditional values, definitively swept away by the war. A new era was about to begin.

In Europe straight after the war, the real needs of the working class and the rejection of the previous bourgeois models led to the architectural debate over *existenz minimum*, with the search for housing solutions equipped with 'modern kitchens'. While the Americans had the task of organizing domestic chores in a Taylorist way, in Europe efforts were made to rationalize the working-class household with the *minimum* kitchen. Erna Meyer (1926, consultant to the 1927 Weissenhof

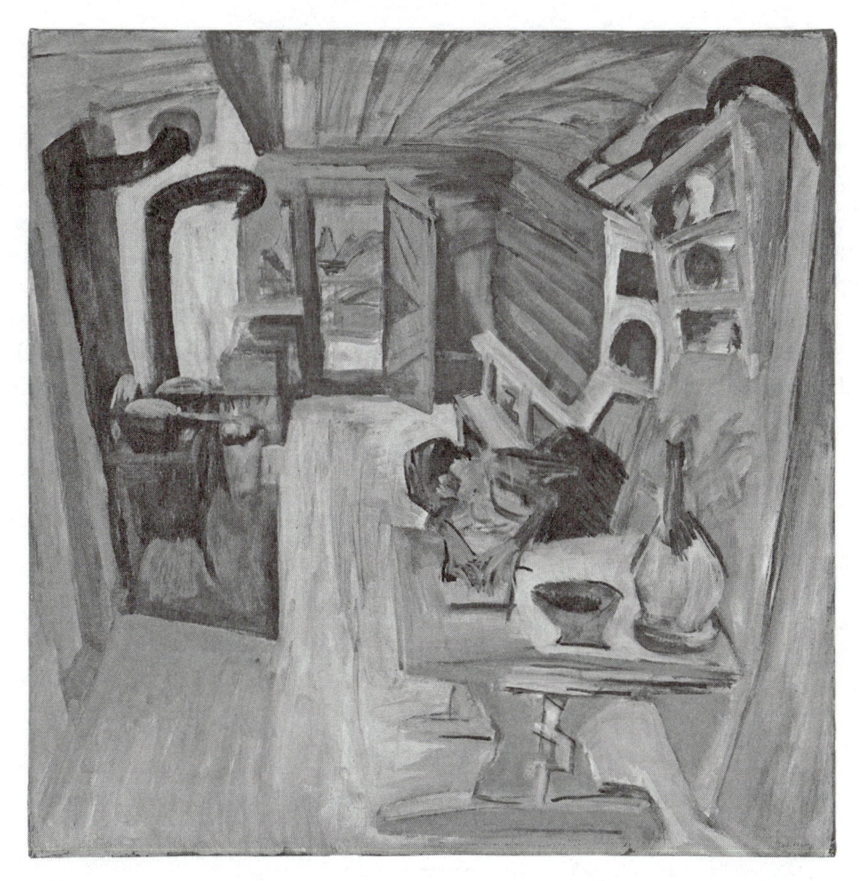

6.3. Ernst Ludwig Kirchner, *Alpine Kitchen*, 1918, oil on canvas. ©Museo Thyssen-Bornemisza, Madrid.

exhibition for J.J.P. Oud houses), Margarete Schütte-Lihotzsky (Frankfurt Kitchen, 1925–6)[40] and Walter Gropius (Dessau kitchen with furniture by Marcel Breuer, 1925–6) were just a few of the protagonists in the debate on the functional kitchen. Located in a specific, small room, the furniture of the Frankfurt Kitchen—the best known prototype of the rationalist kitchens—was arranged in a line and in the corners and included a double, electric-and-gas stove, a sink with a foldaway drip counter, wall cupboards, a dresser and a metal table with drawers.

The first European modular kitchen was made by the Belgian architect Louis H. De Koninck. An initial study (1930) depicted a woman in an apron in the centre of the picture with arms flung out towards the Cubex kitchen. Here, the woman seems to be the moral centre of the space she is destined for, but, above all, she seems to dictate its size. The Cubex kitchen was in fact designed on the basis of a precise modular unit (60-by-60 cm for the base unit, 45 or 60 cm high). While drawing on some *casiers-standard* concepts applied to the kitchen—presented by Le Corbusier, Pierre Jeannaret and Charlotte Perriand at the Salon d'Automne (Paris) of 1928[41]—the Cubex was a model that could actually be made by industry as well as be extremely versatile and flexible (Rüegg 1998: 204). Exhibited at the II International Congress of Modern Architecture (CIAM) in

Brussels (1930), in a show organized by the Belgian national group, its success was so great that it was extensively adopted in Belgium, where it remained in production until 1960.

With the dawn of the 1930s, the continuous kitchen model became internationally established. With its continuous and easily cleaned surfaces, doors with no engravings, lines of containers and not excessively prominent wall cupboards, some scholars emphasized its assonance with the factory assembly line, which is organized into specialized work stations (Lupton and Miller 1992: 41). It was, moreover, Lillian M. Gilbreth who designed the 'Practical Kitchen' (1924–30) for the Brooklyn Borough Gas Company, in which the linear sequence of the cook's tasks is clear.

In Italy, the architect Tomaso Buzzi was the illustrator (with Gio Ponti) for the recipe book by Emma Vanzetti (1931), and his drawing *Galilea o la cuoca meccanica* (Figure 6.4) ironically expressed the contradictions of this 'mechanical bride' who was subjected to the marital yoke as

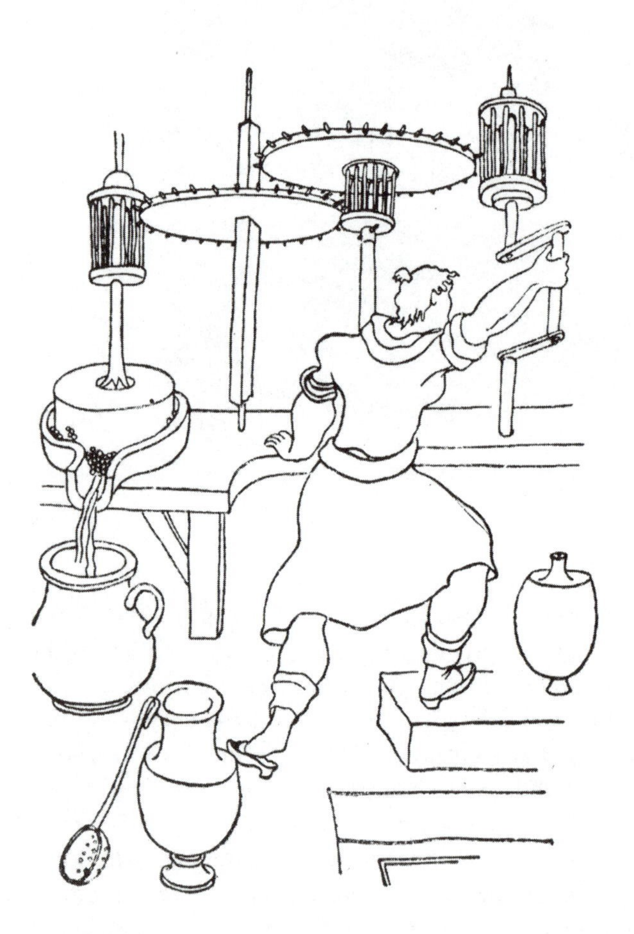

6.4. Tomaso Buzzi, *Galilea o la cuoca meccanica*, 1931, illustration. Courtesy Archivio Tomaso Buzzi, la Scarzuola, Montegabbione (TR), Italy.

much as to the role of perfect housewife,[42] as is clear from the recipe book itself: 'For a conscientious mistress of the house making a meal means tackling the most delicate, most complex and most interesting problem of her ménage. More than a science made of rules, it is an art consisting of nuances' (Vanzetti 1931: 13).[43]

TOMORROW'S KITCHEN: EASIER LIVING

After the Streamlined period, which instigated the remodelling of both the kitchen environment and its appliances with aerodynamic styling, the assembled kitchen once more aroused great interest in American industry: in approximately 1945, user demand steered the market in the direction of brighter and more scenic kitchens, with artificial lighting directed towards work surfaces and the sink, and less rounded surfaces than the streamlining design.

In 1943, George Nelson developed several designs for prefabricated kitchens, which would remain on paper for a long time (Nelson and Wright 1943: 101).[44] Among these, the Food Preparing Unit was a counter for preparing food, structured in units (cold, hot and water), which incorporated the various kitchen appliances. Ten years later, the Kitchen Design Department of General Electric assigned Nelson the position of consultant (until 1962). There were two definite projects (approximately 1960) which would remain in prototype status: the Mini-Max Kitchen, for smaller spaces, and the Mechanical Storage Unit (MSU). This latter was a mechanized cooking and refrigeration system, with components that, thanks to an internal latch mechanism, could be lifted onto the work surface. Strangely, the unit is reminiscent of the complex designs by Thomas Sheraton for writing desks with rising drawers (Harlequin Pembroke Table, approximately 1790).

But it was the articles[45] and the book *Tomorrow's House* by Nelson and Wright (1945) that brought the practicality of the American kitchen into the postwar era. *Tomorrow's House*, aimed at a non-specialist public, was a guide for designing and furnishing one's house that tackled the theme of new demands for the home.[46] It expressed the idea of a 'home-for-everyone' that was within the economic means of the wider public and also in line with their tastes: a house in which average Americans could easily imagine themselves, outside of nostalgic formalisms. A functional distribution of space and attention to the diffusion of light, to ventilation and heating systems and to the storage and cleaning of objects were the basic principles supported. But the book was truly innovative in that it emphasized the need for a human approach to the problem of habitat. Enhancing personal needs, the focus on family life, and avoiding breaks between the worlds of adult and children were some of the methods proposed for constructing a happy 'house-of-the-future'.

In terms of the kitchen, the authors criticized a purely Taylorist vision: 'Efficiency in the home and the well-being of the housewife depend on more factors than steps and minutes' (Nelson and Wright 1945: 71). The response was to design a large space—'possibly the biggest room in the whole house' (Nelson and Wright 1945: 72)—which would mainly be a kitchen plus a living room and a dining room, or rather a 'work centre-social centre', welcoming for the whole family and no longer a workshop that imprisoned the mistress of the house. It was an unusual solution in comparison to the European *machine-à-habiter* in which functional order was openly combined with North American easier living.

Similarly, Mary and Russell Wright acted as promoters of 'good design for everyone'. Russell planned the most revolutionary dinnerware of the postwar period, which came into widespread use in the United States (*American Modern* 1938–40),[47] available in rounded forms and an incredible variety of colours, with no decoration. In 1950, Russell and his wife, Mary, wrote the famous *Guide to Easier Living* (Wright 2003).

The text examined each area of the house in great detail, teaching the public how to organize it and easily keep it tidy. The *Guide* picked up the theme of efficiently performing the domestic chores of the housewife, and from it a style of living according to a new informal way of living for a newly suburban American public emerged. One image (Figure 6.5) in particular made the changes proposed worthwhile: in the kitchen and dining room, the owners of the house and their guests tidy up together smiling, and the caption reads: 'Cleanup can even be a part of the evening's pleasure, if managed properly' (Wright 2003: 176). The kitchen was no longer an aseptic workshop but a space in which to live together, as George Nelson and Harry Wright had written. It was the sign of the most profound change to the *kitchenscape*: the kitchen was no longer the reign or gleaming prison of the woman, but the definitive 'heart of the family'. The 'lived space', of Bachelardian memory, is more a mental *habitus* than a physical one, and has lasted until this day.[48]

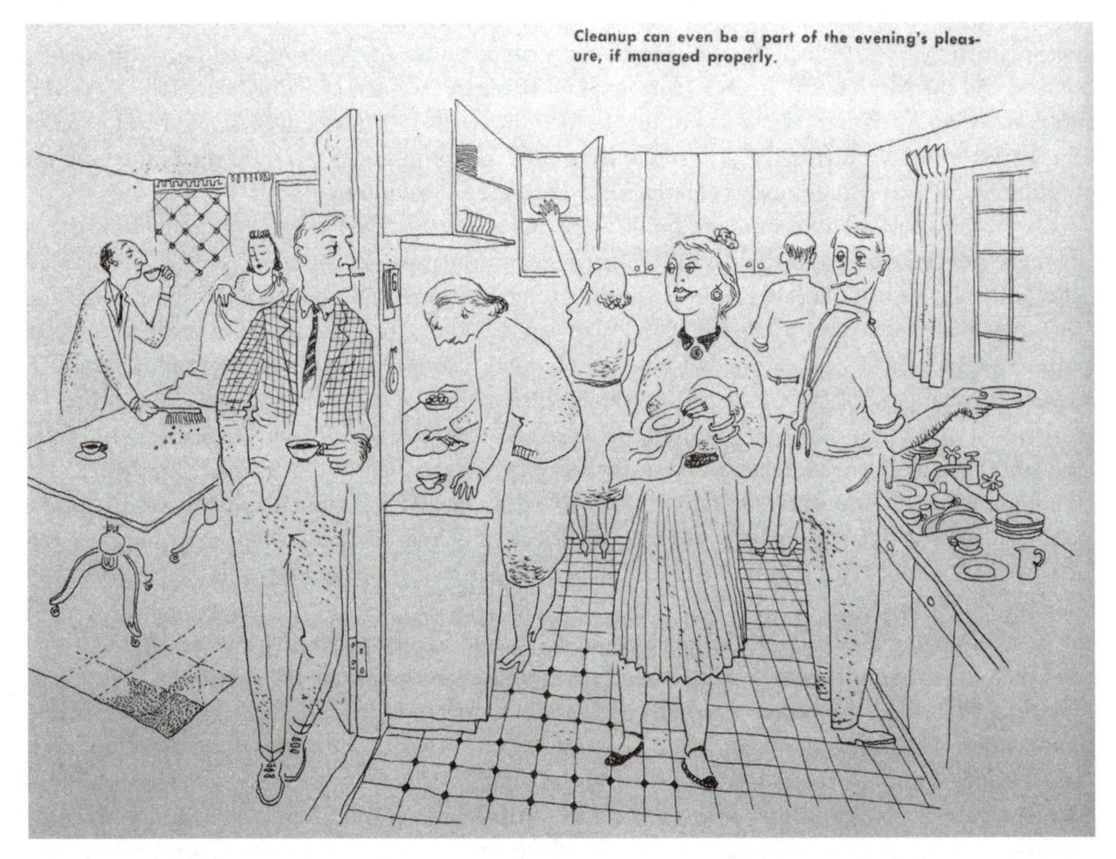

6.5. Russell Wright, *Cleanup with Guests* . . ., 1950, illustration. Courtesy Russell Wright Studios, New York.

NOTES

1. For the figure of the *flâneuse*, see Bruno 2002: 76, and *passim*.
2. Let us recall the case of Swiss Fritz Karl Watel, known as Vatel, who was responsible for the procurement and preparation of the table of Louis II de Bourbon, Prince de Condé. In 1670, on the occasion

of the visit of King Louis XIV, Vatel, terrified by the thought of a possible shortage of fresh fish to cook, committed suicide, unable to stand the dishonour. His legacy to the world was the invention of *Crème Chantilly*.

3. In Medieval times, witches and healers prepared their potions in the kitchen. The accusation of witchcraft, often by jealous doctors, was therefore aimed at women who knew the properties of plants (see Muzzarelli and Tarozzi 2003: 20–1).
4. For a general introduction to this theme, see Bassanini 1990.
5. On the *topophilia* of the house, see Bachelard 1984: 26.
6. Odysseus is greeted by the swineherd Eumaeus on his return to Ithaca (Homer 2008: XIV). The hearth in the Palace of Alcinous (Homer 2008: VII, 160–85) seems instead similar to the perpetually lit fire of the *megaron*. More familiar is the hearth where the parents of Nausicaa sit (Homer: VI, 50), and where King Laertes rests in winter, along with his slaves (Homer: XI, 190). Finally Odysseus waits for Penelope at the hearth, after killing the Suitors (Homer 2008: XXIII, 70).
7. Archaeological excavations have uncovered rooms with hearths and sinks in the homes of Vetti, Pansa and Meleagro (first century AD).
8. In that period, the hearth did not have a hood, meaning the kitchen was full of smoke. It slowly dissipated through the cracks in the ceiling, to then emerge from the roof.
9. An illuminating example of a monumental kitchen is found in the Certosa di San Lorenzo, also known as the Certosa di Padula (approximately 1306–1750), not far from the Italian city of Salerno. Legend has it that a frittata of 1,000 eggs was cooked in the kitchen of the Certosa for Emperor Charles V, on his return from the Conquest of Tunis.
10. Lighting the fire was not actually a simple task: the first matches were invented in 1530; the self-igniting variety was introduced in the nineteenth century. Before that a flint was used, made of a piece of steel and a splinter of flint which were banged together with force.
11. Fresco, Basilica Inferiore, Assisi.
12. Fresco, Cattedrale di Santa Maria Assunta, Atri (Teramo).
13. The problem of smoke in the kitchen seems to have been resolved by Raffaello Sanzio since, in 1520, in the designs of his own palazzo in Via Giulia in Rome, he positioned the kitchen on the *piano nobile*, alongside the living rooms (Pagliara 2001: 43).
14. On the testimonial value of the pictorial sources relating to interiors, furnishings and objects, see Schiaparelli 1908: XI.
15. Oil on canvas, The National Gallery, London.
16. A famous example of *doorkijkje* appears in the work of Emanuel de Witte, *Interior with a Woman at the Virginals*, 1665–70, oil on canvas, Museum Boymans-van Beuningen, Rotterdam.
17. The term *sloth* was used in the Greek age as a synonym for indifference tinged with sadness, while in the Roman age it was a synonym for indolence. During the Middle Ages, it identified a state of melancholic torpor, inertia almost. It was the Catholic interpretation that gave the word its moralistic and negative value of negligence of charitable acts.
18. Oil on canvas, Germanisches Nationalmuseum, Nürberg.
19. Oil on canvas, Rijksmuseum, The Hague. The painting is also known as *The Milkmaid*.
20. The expert in gastronomy (*mangeur* or gourmet) was a figure apart from the cook who emerged in France during the nineteenth century (see on this matter, Aron 1978a).
21. For the conditions of servants during the nineteenth century, see Perrot 1994a: 145–8.
22. Oil on paper, Museo Mario Praz, Roma.
23. The Florentine palazzo, which still exists, is included in the Museo Bardini with other buildings.
24. Oil on canvas, private collection. The letter is from the son of the elderly couple, husband of the young woman, and was written from the battlefield for the Unification of Italy.

25. Oil on canvas, private collection. The painting is also known as *Ascoltando la notizia del giorno*. In the painting, the women are reading a proclamation from the Roman Committee, hoping for the annexation of Rome to the Kingdom of Italy. A similar room is in Domenico Induno (Gerolamo's brother), *La visita alla nutrice*, 1863, oil on canvas, Fondazione Cariplo Collection, Gallerie d'Italia, Milan.
26. In 1844, the Society for Improving the Conditions of the Labouring Classes had been established under the patronage of Queen Victoria and Prince Albert, with Lord Ashley Shaftesbury as president.
27. With the expression 'food topography', Aron (1978b: 221) identifies the spaces where the 'rite' of eating takes place. The social status or way of life of the family changes depending on the number, distribution and importance of these places in the house, and so does the degree of civilization of a food group.
28. In the mid-nineteenth century, the servants called this room for storing food 'the pantry'.
29. Frequently, domestic staff slept in the larder, even in refined residences (Bryson 2011: 110).
30. *The Spectator* published various adverts for the 'tiled kitchen' by Fredk. Edwards & Sons (49, Great Marlborough Street, Regent Street, London) (see *The Spectator* 1870: 1304; *The Spectator* 1872: 1348; *The Spectator* 1878: 456.
31. An electric stove was presented at the World Columbian Exposition in 1893. General Electric began production starting in 1905.
32. *La table de cuisine—Nature morte au panier*, oil on canvas, Musée d'Orsay, Paris.
33. Actually, Cézanne exhibited many of his *Still lives* in his studio. As is well-known, the artist did not realistically represent the forms but used apparently out of scale proportions to balance the general composition of the painting.
34. The text was written in collaboration with Harriet Beecher Stowe, the author's sister. It was preceded by Beecher in 1841.
35. Then collected in Frederick 1913. Frederick 1919 followed, which now emphasized the scientific condition of domestic work rather than home economics.
36. Larsson and his wife, Karin, moved to the cottage in Sundborn in 1889; it was subsequently transformed and expanded by the pair for their large family.
37. For Frampton (2002: 24), Gamble House was the closest piece of American work to European Art Nouveau of the previous decade.
38. Also known as *Intérieur de cuisine*, oil on canvas, Musée National d'Arte Moderne, Centre Georges Pompidou, Paris.
39. Oil on canvas, Museum Thyssen-Bornemisza, Madrid.
40. On German applications of scientific housekeeping, see Bullock 1988.
41. The first *casiers-standards* were exhibited by Le Corbusier and Pierre Jeannaret on the Esprit Nouveau pavilion at the *Exposition Internationale des Arts Décoratifs et Industriels Modernes* (Paris 1925).
42. The word housewife, literally 'she who is married to the house', emphasizes the gender relationship between the woman and the space. In Bruno 2002: 81–3, the theme of the housewife is analysed with reference to the film *Craig's Wife* (1936), taken from the comedy by George Kelly, directed by Dorothy Azner; the main actors were Rosalind Russell, Thomas Mitchell, Jane Darwell.
43. In Italy, architect Alberto Sartoris (1930) released Frankfurt Kitchen. Italian rational kitchens were by Piero Bottoni in the exhibition pavilion 'La Casa Elettrica' (by Luigi Figini and Gino Pollini), IV Triennale di Monza (1930), and in the exhibition *Criteri della casa d'oggi*, VII Triennale di Milano (1940).
44. Here the two architects outlined some considerations that would be drawn on in Nelson and Wright 1945. The same article published some sketches for an experimental kitchen design.
45. In 1940, Nelson wrote fourteen articles on the modern house entitled 'When You Build Your House' for the magazine *Arts & Decoration*; the articles were then collected in Nelson 1946. One of the articles was dedicated to 'Bathrooms and Kitchens' (Nelson 1946: 39–41).

46. The book was illustrated with numerous sketches by Paul Grotz (art director of *Architectural Forum*) and photographs of contemporary interiors (by Frank Lloyd Wright, Marcel Breuer, Walter Gropius, Richard Neutra and the authors themselves).
47. *American Modern* won the American Designers' Institute Award in 1941 for Best Ceramic Design of the Year.
48. Imma Forino's chapter was translated by Victoria Miller, Language Password sas.

REFERENCES

Acton, M. (2008), *Guardare l'arte contemporanea*, Turin: Einaudi.

Aron, J.-P. (1978a), *La Francia a tavola, dall'Ottocento alla Belle Epoque*, Turin: Einaudi.

Aron, J.-P. (1978b), *Cucina.* In *Enciclopedia Einaudi*, vol. 4, Turin: Einaudi, 215–37.

Bachelard, G. (1973), *L'intuizione dell'istante: La psicoanalisi del fuoco*, Bari: Dedalo.

Bachelard, G. (1984), *La poetica dello spazio*, Bari: Dedalo.

Bachelard, G. (1990), *Poetica del fuoco: Frammenti di un lavoro incompiuto*, Como: Red edizioni.

Bassanini, G., ed., (1990), *Tracce silenziose dell'abitare: La donna e la casa*, Milan: FrancoAngeli.

Beecher, C. (1841), *A Treatise on Domestic Economy*, New York: Schocken.

Beecher, C. (1870), *The American Woman's Home: Or, Principles of Domestic Science; Being a Guide to the Formation and Maintenance of Economical, Healthful, Beautiful, and Christians Homes*, New York: J.B. Ford & Co.

Benton, T. (2006), 'The Twentieth-Century Architectural Interior: Representing Modernity', in J. Aynsley and C. Grant, eds., *Imagined Interiors: Representing the Domestic Interior Since the Renaissance*, London: V&A Publications.

Bruno, G. (2002), *Atlante delle emozioni: In viaggio tra arte, architettura e cinema*, Milan: Bruno Mondadori.

Bryson, B. (2011), *Breve storia della vita privata*, Parma: Ugo Guanda Editore.

Bullock, N. (1988), 'First the Kitchen—Then the Façade', *Journal of Design History*, 1/3–4: 177–92.

Carter, A. (1985), 'The Kitchen Child', in S. Bortolussi, trans., *Black Venus*, London: Chatto & Windus.

Contaime, P. (1993), 'L'organizzazione dello spazio privato: Secc. XIV–XV', in P. Ariès and G. Duby, eds., *La vita privata: Dal Feudalesimo al Rinascimento*, Milan: Mondadori.

Farè, I. (1990), 'Quando diciamo privato', in G. Bassanini, ed., *Tracce silenziose dell'abitare: La donna e la casa*, Milan: FrancoAngeli.

Flandrin, J.-L. (1993), 'La distinzione attraverso il gusto', in P. Ariès and G. Duby, eds., *La vita privata: Dal Rinascimento all'Illuminismo*, Milan: Mondadori.

Frampton, K. (1978), *Ambiente e tecnica nell'architettura moderna*, Bologna: Zanichelli.

Frampton, K. (2002), *Capolavori dell'architettura Americana: La casa del XX secolo*, Milan: Skira-Rizzoli.

Frederick, C. (1913), *The New Housekeeping: Efficiency Studies in Home Management*, Garden City, NY: Doubleday.

Frederick, C. (1919), *Household Engineering: Scientific Management in the Home*, Chicago: American School of Home Economics.

Giedion, S. (1967), *L'era della meccanizzazione*, Milan: Feltrinelli.

Hall, C. (1994), 'Dolce casa', in P. Ariès and G. Duby, eds., *La vita privata: L'Ottocento*, Milan: Mondadori.

Homer (2008), *Odissea*, Milan: BUR.

Kerr, R. (1972), *The Gentleman's House: Or, How to Plan English Residences, from the parsonage to the palace; with tables of accommodation and cost, and a series of selected plans*, London: Johnson Reprint.

La Roncière, C., de (1993), 'La vita privata dei notabili toscani', in P. Ariès and G. Duby, eds, *La vita privata: Dal Feudalesimo al Rinascimento*, Milan: Mondadori.

Lasdun, S. (1981), *Vita di casa nell'età vittoriana*, Florence: Passigli.

Lupton, E., and Miller, A. J. (1992), *The Bathroom, the Kitchen and the Aesthetics of Waste: A Process of Elimination*, New York: Kiosk

Maiuri, A. (2000), *La casa pompeiana: Struttura, ambienti, storia nella magistrale descrizione d'un grande archeologo*, Naples: Generoso Procaccino.
Maldonado, T. (1987), *Il futuro della modernità*, Milan: Feltrinelli.
Meyer, E. (1926), *Der neue Haushalt: Ein Wegweiser zur wirtschaftlichen Betriebsführung*, Stuttgart: Franck'sche Verlagshandlung.
Mumford, L. (1999), *La cultura delle città*, Turin: Edizioni di Comunità.
Muzzarelli, M. G., and Tarozzi, F. (2003), *Donne e cibo: Una relazione nella storia*, Milan: Bruno Mondadori.
Nelson, G. (1946), 'When You Build Your House', in M. Reid, ed., *When You Build*, New York: Robert M. McBride.
Nelson, G., and Wright, H. (1943), 'Houses for Human Beings', *Fortune,* 4: 100–5.
Nelson, G., and Wright, H. (1945), *Tomorrow's House: A Complete Guide for the Home-Builder*, New York: Simon & Schuster.
Pagliara, P. N. (2001), '"Destri" e cucine nell'abitazione del XV e XVI secolo, in specie a Roma', in A. Scotti. Tosini, ed., *Aspetti dell'abitare in Italia tra XV e XVI secolo: Distribuzione, funzione, impianti*, Milan: Unicopli.
Pennell, S. (1998), '"Pots and Pans History": The Material Culture of the Kitchen in Early Modern England', *Journal of Design History*, 11/3: 201–16.
Perrot, M. (1994a), 'Figure e compiti', in P. Ariès and G. Duby, eds, *La vita privata: L'Ottocento*, Milan: Mondadori.
Perrot, M. (1994b), 'Modi di abitare', in P. Ariès and Georges D., eds., *La vita privata: L'Ottocento*, Milan: Mondadori.
Praz, M. (1964), *La filosofia dell'arredamento: I mutamenti nel gusto della decorazione interna attraverso i secoli dall'antica Roma ai nostri tempi*, Milan: Longanesi & C.
Praz, M. (2003), *La Casa della Vita*, Milan: Adelphi.
Rüegg, A. (1998), 'De Konink, créateur de mobilier. De Koenick's Furniture Design', in C. Mierop and A. Van Loo, eds,, *Louis Herman De Konink: Architects des années moderns. Architects of Modern Times*, Bruxelles: A.A.M. Éditions.
Rybczynski, W. (1989), *La casa: Intimità, stile, benessere*, Milan: Rusconi.
Sarti, R. (2006), *Vita di casa: Abitare, mangiare, vestire nell'Europa moderna*, Roma-Bari: Laterza.
Sartoris, A. (1930), 'Intorno alla cucina standardizzata di Francoforte', *La Casa bella,* 26: 59–60.
Schiaparelli, A. (1908), *La Casa fiorentina e i suoi arredi nei secoli XIV e XV*, 2 vols., Florence: G.C. Sansoni.
Senise, M., and Buscagliene, S. (1980), 'La cucina nell'arte', *Ottagono*, 15/56: 108–11.
Sparke, P. (2008), *The Modern Interior*, London: Reaktion Books.
The Spectator (1870), 43: 1304.
The Spectator (1872), 45: 1348.
The Spectator (1878), 51: 456.
Thornton, P. (1992), *Interni del Rinascimento italiano, 1400–1600*, Milan: Leonardo.
Vanzetti, E. (1931), *Il Quattrova illustrato ovvero La cucina elegante. Con prefazione di Piero Gadda e disegni di Tomaso Buzzi e Gio Ponti*, Milan: Domus S. A. Editoriale.
Wedd, K. (2002), *The Victorian House*, London: Aurum Press.
Wright, R., and Wright, M. (2003), *Guide to Easier Living*, New York: Simon & Schuster.

7.

BATHROOMS: PLUMBING THE CANON—THE BATHTUB NUDES OF ALFRED STEVENS, EDGAR DEGAS AND PIERRE BONNARD RECONSIDERED

georgina downey

In the late nineteenth- and early twentieth-century European painting eroticized images of female bath time are so pervasive that American art historian Linda Nochlin, in *Bathers, Bodies, Beauty*, is given pause, wondering, 'Why in this period, did the female naked figure, in or near water, become *so* important?' (Nochlin 2006: 17). Nochlin examines the rise of the 'highly idealised and aesthetically specific female bathers' such as Renoir's *The Bathers* (1884–7), and she notes how in these paintings women's bathing practices were '*strenuously* removed from any context that would suggest contemporaneity or the realities of urban existence' (Nochlin 2006: 17).[1] However, a closer look at some celebrating paintings of female bath time by Renoir's contemporaries, as well as from the Post Impressionist canon, reveals that 'the realities of urban existence' and in particular modern regimes of hygiene, were fully present in the art of the period.

Images of female bath time thus have a lot to tell us about attitudes towards the advances of modernity, as they are encoded in bathing technologies. I will explore well-known representations of female bath time *through* the technology of bathing to see what these might suggest about contemporary practices around cleanliness, smell, maintenance and attitudes towards the feminine body.

METHODS AND REVIEW OF LITERATURE

Three groups of literature bear upon this reading of the representation of female bath time in modern art. The first body of literature consists of histories of bathing practice. The authors here are generally in agreement that the technological advances, while intriguing, are in fact, the by-products of popular *mentalitiés* about the body. These texts are therefore outlined here for the purpose that, as well as providing relevant accounts of changes in bathing, they also reflect underlying notions of bodily health within everyday practices, especially as these notions refer to the feminine body.

Siegfried Giedion commences his *The Mechanisation of the Bath* by proposing that the Minoans were the world's originators of the practice of relaxing in a hot tub, and that for them regenerative, social bathing required the development of sophisticated public water heating and sewerage systems. He explains his notion of the 'total regeneration' style of bathing of the Ancients, and contrasts this with the 'mere surface ablution' regimes of the modern period (Giedion 1948).

Lawrence Wright, in *Clean and Decent: The Fascinating History of the Bathroom and Water-closet*, reveals how for the Greeks and Romans the concept of *sanitas* referred to healthful practices, not sanitisation or the removal of dirt as we might understand it (Wright 1960: 2). He explains that in the ancient world, bathing was both a pleasure and a social ritual that was practised communally. It only incidentally resulted in a bodily state that the modern period would deem 'hygienically clean'. He explains how the Romans believed that it was every man, woman and child's natural right (freeborn or slave) to bathe in every twenty-four-hour period. Thus the Romans built elaborate, costly and technically sophisticated bathhouses, both on home territory and in their colonies, that were accessible to all (Wright 1960: 14).

After the fall of the Roman Empire, bathing continued to be practiced, but on a much reduced scale, with early Christians believing that face, hands and even full body washing was a sign of respect to God rather than a pleasure for the individual. Monasteries across Europe installed sophisticated plumbing technologies that served communal bathing stalls and drained privies (Wright 1960: 24). Between the twelfth and fourteenth centuries, steam was believed to be relaxing and cleansing, and the medieval townsfolk of Europe, on an at least a weekly basis, visited steam or spa bath facilities—a bathing regime that challenges our contemporary stereotyped view of the 'filthy' peasants of this period (Wright 1960: 39–45).

Art historian Christopher Wood describes Durer's *Women's Bathhouse* (c. 1496) as the first studio nude, but it is also for our purposes an early and influential female bather scene (Wood 2005: 65; see Figure 7.1). Wood suggests that bathing houses could be likened to studios. Both spaces privileged the novel practice of life drawing that arose in the Renaissance:

> Durer figures the bath house as a parable of the intrusion of life drawing into the painter's workshop . . . The 'work' of the sauna—sponging, brushing, scrubbing, combing, kneading, birching—is a preparation for the display of the body, a preparation of the body so it can be admired. (Wood 2005: 65)

The *Women's Bathhouse*, according to George Vigarello, underscores how bathing in the medieval period in Europe was dominated by notions of play. Town criers summoned city folk to steam baths and bathhouses in the thirteenth century for festive events that doubled as 'feasts of pleasure', involving not only bathing but also food, socializing and sex, and only incidentally, cleanliness (Vigarello 1988: 157).

In the fourteenth century when the Black Death spread through Northern Europe, bathhouses were blamed for the spread of infection, and public bathing ceased across Europe with a dramatic suddenness, ushering in what Lawrence Wright refers to as 'two rather insanitary centuries'—the sixteenth and seventeenth. During this period it was believed that cleaning or scrubbing the skin left it vulnerable to disease. The only parts in these two centuries that required cleaning were the

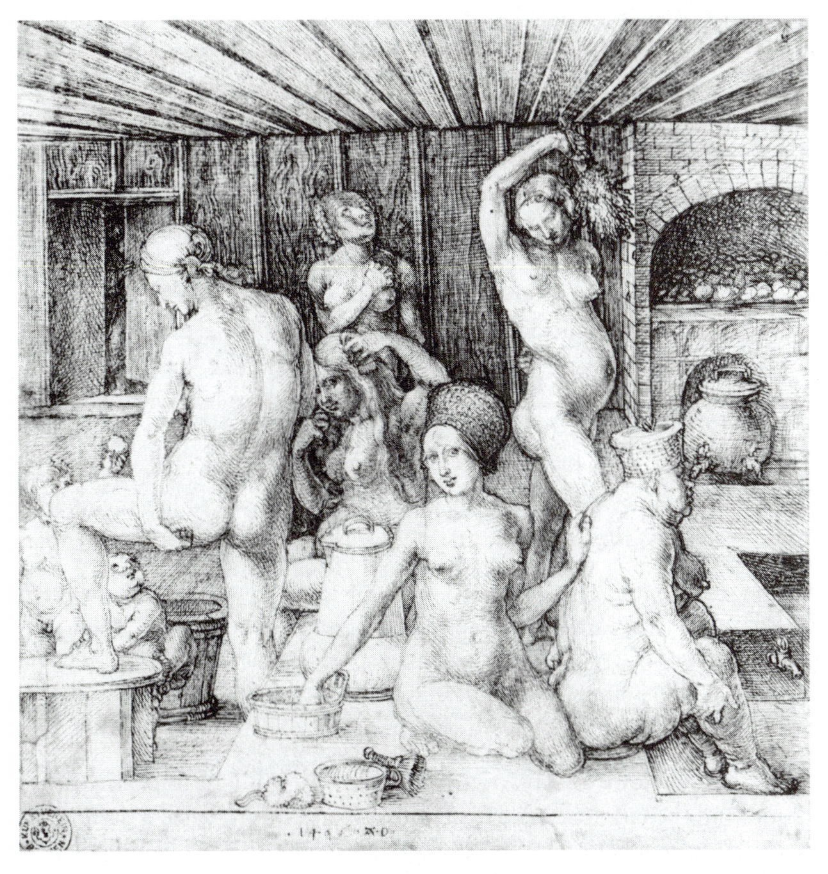

7.1. Albrecht Dürer, *Women's Bath House*, engraving, c. 1496, Kunsthalle Bremen, Photo: Karen Blindow.

face, hands (before eating) and, occasionally, the feet. Clean linen in the form of undergarments were understood to clean and freshen the body by absorbing and wicking away smells and grime, so the well-to-do changed their *chemises*, or undershirts, several times a day, without ever washing their bodies from one year to the next. Wright and Ashenberg both cite the notorious example of James I, successor of Queen Elizabeth, who, over a lifetime, 'reportedly washed only his fingers', but who changed his linen five times a day (Ashenberg 2007: 99). We might surmise that cleanliness, unlike Godliness, was not even skin deep.

In the late eighteenth century, bathing for Roman-style bodily regeneration came back into practice, not only through the general revival of interest in classical culture, but also because it became fashionable for members of the European courts to visit hot spas and undertake sea bathing for health reasons. This led to the installation of baths in the houses of the more stylish aristocrats. Queen Marie Antoinette also provided a leading example, with her habit of taking a daily bath (Wright 1960: 100).

Entering the nineteenth century, public health became a focus. The wave of waterborne diseases in the mid-nineteenth century such as typhoid and cholera were initially attributed to miasmas, or rising smells around stagnant water. However, Pasteur's discovery of the role of germs in causing disease further prompted civic authorities to undertake projects to cover and control open sewers and to ensure the availability of fresh water to metropolitan populations. Theories of health and the modern body served to highlight the importance of daily bathing, and authorities in major cities began to install running water to whole suburbs of 'subscribers', usually the wealthiest suburbs being connected first. Piped water within houses that connected to public sewerage systems became increasingly prevalent across the major European and American cities.

In *The Great Stink of Paris and the Nineteenth-Century Struggle against Filth and Germs*, David Barnes looks at the period of the 1870s and 1880s which merged the miasma theory of the spread of disease (pestilent fogs)—with bacteriologically based theories. He shows that while Pasteurian theory emerged in the 1880s, it did not displace previous beliefs straight away, and that for a while in the fin-de-siècle (on both sides of the English Channel and the Atlantic), people continued to associate bad odour with disease and a clean-smelling body with its absence (Barnes 2006: 104).

Mrs Beeton's advice of a daily bath in the early 1860s reflects a regime of cleanliness that was ahead of its time, but running water was only affordable by those in high-income households. In her classic *Book of Household Management*, first published in 1859, she recommends:

> Health and strength cannot be long continued unless the skin—all the skin—is washed frequently with a sponge or other means. Every morning is best; . . . it brings blood to the surface, and causes it to circulate well through fine capillary vessels . . . this insensible perspiration cannot escape well if the skin is not clean as the pores get choked up. (Beeton 1859–62: 1095–6)

In America, Catharine Stowe and Harriet Beecher Stowe brought to bear their own advice on bathing techniques and the rationale for daily bathing—and this revealed a quite sophisticated understanding of the body, in a period when 'humeral' medicine was still being practised. Jacqueline Wilkie explains how the Beecher Stowes delineated the structure of the body in terms of pores, nerve endings, hair follicles and blood vessels: 'They pictured the skin as a vital organ . . . [thus] the true purpose of bathing was to rinse off . . . perspiration, not to remove dirt or sensually satisfy the body. Therefore . . . the most appropriate form of bathing consisted of a cold plunge for a few seconds, followed by brisk towelling' (Wilkie 1986: 651).

Moving on into the twentieth century, Giedion considered that the mechanics of bathing provided an important insight into the inner nature of early-twentieth-century Western culture. In particular, bathing mechanics reflected changing attitudes toward relaxation and toward dwelling in harmony with the body. He traces the nomadic journey of the modern double shell porcelain tub, through various stages of 'mechanisation', towards its current fixed position in its own dedicated space in the modern home. He contended (somewhat despondently) that Western societies' eventual choice of 'the bath *cell* with hot and cold running water', after decades of 'a Darwinian contest of forms'—delivered mass hygiene at the cost of true bodily and mental regeneration (Giedion 1948: 682). Other commentators on modernity were also interested in the 'antiseptisation' of households, bodies and bathrooms. In 1904, Herman Muthesius could marvel at how 'a modern bathroom . . . is like a piece of scientific apparatus' (quoted in Long 1996: 98).

In Giedion's view, the forfeiting, in the twentieth century, of the Roman notion of a hot *communal* bath taken to restore the body's equilibrium once within a twenty-four-hour cycle has been a profound social loss. He considers that that the modern, fully mechanized bath *cell*, with its complex plumbing, enamelled tub and chromium taps, appended to the bedroom, is *no substitute* for a social (regenerative) type of bathing (Giedion 1948: 711). This is because the cell serves only mere surface ablution, taken in solitude, with no time for the individual to talk, relax and dream (Giedion 1948: 712). Time to regenerate, time to think, formed part of his concept of 'man in equipoise' for whom communal leisurely bathing would offset the 'mechanised barbarism' of the early twentieth century—a period in which, he contends, had the most advanced technology but was neither happier nor fairer than the nineteenth century (Giedion 1948: 715).

Fifty years before Giedion, Adolf Loos had argued in 'Plumbers', written for the *Neue Freie Presse* in 1898, that the plumber was the 'quartermaster of civilisation'. Here he expresses precisely what Giedion later elaborates on: that there is an explicit link between the idea of universal plumbing and the advance of modern civilisation, and here Loos is particularly concerned with the impedance of the advance of German culture because of its stingy use of water. Loos therefore urged Germans to follow the English and the Americans to adopt civilization through plumbing, 'for only that nation that approaches the English in water usage can keep pace with them economically; only that nation that exceeds the English in water usage is chosen to overtake them in world dominance' (quoted in Lahiji and Friedman 1997: 18).

Taking Loos at his word in regard to lavish water consumption, Alfred Stevens's *The Bath* shows us a full-length French zinc tub filled to the brim. *The Bath* (see Figure 7.2) is a departure for Stevens, whose subjects are usually seen fully dressed in lavish interiors. Known for his paintings of Paris's fashionable women, Stevens was interested in psychological interiority, and often caught his subjects in moments of frustration, boredom or longing. His were contemporary women, who liked precious objects and dwelt in luxuriously decorated salons or boudoirs. He painted both society women and *cocottes* or *demi-mondaines*, *femmes* both *fragile* and *fatale*, and his approach was sensitive and objective, sensual and almost documentary in style, leaving clues for his fashion-conscious audiences to pick up on—subtle narrative threads laid down in details of dress, décor, and pose.

The woman in Stevens's *The Bath* is in a state of interiority that is palpable, an idea conveyed by the novel placed half-finished on a stand by the bath (she has been doubly immersed, in bath water and text). But she has put the novel down, perhaps either because her reading has triggered

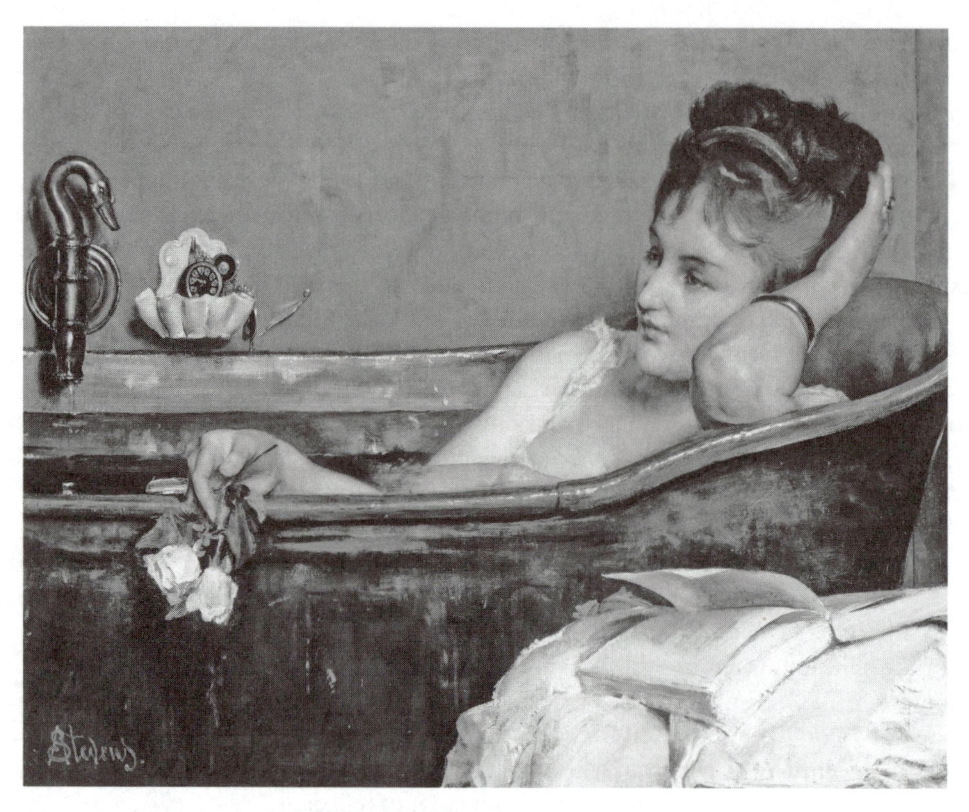

7.2. Alfred Stevens, *The Bath*, 1873–74. © Art Renewal Centre.

a memory or because she's been too distracted to concentrate on it. The water in the bath is clear (more on that later) and still, as might be expected from a scene in which the bather is in a state of motionless reflection. She touches her left hand to the back of her head, and her facial expression is dreamy and absorbed as the warm water envelopes her and creates a Freudian sense of oceanic boundarylessness.

The white roses she holds in her right hand dangle over the edge of the tub and could be viewed as symbols of love and beauty; furthermore, the fact that there are two blooms evokes notions of being part of a pair, and the fact that she holds them pointing heads down indicated to knowing audiences that she is indeed 'off the market'. The bath tap, in the shape of a swan's head, is based on a classic Roman design that is still popular and available today from plumbing suppliers. The inclusion of the swan-shaped tap also refers to the classical myth of Leda and heightens the erotic subtext in the painting. The bathing woman wears the gold bracelet of the successful artist's model, and her red hair, distinctive facial features and known friendship with Stevens suggests the model may have been Victorine Meurent, the model Manet used for his *Olympia* in 1863 and whom Picasso used for his *Celestine* in the 1900s.

The viewing dynamic Stevens established here locates the viewer as a desiring heterosexual male lover, placed at an almost intrusively intimate nearness to her. *The Bath* operates in a manner not unlike another work of that time, Fantin-Latour's *Woman Reading*. Of this picture, Michael Fried has written that it functions within an absorptive framework and tradition. In this framework, the preoccupied face of the sitter is composed in such a way that our role as beholders is denied; a proposal is being constructed (through a range of conventions or *effets de real*) that suggests that the scene before us is 'real' and that there are no barriers in our observational relationship with the sitter. We observe her state of mind in a manner that is as natural and as unmediated as it might be in real life, while at the same time appreciating this 'effect' as it has been mastered by the artist (Fried 1992: 52).

Here Stevens has turned the bathroom into a cloister, and the dreamy meditations of this bather have been encouraged by her access to endless hot running water. That she has been meditating for some time is gently underscored by the fob watch in the soap holder in the centre of the picture. Social historian Michael Adcock makes the astute point that the bathroom is now aspiring to the status of the boudoir. Moreover:

> for the first time, bathing could become a regular rather than an occasional occurrence, and the bathroom began to change form from being the site of rather awkward and make-shift ablutions to being a place of stylishness and comfort . . . The bathroom was now a place to tarry and to relax, and has taken on some of the intimate and romantic connotations of the boudoir. (Adcock 1996: 34)

Thus the bathroom took on some of the connotations of the boudoir, especially with the advent of the popular 'en suit', where the one space flowed into the other architecturally.

In Paris, the concept of public health and its relationship to fresh running water and hygiene underwrote Baron Haussmann's plans for the city's regeneration at the earliest of stages (Adcock 1996:34). Haussmann decried the 'old' unhygienic waters of the Seine and decreed that his modern Paris would be fed by pure new waters, supplied by an aqueduct fed from springs eighty miles away in the Marne Valley. Henceforth, according to Michael Adcock:

> Water from the Seine was called 'old water' and was distributed though one network servicing public facilities [the washing out of gutters was one of its purposes] . . . The second type of water, 'new water' was distributed through a separate system of mains that would be piped beneath every street of Paris . . . it would rise to every level of Parisian apartments . . . In the end Haussmann managed to increase the number of houses with piped water from 6,000 to 34,000. (Adcock 1996: 34)

Thus, of Stevens's *The Bath* Adcock points out that the red-haired woman bathing is modern not only because of her connection to the mains, her fixed bath, her stylish taps and her water heater, but also because she is bathing in literally 'new' water. Thus, because of this supply of new water Stevens is able to geographically locate the woman and her bath in one of the new Haussmannised suburbs of Paris, and this use of plumbing to do so would have been read and understood by his sophisticated and wealthy patrons.

Methods of bathing contemporaneous to *The Bath* were quite varied. Giedion and his fellow historians of the bath, Wright and Ashenberg, take us through the late nineteenth century panoply, from Swiss doctor Rikli's 'sun' bathing (ray therapy) and regime of outdoor cold-water showers, to snow bathing, air bathing, steam bathing ('Turkish' baths), public bathing, spas, transportable baths and, for an indulgent moment in Paris, hot baths delivered to the door (Ashenberg 2007: 187).

From the date of Haussman's connection of the wealthier parts of Paris to 'new' water (1865), and from Steven's elegant reference to it in *The Bath* of 1873, it is evident that progress was being made.

By the 1880s, mains, with connections to water and sewerage systems, water heaters and comfortable double shell porcelain baths were all on their way in the large cities of the developed world to produce the modern bath cell and its accompanying hygienic regimes and social attitudes to the body.

The growth of modern plumbing and sewerage systems in metropolitan centres in Europe, the ex-colonies and the Americas were represented in a new addition to the bathtub motif. There are not many examples of these in oil painting—and I am not focusing on them in any detail here, but they are worth noting for the imagery they anticipate. Neither a development from the nude in the landscape or the studio nude—this small but fascinating group of paintings have, as their point, the proud display of modern plumbing—for what is at stake is not the usual sticky web of gaze-oriented erotic provocations, but rather, the promotion of the technology itself, with all of its underpinning assumptions about cleanliness and gender, class and race. The figures (customarily female, usually clothed and in the act of running a bath), are showing us how the plumbed-in bathroom is operated and enjoyed, but with an aesthetic element that suggests the topic was considered fit for the medium of oils.

Carl Larsson's *Lisbeth Prepares a Bath*, 1909, shows a woman in a *peignoir* standing in front of a full bathtub with exposed pipes in a trombone figuration in a purpose-build bathroom with a wood-slatted mat, a potted flower and curtain behind her. She meets our gaze directly as a modern women competently operating her modern bathing technology. Ramon Casa' *Preparing the Bath* from his series *Escenas de interior* (c. 1900) shows a dressed woman, her back turned to the viewer, operating the taps on a similarly plumbed modern tub in Spain, in a spacious bathroom side-lit with a golden filtered light. There is a companion image where the same woman, now undressed, turns the tap off and prepares to bathe. Jules Scalbert's *Young Woman Preparing a Bath*, 1910, shows a woman getting her bath read, her hand turning a tap bath, but this time as she does, she meets our gaze through a mirror over the tub. Thus the lesser known images are important in a continuum of visual elements comprising modern bath technology + the figure + the bath *room* in the late nineteenth and early twentieth centuries.

Ashenberg notes, 'By the 1880s, solidly middle class apartments [in Paris] often had running water' (2007: 187). However, not everyone was connected to the 'matrix'. Services and fittings were expensive and getting them at all depended on where one lived. Given what we know of municipal advances in connecting households and suburbs to running water, to and from the dwelling, the primitive plumbing arrangements depicted in Degas's controversial *baigneuses* would thus seem somewhat retrograde. But the representation of a woman in the act of washing, whether in a washbowl or full-length zinc tub, plumbed-in or not, as we shall see, had powerful meanings for audiences about the control of the female body, specifically in terms of hygiene practices in bathing (see Figure 7.3).

Degas's *Woman in a Bath Sponging Her Leg* shows us the physical effort (the work, in muscular terms) of cleansing each part of the skin. *Woman in a Bath Sponging Her Leg* (1884) is part of a series of bather images that have attracted an enormous amount of scholarly attention (see Figure 7.3). Interestingly, this pastel drawing is one of the few in the series from the mid- to late 1880s that depicts a bather fully immersed in deep water. Most from the other pastels show bathers in shallow transportable bathing dishes, such as *The Tub* (1886) and *Woman Bathing in a Shallow Tub* (1885–6). These devices, the shallow tubs, were enlarged washbowls called *bains partiel* in France and *sponge baths* in England. Other images in the suite show women bathing, washing, drying, wiping themselves and combing their hair or having it combed.

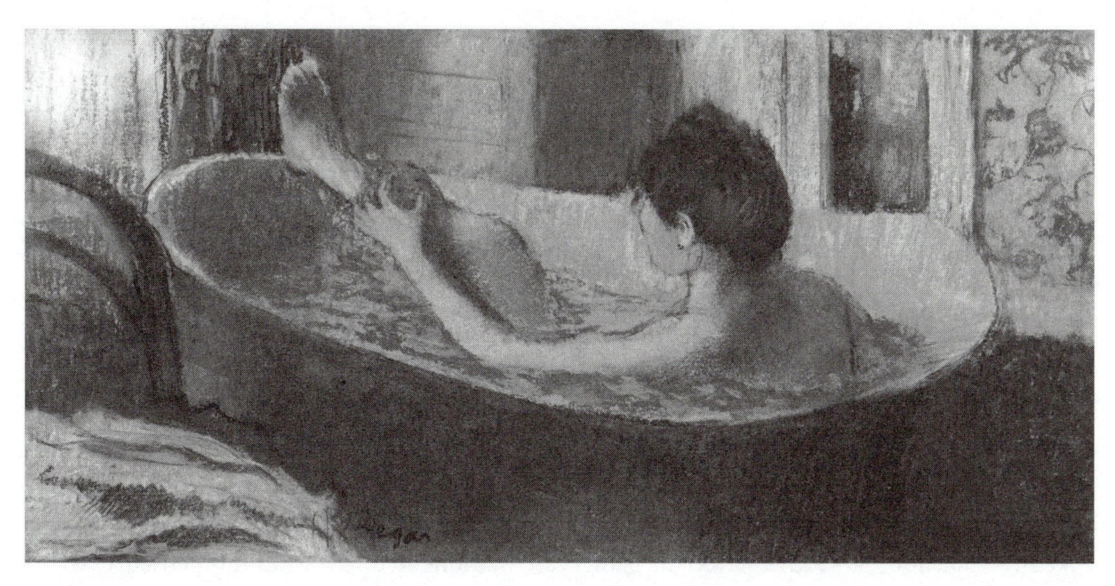

7.3. Edgar Degas, *Woman in a Bath Sponging Her Leg*, pastel, 1884, © RMN Musée d'Orsay. Picture credit: Hervé Lewandowski.

Degas has depicted a bather in a full and capacious zinc bathtub, of a type and shape common in France in the 1880s. It was hand filled with water, but designed to include a drain hole and plug at one end to save the effort of removing the used water by hand. This classic design can still be purchased through top-end antique and salvage Web sites. The bather is up to her underarms in water, and Degas is keen to show us this via the use of darker wriggling strokes of chalk that indicate that the water is swirling around as the bather raises her left leg and sponges her shin carefully. The effort of this is shown through the tensed muscles along her left shoulder and arm and the attentive tilt of her head. Her dark brownish-red hair has been twisted up out of the way of the water, allowing us to see the play of muscle and bone in counterbalancing herself through the right side of her body in the water.

There is a sense of fittingness between the proportions of the tub and the bather's body. The manner in which both points towards the window indicate the possibility of a protected and womb-like view out into the wider world. Patterned wallpaper, a mirror or glass surface (a picture tilted against the wall?) just to the right of the bather's head, a chest of drawers behind her raised leg and a chair covered in linen protruding at the bottom front edge of the composition (and forcing its way into the viewer's space) inscribe the scene as most likely a studio corner set up to depict a domestic space, a guise supported by the light-drenched net curtain over the window at the far left and the domestic dimensions of the room.

Many have commented—Degas's contemporaries and since—on how his mode of address places the viewer as if he or she were looking through a key hole at this private scene. Degas agreed with this observation, and said himself, 'Hitherto the nude has always been represented in poses that presuppose an audience, but these women of mine are honest, simple folk . . . Here is another; she is washing her feet. It is as if you looked through the keyhole.'[2] However, while there is much that is ambiguous in terms of locating the interior on a class level, there is nothing to suggest that this is the interior of a brothel, which is how some audiences then and now have interpreted the setting. It would seem that the narrow range of narrative clues in the décor opened a range of readings, a strategy of ambiguity on the part of Degas that provoked a furore of confusion, projections and anxieties that greeted the display of the 'bather' pastels at the last Impressionist exhibition of 1886. In *Degas's Brothels: Voyeurism and Ideology*, Charles Bernheimer notes:

> The voyeuristic perspective [of the bathers] was felt by the critics to reveal woman as instinctual animal. Only one critic, Octave Maus, in *L'Art moderne* (Brussels), 27 June 1886, was able to see anything positive about the exposure of woman's unself-conscious physicality. He imagined the bathers as domestic cats cleaning themselves, whereas the majority of the critics chose to compare their gestures to the wild movements of monkeys or frogs. (1989a: 181)

One of the reasons for the conflations of Degas's bathers with prostitutes and/or animals is the fact that they were exhibited at the same time and thus likened to Degas's brothel monotypes, a series of prints produced just before the suite of ten *baigneuses* (Broude 1988: 653). However, unlike the women in the brothel series, the bathers are washing themselves and this particular act attracted its own set of assumptions and projections, linking the more 'arty' and aesthetic bathing scenes with the more explicit and pornographic brothel series. Anthea Callen examines the bathers in terms of personal hygiene in the context of late-nineteenth-century Paris, and she contends:

> Attempts to encourage feminine hygiene were fraught with taboos . . . [and] bathing was directly associated with lascivious sexual activity, in particular with prostitution; [and most apposite for our submerged bather] . . . Water was feared not simply because of its old association with disease [miasmas]. Writers both for and against intimate hygiene for women recognised the sensuality of water. They likened immersion in it and its intimate contact with every bodily crevice to the sexual act itself; water was perceived as a surrogate lover. (Callen 1992: 173)

Callen goes on: 'Arguments for and against woman washing their genitals were by no means clear cut. Religious moralists inveighed against the practice on the grounds that it promoted indecent bodily self-awareness and masturbation. However the popular advice literature advocated regular use of the bidet—particularly after menstruation—to prevent the harbouring and spread of disease' (Callen 1992: 173). But above all, 'In the attitudes of middle class contemporary viewers the unregulated body-care of the naked woman marks the prelude to her sexual aggression' (Callen 1992: 174). It is this direct link between washing and sex and Degas's emphatic staging of women's bathing that explains the hostility and confusion that met their public unveiling.

But who is the woman sponging her leg, and who were the others in the later images? They were assumed to be prostitutes *because* they were bathing. J. K. Huysmans, in his review of the 1886 exhibition, described them as such, busy '[removing] the filth from their bodies' after the sexual act (quoted in Callen 1992: 174). The woman washing herself, with no other narrative fact or telling detail, aroused the fears outlined above, and not only at the level of fear of the dirty woman, but fear also of the woman who was 'too clean'—who aped respectability by having an immaculate and sweet-smelling face, hands, hair, feet and genitals. Notwithstanding, Degas's bathers retain a sense of modern, everyday reality, staged through their 'self-sufficient dignity' as noted by Charles Bernheimer in his seminal work on the representation of prostitution in nineteenth-century French art

(Bernheimer 1989b: 163). Degas himself merely commented disingenuously: 'Two centuries ago I would have painted *Susannah at her Bath*. Now I just paint a woman bathing' (Halévy 1960: 233).

Degas did, however, stage these scenes. They are not documents of the daily bathing experiences of Parisian women. Accounts from his models suggest that his late bather images were, in fact, carefully constructed in the studio. Heather Dawkins proposes this possibility in her discussion of Degas in the light of the personal memoirs of one of his models, Alice Michel. Dawkins cites Michel's accounts of 'managing Degas's, of striking and maintaining the difficult poses he insisted on' (Dawkins 1992a: 205). Dawkins uses Michel's memoir to affirm that the women in the bather drawings were not, as some critics assumed, either prostitutes or the wives of friends. Further evidence of the staged nature of the baigneuses comes from John Rewald who quotes an eyewitness (most probably Alice Michel) in a chapter on Degas's sculpture and describes his studio as containing 'sculptor's easels, tables, armchairs, stools, several screens, and even a bathtub which Degas used for his *baigneuses*' (Rewald 2002: 280). Degas may well have had both kinds of baths, the shallow dish and full-length tub, as props. As a man by now of some wealth, it is extremely likely he made his own bathing arrangements on the third or fourth floor of his house in the rue Victor Massé; clearly, such atavistic forms of bathing were not for his personal use. We know also that as his sight failed he worked more and more in the studio. And for models that studio time with Degas was rigorous:

> He engaged his models four or five times a week, sometimes twice a day, and often continued to work after their departure . . . Posing for Degas was not easy; the hours were long, and the artist was so exacting that some models refused to work for him . . . He had a profound aversion for all so-called graceful poses, which were so popular in other studios, and nearly always insisted on poses that were full of action. (Rewald 2002: 278)

Degas's preoccupation with anatomy and movement is borne out by his pastel work and small maquettes of horses in states of torsion not unlike what he sought from his bathers; the horses rearing, twisting, jumping, all their weight borne on hind limbs in a manner reveal the beauty of the mechanics of the supporting skeletal muscular structures. However, these are movements that cannot be held for long without injury. It is a harsh, fleeting but exact kind of beauty Degas seems to pursue here. He said himself of the equine wax maquettes and pastels, 'I didn't make enough horses. It is necessary that the women wait in their basins' (quoted in Guérin 1945: 127).

Since 1886, the *baigneuses* drawings have attracted a weighty collection of contradictory readings, many concerning Degas's alleged misogyny. However, what matters more here is how he understood modern bathing regimes and technologies of the bath and how these reflected attitudes to the female body and identity. This reading of Degas's *Woman Sponging Her Leg* proposes that Degas was less interested in hygiene than in how the body moves, and how this knowledge might serve a Realist metaphysic, and he raises these ideas about the conventions of Realism through his use of the tub as a kind of accessory, used in a way similar to the jumps he put his horses over for sketches made at the race course. Given this context, we might conclude that Degas has depicted the woman sponging her leg as *posing* as a bather and thus getting clean inadvertently, which in turn returns us to the trope of the studio nude and its relationship to the discovery of truth through the senses without the distortion of personal bias, interpretation or conceptual schemes. Because female bath time is a trope that compels the artist and viewer to close observation, it is used here by Degas much like the wires and armature he used to hold together his wax maquettes of the same subject—as a framework to invigorate the stale subject of the studio nude.

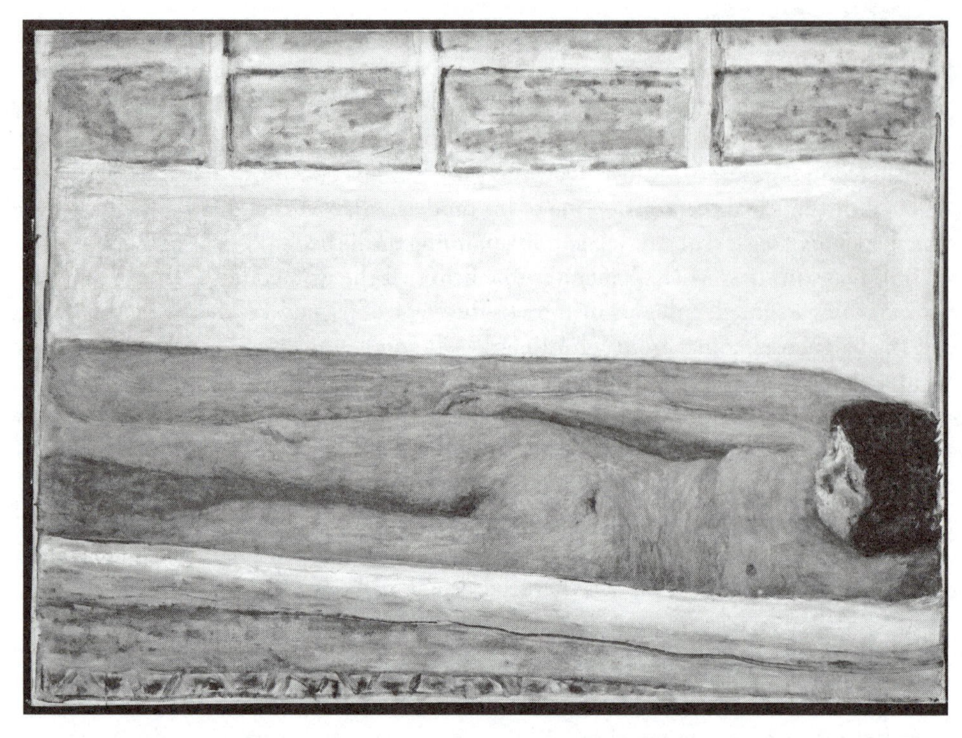

7.4. Pierre Bonnard, *The Bath*, 1925, oil on canvas, ©Tate Gallery London.

The next bathing representation bears many similarities to Degas's *Woman Sponging Her Leg*. Bonnard's *The Bath* of 1925 (see Figure 7.4) emerges from a similarly radical, avant-garde milieu. However, the two works present quite a different set of concerns and implications for the figuring of female bath time. Containing the same compositional elements of woman, bathtub and transparent water depicted from an intimate viewing distance, but painted twenty-five years after the Degas, Bonnard's painting takes female bath time in a dark and poignant direction.

In Bonnard's *The Bath*, we see a woman, the artist's wife Marthe lying motionless in a bath full of water. The two curved ends of the bathtub have been cropped, removing the woman's feet from view at one end and the bath taps at the other. This odd framing serves to universalize the bathing scene, disconnecting it from the quotidian world.

Unlike the woman in the Degas, we see Marthe's face in profile over the edge of a full-length tub. Yet this tells us little of her character. In fact, here we witness a new stratagem—a nude who is not just absorbed but detached from the whole business of looking and being looked at. This detachment makes the figure seem remote. Her legs and arms seem to float lightly beneath the water. She looks down towards her feet and her bodily position is 'hunkered down' in the water as if it were a shielding element, but perhaps she is also trying to conserve comfort in the lowering temperature of the bath. The posing of Marthe's body in this way emphasizes the 'time' of the painting.

From the sandy-coloured ceramic tiles on the wall behind the bath, and the pristine good quality porcelain of the tub itself as well as sufficient natural light, it's obvious this bathroom was well appointed with the latest fittings. It is sometimes assumed that this bathroom was the one at 'Le Bosquet' (the Thicket), the house Bonnard purchased in the Antibes at Le Cannet in 1926, and where he and Marthe lived until their deaths in 1942 and 1947 respectively. However, *The Bath* is dated a year before their permanent move south, so it must have been set in either their Paris apartment in 48 boulevard des Batignolles or at one of the rented villas Bonnard and Marthe stayed at in Arcachon, Deauville or Vernon throughout the early to mid-1920s.[3] The attractiveness of the space of both this particular bathroom and the later one renovated with a quiet luxury at Le Cannet suggests Marthe may have taken her ideas of the modern hygienic bathroom (with its laboratory aesthetic and associated regimes of cleansing the body of germs) from the various sanatoria she visited for her health.

The confusion over the site has no doubt come through the fact that this 1925 bathtub nude is the precursor, in all its critical visual elements, to four late, great full-length nudes in the tub that are indisputably set at Le Cannet; these latter four pictures expand in a masterly fashion on the complex, historically loaded and seemingly endlessly challenging problem of depicting an intimately known body lying in a complex watery space tightly contained by the commanding shape of the full-length double shell porcelain tub. Of the late full-length tub paintings Sarah Whitfield has written:

> The contemplation of loss, which is prefigured in *The Bath*, is made more absolute in these . . . late masterpieces in which colour accumulates in a rich and jewel-like brightness evoking the splendours of ancient tombs and Early Christian mosaics. Here the longing has ceased to be for a person, for a life that has been slowly erased by illness, for a time that has long since passed. The longing is now for a death that comes as a release . . . They are 'a lament for transience.' (Whitfield 2006: 29)

The question of 'seeing' Bonnard and how modern he was in the way he used sensory and perceptual shifts to destabilize and disrupt 'reality' has already been dealt with at length elsewhere (see Clair 1975; Cogeval 1993; Hyman 1998; Whitfield 1998, 2006; Elderfield 1998; Nochlin 2006; Bois 2006; Rocques 2006; and Munck 2006). Most of these accounts focus on the late interiors and particularly the full-length tub nudes. Naturally, Bonnard's scholars have pondered over the prevalence of bathing themes in his oeuvre, and they have associated it with the opportunities on hand in his home provided by the ritualistic bathing practices of his companion, Marthe Boursin, who suffered a lifetime of ill health that required her to take curative or restorative baths.

Their long relationship, his painting, and her role as model, muse and patient are mutually imbricated in the late bathtub nudes, so without slipping into a biographical framework solely for reading *The Bath*, it is worth briefly reiterating some of the salient details. It is unclear what the precise nature of Marthe's illness was. Bonnard's diaries and letters do not specifically name it. Sarah Whitfield has plumbed these primary sources and proposes convincingly that Marthe suffered from tuberculosis and, later in life, 'a nervous disorder' (Whitfield 1998: 27). Whitfield proposes:

> Marthe's meticulous attention to hygiene could . . . well fit the pattern of someone carefully following popular medical advice of the day' and she quotes a tuberculosis specialist of the 1920s, Dr Elisée Ribard who recommended that 'the whole body should be soaped daily, in favourable conditions, after which it should be a massaged quite energetically'. (Whitfield 1998: 28)[4]

In her essay 'Fragments of an Identical World', Whitfield makes a convincing case for the likelihood that Bonnard acted for Marthe as a preoccupied but, nonetheless, consistent and loving carer—an insight that gives his late bathing paintings of her an aching poignancy. Thus it seems likely that this important ritual, around which daily domestic routine was no doubt arranged, provided a motif for Bonnard, who, with his capacity for infinitely patient, close looking, took it far beyond the usual parameters of 'female bath time'. However, the purpose here is not to reiterate Bonnard in terms of the 'transcribed adventures of the optic nerve' (what Bonnard himself said painting was; quoted by Elderfield 1998: 33) nor to diagnose Marthe as part of a biographical reading of the work. Rather, it is to interrogate the technologies of bathing, linking these to the placement and posing of her figure and other compositional elements in order to explore the bathroom as a viewing mechanism that reflects the encoded advances of modernity.

Looking at *The Bath* in these terms, there is a sense here that Bonnard departs quite deliberately from the separate representational traditions of the nude and the interior. He makes an intervention such that what he was rejecting is (almost) as important as what he includes. For a start, he rejects the 'time' of the typical nude in the interior, specifically the trope of the *femme à sa toilette*, which up until the late nineteenth century was invariably the before or after bathing phase, in which the feminine body could be displayed attractively *deshabillé*. What Bonnard has done instead is to almost eradicate the very thought (while looking at this painting) of any kind of 'before' or 'after' moment. With her immobility, the mottled tones of her skin, and the absence of clothing nearby, this bath seems to have been going on for hours.

Bonnard was highly aware of the Impressionist modernisations of the female bath time, and he greatly admired Degas's *baigneuses*. Like Degas, he domesticates the traditional subject of the bather by bringing her indoors. The dozens of pastels and paintings Bonnard produced in the early 1910s of Marthe in sculpting light, sponging herself while standing or kneeling in a shallow zinc *bain partiel*, are doubtless a form of both personal exploration and a tribute to Degas (Whitfield 1998: 22). However, what marks out the difference between Degas's bathers and Bonnard's nudes in the tub is that, for Bonnard, the bathtub is not a pretext for a kind of exegesis on the nude in the interior; here the bath itself, its shape, its water, its 'time', is a central subject. The Bonnard nudes in the tub, as well as being 'a lament for transience', are also about the rituals, pleasures, technologies and failures of curative bathing.

The other conventional tradition in the representation of female bath time that Bonnard departs from in *The Bath* is that his nude is not the universal 'nude' wrung from the hard work of the professional model, but rather she is someone intimately well-known and familiar. Sarah Whitfield points out Bonnard's preference was for models who just 'walked around' and 'lived' in front of him, striking natural poses that reminded him of antique sculpture, both Western and Eastern (Whitfield 1998: 23). He was also shy about painting directly in front of the model, which explains his adherence to intimate daily home life for his subject matter. So, departing in this way from the usual nude in the interior schema, we gain a sense of intimacy. While Bonnard occasionally did use professional models and also often based poses on classical sculpture, what's far more noteworthy is his commitment to Marthe as a lifelong muse. This repetitive, almost ritualistic use of the same person in his interiors suggests he was interested in destabilising the female bath time paradigm, and is yet another intriguing aspect of his approach to the nude in the bathtub. In any case, it would have been anomalous to his usual mode of working to have a professional model undress and lie still in a bath for such a length of time. His practice of slow, inexorable, almost metaphysical 'looking' required daily interaction and familiarity with another's habits; this is what allowed him to sketch, compose and paint his models with the degree of intimacy he did.

More destabilisations follow. Bonnard elides the conventional tactile and sensual agendas contained in the nude. This nude is not a 'busy' bathing body; she's the opposite, in fact. There is a meditative stillness about *The Bath* that suggests that this is a long and contemplative bath, not a display. While he shows us a slender, attractive female body (indeed he places Marthe's pubic area just below the centre point of the composition), this tub-framed nude is not, in the way Bonnard's many *femmes à ses toilettes* often are, playful or titillating.

The stillness of the bath water, suggested by the tight, slightly darker 'meniscus' line around the edge of the bath and around Marthe's chin line, further emphasizes the extreme motionlessness of her body. Sarah Whitfield notes how Marthe's body here looks 'so relaxed that it is almost lifeless. The wall and the rim of the white porcelain encasing the body in *The Bath* seem to play deliberately on the similarity between the shape of a sarcophagus and the shape of a bathtub, and so reinforce the painting's death-like stillness, its sense of presence-absence' (Whitfield and Elderfield 2006: 28).

Bonnard's interest in extending the *dureé* or time of viewing, the soaking body and viewer's eye simultaneously soaking into the image, suggests that here he has taken Gideon's lament over replacing 'total regeneration of the body with surface ablution' to its logical, lonely conclusion. It looks as if the bathing being done here is regenerative (or at least that is the expected transformation). The treatment of the figure in the water itself underscores this and invokes the viewer's own bodily awareness of being submerged in warm water; the slowness of it, the way that bath water, when it is over one's ears, slows the apperception of sounds—they become muted and 'far off'—as it also slows the apperception of time, as the relaxation deepens and each muscle relaxes—safely, within the walls of the bath that form a protective barrier against all that is 'out there' in the world.

This notion of being barricaded against social contact is implicit in a line from a letter Bonnard wrote to his friend George Besson in the winter of 1930–1, and it is oft quoted since it constitutes one of Bonnard's few direct references to Marthe's state of mind in the last fifteen years of their lives together. Bonnard writes, 'For quite some time now I have been living a very secluded life as Marthe has become completely antisocial' (Whitfield 1998: 27).

Looking again at *The Bath* with the situation above in mind, it is as if Marthe has been imagined at the epicentre of many containers which expand in a spatial sense out to the infinite. This awareness of there being something extremely powerful 'beyond what we see' is a clear legacy of Bonnard's years as a Symbolist in the Nabi Brotherhood. Like Vuillard, Vallotton and Denis, in fin-de-siecle Paris, Bonnard was influenced by Belgian Symbolist playwright, poet and essayist Maurice Maeterlinck's theories of the power of suggestion. Maeterlinck believed that art should be a receptacle for the uncanny; it should bear witness to and embody the mysteries of sex and death; it should, above all, summon up the 'faceless unknown', a mystical force of both life and death that is repressed in everyday consciousness.[5]

There can be little doubt that through her immersion in warm water, in an enamel tub, this small, self-absorbed female figure here is hoping to be 'regenerated'. However, Marthe's bathing, since it is being performed under the 'logic' of work and [medical] function—and worse, in an entirely private and specialized room—cannot be redemptive according to Giedion (Giedion 1948: 712). Yet we keep looking and hoping. It is Bonnard's genius that he manages to keep perceptual recognition at bay without 'allowing us to give up the quest for it' (Read 2012: np). Doubtless one aspect of our quest here is the ever-dwindling hope that the slender, bruised-looking figure in the bath will bloom into health.

In summing up Giedion's contribution to the theory of the tub going into the twentieth century, William Braham concludes, 'The . . . tub [is] conceived as both an enduring hygienic artefact and as the site of transformation that it cannot guarantee, but which it dreams of accommodating' (Braham 1997: 220). The modern tub as a site of longed-for transformation is nowhere more surely underscored than in David Scherman's well-known 1945 photograph of American reporter Lee Miller in Adolf Hitler's tub in his Munich apartment in the weeks after the end of World War II. Here, the beautiful American photographer, who had earlier that day walked through the camp at Dachau, has taken off her muddy boots, placed them carefully on the bath mat and washed, or attempted to wash, the most horrendous chapter of human history off her body in the modest, neatly tiled bathroom where these horrors may well have been planned. Here, transformation may be promised, but it was in no way guaranteed.

In sum, the nude in the bath bears a more than passing resemblance to the earlier tradition of the nude in the interior, but with one crucial difference: pictorial representations of female bath time, since the late nineteenth century, have *had* to take account of the bath and its room as an apparatus through which modernity's advance is inevitably embedded. Paintings of female bath time bring the social, the traditional and the modern into a dynamic interaction. This is especially evident at the turn of the last century where there was no consistent universal schema yet in place to identify the bathroom with its attendant modern regimes. The industrial West hadn't yet settled on the bathing cell, with the double shell plumbed-in porcelain tub as the dominant model or 'metric'.

Paintings dated after the municipal installation of universal mains water and sewerage systems in major cities muddy the waters by featuring old fashioned washbowls; in other examples, the sophistication of bathing technology that the wealthy had access to in the 1870s predates what we might assume to be modern plumbing arrangements, as we see with the Stevens bather. Thus, these representations also defy attempts to construe a straightforward visual chronology of progression. The bath, in the bathroom with its attendant fixtures, fittings and pipes, introduces elements of uncanniness, as with the Bonnard. Yet each example given here reflects how the technology of bathing (it's 'mechanisation', in Giedion's terms) was represented in late-nineteenth- and early-twentieth-century art. We see in particular how the space *around* the bathing figure begins to shape our readings by adding complex additional layers of meaning.

The bathroom is thus a far from neutral setting; it has its own allegorical power both within and beyond the picture plane. At the turn of the last century, the popularity of images of women in or near water turns not only on increasingly modern 'mechanics' but also on an enduring iconography. While 'femininity' has been seen as emblematic of modernity itself (Huyssen 1987), water has, for a much longer period, been seen as emblematic of change and transformation. When brought together, they form a persuasive ensemble and enduring trope in which the figure and the (relatively new) purpose-built bathroom are seamlessly intertwined in the representation of a now unassailably private act of modern bathing.

NOTES

1. These pastoral female bathers were produced by the entire field of artistic ideology in the period, from 'the erstwhile vanguard' to the 'most conservative official specialists'. Nochlin concludes that the function of these pastoral female bathers was to propose a *rappel à l'ordre* (Nochlin 2006: 17–20.
2. Jonathan Jones (2004), 'Through a Keyhole', *The Guardian,* 30 October, <http://www.guardian.co.uk/culture/2004/oct/30/1> accessed 10 Dec. 2011. The original quote was recorded by George Moore in conversation with Degas (1891), *Impressions and Opinions*: 'Hitherto the nude has always been represented in poses which presuppose an audience; but these women of mine are honest, simple folk, unconcerned by any other interests than those involved in their physical condition. Here is another; she is washing her feet. It is as if you looked through a key-hole' (Moore 1891: 232).
3. Pagé, Whitfield and Elderfield, in their respective catalogues, describe this work as having been started at the Boulevard des Batignolles where Bonnard and Marthe were living in 1925 or in one of the bathrooms of the villas they rented outside of Paris that year.
4. We see this therapeutic 'massage' process after the bath with almost documentary clarity in another portrait of Marthe by Bonnard: the *Nude with Blue Glove* (1916).
5. Source: <http://fr.wikipedia.org/wiki/Maurice_Maeterlinck> accessed 8 Dec. 2011. Verlaine summed up the significance of 'in definability' in his poem *The Echo* of 1882: '*Rien de plus chere que la chanson grise, ou l'indecis au precis se jointe.*' ('Nothing is more precious than the twilight song in which the uncertain is joined to the precise'.)

BIBLIOGRAPHY

Adcock, M. (1996), 'Remaking Urban Space: Baron Haussmann and the Rebuilding of Paris, 1851–1870', *University of Melbourne Library Journal,* 2/2, <www.unimelb.edu.au/culturalcollections/research/ . . . / adcock.pdf> accessed 24 Oct. 2011.

Ashenberg, K. (2007), *The Dirt on Clean: An Unsanitized History*, New York: North Point Press.

Barnes, D. (2006), *The Great Stink of Paris and the Nineteenth-Century Struggle against Filth and Germs*, Baltimore: Johns Hopkins University Press.

Beeton, I. (1859–62), *Mrs Beeton's Book of Household Management*, Hungary: Chancellor Press.

Bernheimer, C. (1989a), 'Degas's Brothels: Voyeurism and Ideology', in R. H. Bloch and F. Ferguson, eds., *Misogyny, Misandry, and Misanthropy*, Berkeley: University of California Press.

Bois, Y.-A. (2006), 'Bonnard's Passivity', in Suzanne Pagé, ed., *Pierre Bonnard: The Work of Art: Suspending Time*, Paris: Lund Humphries.

Braham, W. W. (1997), 'Siegfried Giedion and the Fascination of the Tub', in N. Lahiji and D. S. Friedman, eds., *Plumbing: Sounding Modern Architecture*, New York: Princeton Architectural Press.

Broude, N. (1988), 'Edgar Degas and French Feminism ca. 1880: "The Young Spartans" the Brothel monotypes and the Bathers Revisited', *The Art Bulletin*, 70/4: 640–59.

Callen, A. (1992), '*Degas's Bathers: Hygiene* and *Dirt / Gaze and Touch*', in R. Kendall and G. Pollock, eds., *Dealing with Degas: Representations of Women and the Politics of Vision*, New York: Viking Press.

Clair, J. (1975), 'Le Peintre et L'Homme', in *Bonnard*, Paris: Hazan.

Cogeval, G. (1993), 'Series: Les Chefs d'Oeuvre,' in *Bonnard*, Paris: Hazan.

Dawkins, H. (1992a), 'Frogs, Monkeys, and Women: A History of Identifications across a Phantastic Body' in R. Kendall and G. Pollock, eds., *Dealing with Degas*, New York: Universe.

Dawkins, H. (1992b), 'Grief and Fascination', *Differences*, 4/3: 66.

Elderfield, J. (1998), 'Seeing Bonnard', in S. Whitfield, ed., *Bonnard*, London: Tate Gallery Publishing.

Fried, M. (1992), 'Manet in His Generation: The Face of Painting in the 1860s', *Critical Inquiry*, 19/1: 22–69.

Giedion, S. (1948), *Mechanisation Takes Command: A Contribution To Anonymous History*, Oxford: Oxford University Press.
Guérin, M., ed., (1945), *Lettres de Degas*, Paris: Bernard Grasset.
Halévy, D. (1960), *Degas Parle*, Geneva: La Palatine.
Huyssen, A. (1987), *After the Great Divide: Modernism, Mass Culture, Postmodernism*, Bloomington: Indiana University Press.
Hyman, T. (1998), *Bonnard*, New York: Thames and Hudson
Lahiji, N., and Friedman, D. S., eds., (1997), *Plumbing: Sounding Modern Architecture*, New York: Princeton Architectural Press.
Long, H. (1996), *The Edwardian House*, Manchester: Manchester University Press.
Loos, A. (1898), 'Plumbers', in N. Lahiji and D. S. Friedman, eds, *Plumbing: Sounding Modern Architecture*, New York: Princeton Architectural Press.
Moore, G. (1891), *Impressions and Opinions*, New York: Brentano.
Munck, J. (2006), 'Bonnard, by default', in S. Pagé, ed., *Pierre Bonnard: The Work of Art, Suspending Time*, exhibit catalogue, Ghent: Musée d'Art Moderne de la Ville de Paris.
Nochlin, L. (2006), *Bathers, Bodies, Beauty: The Visceral Eye*, Cambridge, MA: Harvard University Press.
Read, R. (2012), Personal communication, April 18, 2012.
Rewald, J. (2002), 'Degas at Work', in J. S. Czestochowski and A. Pingeot, eds., *Degas Sculptures: A Catalogue Raisonné Of The Bronzes*, Iowa City: Torch Press and International Arts.
Roque, G. (2006), *La Stratégie de Bonnard: Couleur, Lumière, Regard*, Paris: Gallimard.
Vigarello, G. (1988), *Concepts of Cleanliness: Changing Attitudes in France since the Middle Ages*, New York: Cambridge University Press.
Whitfield, S. (1998), *Bonnard*, London: Tate Gallery.
Whitfield, S. (2006), 'The Problem of Belonging', in G. Roque, S. Whitfield, and Y.-A. Bois, eds., *Bonnard: The Work of Art: Suspending Time*, London: Lund Humphries.
Wilkie, J. (1986), 'Submerged Sensuality: Technology and Perceptions of Bathing', *Journal of Social History*, 19/ 4: 649–64.
Wood, C. (2005), 'Indoor-Outdoor: The Studio around 1500', in M. Cole and M. Pardo, eds., *Inventions of the Studio, Renaissance to Romanticism*, Chapel Hill: University of North Carolina Press.
Wright, L. (1960), *Clean and Decent: The Fascinating History of the Bathroom and the Water Closet*, London: Penguin.
Zola, É. (1922), *Nana*, New York: A. A. Knopf.

8.

BEDROOMS: CORPOREALITY AND SUBJECTIVITY

francesca berry

> The bedroom, do not forget, is above all the asylum of mysterious actions, of large and small secrets, and the refuge of memories. In the home, it is a veritable sanctuary, the fateful place where powerful and humble alike find themselves alone, facing their self; it is where the truth, so often betrayed, disguised and banished, abruptly reveals itself in all its, often unflattering, undress; where during the night, which brings counsel, the mind gathers the wandering imagination, relives the past, evokes vanished images, calculates, computes, seeks to predict, combines, arranges, decides and finally, prepares for the future. (Havard 1887: 180)[1]

In 1887, the leading French interior decoration author Henry Havard identified the bedroom as the location for an authentic and intimate, if not always comfortable, encounter with self; a self imagined in distinct, but related, terms as corporeal and psychological. At once secretive and mnemonic, Havard's bedroom is also the place where the truth of the body is revealed disconcertingly in undress. Moreover, it is where sleep unveils the unconscious as the means to rationalize consciousness: a distinctly pre-Freudian understanding of the function of dreaming. Unsurprisingly, Havard advised an intimate and soothing décor capable of sheltering these functions and experiences. With his definitively epochal attention to the categories of the corporeal and the psychological, Havard provides a suitable starting point for this chapter, which pursues the themes of the body and subjectivity in the artistic and broader visual culture of the bedroom between the 1870s and 1920s, principally in France and Britain. Specifically, this chapter will analyse these themes in relation to three pictorial motifs that became more and less significant during the bedroom's representational journey from the Victorians to the moderns. Firstly, it will analyse the domestic bedroom scene favoured in the 1870s and 1880s by French modern-life artists who intimately staged the veiled female body as an implicitly erotic object on the bourgeois bed. Secondly, it will consider the bedsit scene, which at the beginning of the twentieth century attained a new currency in the work of female artists as a space of subjective experience and potentiality. Finally, the chapter will culminate with an analysis of the representation of the child's bedroom in early-twentieth-century illustrations for children. This chapter will argue that images of the child's bedroom brought together—but in relation to a new subject and with new implications—the issues of corporeality and subjectivity already familiar to the bedroom scene.

SLEEPING IN DAYLIGHT

The social history of the bedroom in nineteenth-century France was marked by two key ideological changes. Firstly, the dominant conceptualization of the marital bedroom shifted from, at the beginning of the century, the aristocratic model of separate bedrooms for husband and wife to, at the century's close, the bourgeois model of the conjugal bedroom (Martin-Fugier 1990: 321; Musée des Arts Décoratifs 1995: 105). In the process, the style and location of beds in bedrooms altered. The *lit à travers*, a small curtained bed with one longer side abutting the wall, was exchanged for the centrally located *lit au milieu*, the more familiar double bed with headboard located against the wall; the latter a shrine to bourgeois marital fertility, often purchased upon marriage (Walton 1992: 88). Equally, the old, aristocratic conceptualization and use of the bedroom as a public space for the reception of guests gave way to the bourgeois model of the bedroom as a private space (Guerrand 1990: 368), its doors firmly closed to visitors (and only opened to other family members, including children, on a restricted basis). Of course, historical practices are always more complex than contemporaneous prescription and retrospective generalization allow, not least with reference to the complexly stratified French bourgeoisie. Although bourgeois households were, during the nineteenth century, increasingly marked by greater room specialization, inventory-based research demonstrates that, at mid century, it was perfectly possible that the conjugal bed of a modest bourgeois couple might be located behind a curtain in the salon (Walton 1992: 75). And, of course, working-class domesticity was, with justification, popularly characterized throughout the century by a *pot-au-feu,* or stew, cooking in a bedroom (Brisset 1853: 250; Musée des Arts Décoratifs 1995: 110).

Given the dominance of the bourgeois model of the conjugal bedroom, it is surprising to find how equivocally the concept of conjugality was represented in relation to the bedroom in the second half of the nineteenth century. A number of leading interior decoration manuals retained, both in text and illustration, the aristocratic pretension of separate bedrooms for husband and wife (Cardon 1884; Noussanne 1896). And, despite otherwise being fascinated by the allure of the domestic bedroom, modern-life artists rarely chose to represent couples occupying these spaces. The few paintings that did figure a couple in a domestic bedroom, most significantly Edgar Degas's *Interior* (1868–9) and Pierre Bonnard's *Man and Woman* (1900), are neither obviously representations of married couples, nor do they present bedroom relations between a man and woman in terms other than might be deemed ambiguous. A yawning void, punctured by a discarded corset, pushes the dejected and semi-clothed female figure and its tensely poised male counterpart to the margins of Degas's bedroom (Sidlauskas 2000: 20–60). Meanwhile, in Bonnard's painting, a folding screen that might elsewhere function as pictorial shorthand for physical intimacy remains firmly closed between the nude couple—the standing male figure (a self-portrait) resisting the lassitude signified by the female figure petting a cat on the bed. Indeed, in visual representation, the promise of sexual pleasure predominantly resided on beds located outside the bourgeois home—in the many erotic and pornographic nudes, including male and female couples, staged on photographic-studio beds and in the prostitutional paintings and prints favoured by modern-life artists; Henri Gervex's *Rolla* (1878) is a pertinent example. This is hardly surprising given that bourgeois marriage and sexual pleasure were considered uneasy bedfellows, as symbolized by Pierre-Joseph Proudhon's notorious 1846 statement: 'Housewife or harlot, I see no middle ground' (quoted in Mesch 2009: 71). But the visual invisibility of easy bedroom conjugality might also have been related to the fact that the newly dominant model of the conjugal bedroom did not, in itself, add up to a perceived equality of male and female access to, or identification with, the bedroom. In France and Britain alike, the bourgeois conjugal bedroom was constructed as and for the feminine—a room that husbands occupied merely as guests.[2] We might ask why it was so. It may be related to the ideological gendering of public and private space: if the conjugal bedroom was one of the home's most private spaces, it 'naturally' fell within the territory of the feminine. Moreover, in a culture that leant gendered significance to decorative styles and materials (Auslander 1996: 286–9), the soft material culture of the bedroom—its mattresses, pillows, eiderdowns, blankets, sheets and curtains—aligned it with the feminine. Indeed, the fabric of the bed could stand in for the female body and its interiorized sexuality, or facilitate fantasies of revealing, caressing and even penetrating the female body; a metaphorical association persistently exploited by the producers of erotic photographs who, for example, found it hard to resist juxtaposing the curves and recesses of feminine buttocks with sets of parted bed curtains. Conversely, and as will be established in more detail later, it seemed, at a broad cultural level, simply impossible to imagine or picture a male body lingering in a bedroom, let alone reclining on a bed.

Equivocal about the motif of the conjugal bedroom and the place of the couple within it, modern-life artists more confidently and persistently staged the lone, sleeping or waking, youthful female figure as an implicitly erotic object on a bed in the bourgeois bedroom. Federigo Zandomeneghi's *In Bed* (1878; Figure 8.1), painted by the Italian artist whilst living in Paris and associating with the Impressionists, including Degas, is an appropriate example of this genre. It is my contention that such paintings are structured by an erotic dynamic of frustrating restriction and privileged access to the normally private feminized bedroom and, by association, the veiled female body. A symptom of masculine heterosexuality and long-established in nineteenth-century erotica and pornography, this dynamic also featured euphemistically in interior decoration guides such as Emile Cardon's *L'Art au foyer domestique*: 'Madame's bedroom is a sacred place that nothing should penetrate . . . [but] as hermetically sealed as Madame's bedroom may be, we will, for a moment, enter it' (1884: 28).[3] Moreover, characterization of the feminine bedroom as an inviolable room to be penetrated found reinforcement in the narrative structure of most interior decoration guides (and indeed, this present volume) which, in the manner of the striptease that Roland Barthes compared to traditional narrative (1975: 10–11), tended to leave revelation of a home's most private spaces to the final chapters. Whilst disavowing the commodified female sexuality on display in the bedroom scenes of photographic pornography and naturalistic novels, Cardon's and Zandomenghi's domestic bedroom scenes traded implicitly in the erotic dynamics of their more illicit counterparts.

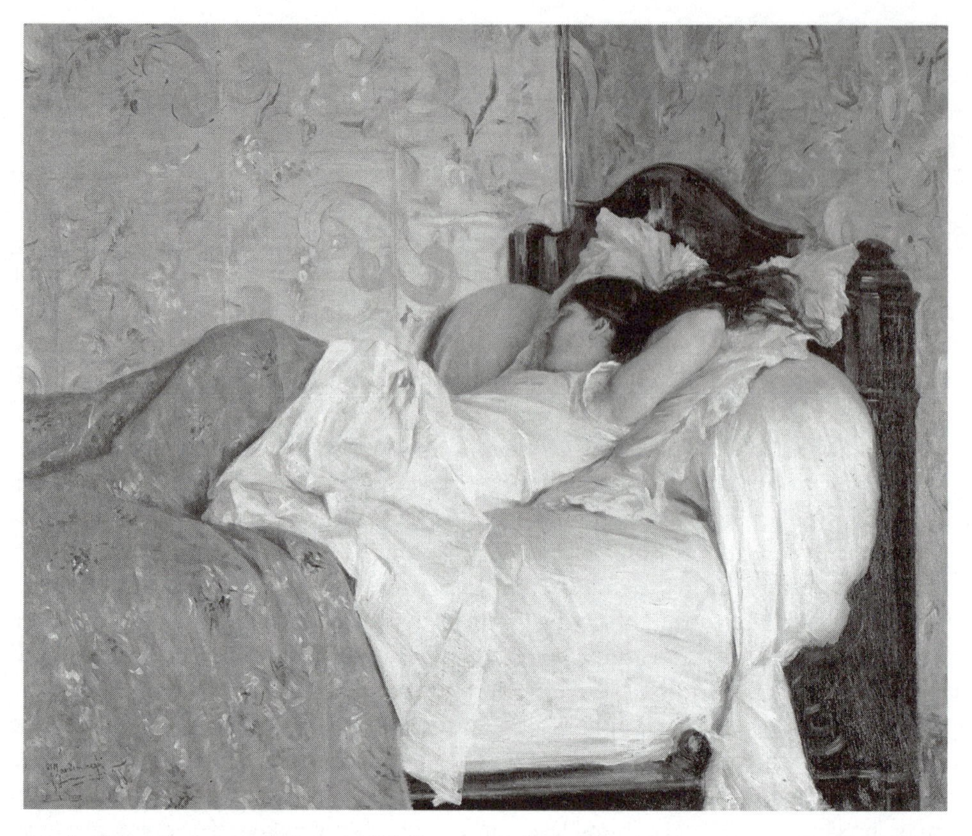

8.1. Federigo Zandomeneghi, *In Bed*, 1878. Florence, Galleria d'Arte Moderna, Palazzo Pitti (Alinari/The Bridgeman Art Library).

In Bed features a female figure sleeping, perhaps unconvincingly, though not unusually for this type of bedroom scene, in full daylight. Here, light operates as the agent of intimate knowledge of a lightly veiled femininity. Indeed, it streams through an unseen window at right foreground; a window implicitly located close to the implied viewing position of the viewer who might, as a result, imagine himself or herself similarly attached to the unseen wall, yet still in close proximity to the bed. Light shimmers across the luxurious silk wallpaper of the perpendicular wall, bouncing off the brass corner rod. The same light more gently sculpts the generously proportioned single mahogany bed and dissolves across the sheets, which, together with the figure's chemise, offer a virtuoso performance of crafting textural and tonal nuance from loose brushwork and complementary colour. In subtle contrast to the sheets, but echoing the palette of the wallpaper, are the pinkish tones of the figure's lightly flushed cheek and the yellow and green tones of the flesh of its left arm, and, in stronger contrast, the auburn tones of its extravagantly splayed hair. With head turned away, inconsequential breasts contained beneath the chemise, right arm obscured and raised knees hidden beneath the eiderdown, this bourgeois bedroom body seems perfectly demure. And yet, the sleeping figure's emphatically raised left arm 'inadvertently' reveals to the viewer a highly intimate, and normally unseen, part of the bourgeois female body—underarm hair. And, of course, without directly revealing the difficult genital truth posed by the female body, the sight of this body hair invites imaginative contemplation of the pubic hair concealed beneath the sheet and between the figure's raised thighs. Whilst resisting the distressing vision of complete undress posed at the beginning of this chapter by Henry Havard, this body is more suggestively corporeal and erotic than it might at first appear. But it is also, in the manner of Havard, a body that appears to be dreaming. The floral motifs that ripple across the eiderdown and shimmer on the walls might be read as symbolic projections of the fluidity of the relaxed mind, a theory emergent in neurology (Silverman 1989: 79, 84) and suggested in contemporaneous paintings of sleeping figures, including Paul Gauguin's 1881 painting of his sleeping daughter, *The Little Dreamer* (McLean 2008: 102). Indeed, just above the bolster, at the wallpaper's most iridescent point, a silvery arabesque dramatically rises and falls, closely echoing the rise and fall of the figure's legs beneath it. For all its fluidity, this tongue-like, even phallic, motif appears irrepressibly corporeal. As is, moreover, the bulging underside of the figure's upper arm which seems, when isolated together with the underarm hair at its base, perversely penile. In the same year as the publication of the second volume of the *Iconographie photographique de la Salpêtrière*, a book featuring photographs of a young woman named Augustine on a bed somatically performing her psycho-sexual 'disorder' (Didi-Huberman 2003: 115–74), Zandomeneghi's painting provides the viewer with a more soothing, but perhaps not unrelated, fantasy of youthful feminine sexual desire bubbling just under the corporeal and decorative surfaces of the bourgeois bedroom.

The 'in bed' scene and the intimate staging of the female body as veiled erotic object within it did not hold the allure for early-twentieth-century artists and their audiences that it had held for their nineteenth-century predecessors. The artist's studio featuring the unveiled working-class model usurped the bedroom as the preferred erotic setting as early-twentieth-century avant-gardists, including Henri Matisse and Pablo Picasso, rejected the domesticated sexuality that had been signified in the bedroom scene. Indeed, the implicitly erotic bourgeois bedroom scene became something of an artistic cliché in the early twentieth century. It is my contention that a generation of artists, sometimes labelled 'Intimists', that came to prominence in the early 1890s, including Bonnard, but also Félix Vallotton and Édouard Vuillard, helped to undermine the bourgeois bedroom scene. In the case of Vallotton and Bonnard, it was by explicitly identifying bourgeois domestic space itself as the location for (sometimes pleasurable) adulterous and illicit sexual encounters; in the example of Vuillard, it was by presenting the sleeping female body for what it is. In 1892, the latter exhibited a small painting, *Sleep* (1892; Figure 8.2), at the Le Barc de Boutteville gallery in Paris. It offers very different interpretations of the female figure sleeping in a domestic bedroom than that presented some fourteen years previously by Zandomeneghi. Moreover, these differences amount to more than a stylistic shift from Zandomeneghi's Impressionist naturalism to Vuillard's pared-down Synthetism.

In Vuillard's *Sleep*, a female figure reclines on its side in a single bed. Though some artificial light falls from upper right upon the figure's head and pillow, demonstrably this is a night scene. Next to the bed is a pair of shoes, whilst other generic garments rest, perfunctorily, on a low chair. But whilst the process of undressing is signified by these elements, the sheet and two blankets that, apart from the head, entirely cover the body, work hard to avoid the erotic narrative that discarded clothes and a reclining female figure conventionally invoked. Vuillard's painting simply negates the terms of that narrative and, as a result, provoked a surprisingly violent critical response. On 26 November 1892, the *Le Journal* newspaper published a page of cartoon responses by 'Mirliton' to

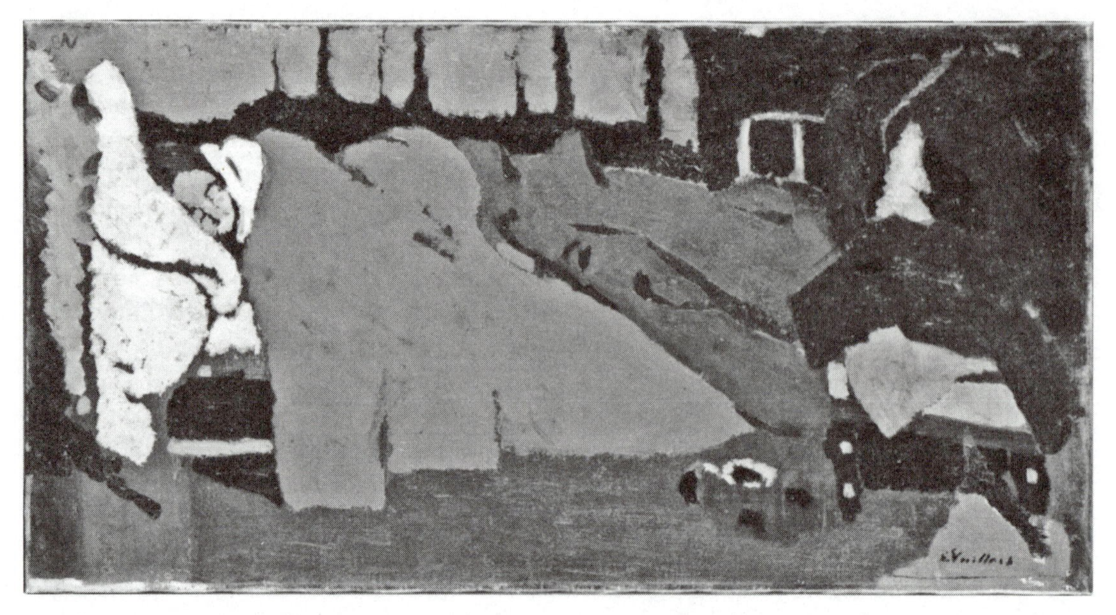

8.2. Édouard Vuillard, *Sleep*, 1892. Paris, Musée d'Orsay (RMN-GP [Musée d'Orsay] / Hervé Lewandowski) ©RMN-GP.

paintings on show in the Le Barc de Boutteville exhibition (1892: 1). One of the cartoons concerns Vuillard's *Sleep,* exhibited under the artist's original title of *Femme couchée* (*Woman Reclining*). In the cartoon, a clothed and lumpen female figure lies on its front on a single bed, its body having been dramatically cut into six separate pieces at wrist, waist, knee and ankles. Beneath the bed lies an amputated hand and at the end of the bed a foot splashes into an ominous basin of dark liquid. Beneath the cartoon, Vuillard's original title of *Femme couchée* has been elongated to 'Femme couchée en morceaux' or 'Woman reclining in pieces'. Significantly, this caption echoed a sensationalist newspaper headline, 'La femme coupée en morceaux' ('The woman cut into pieces'), that had been circulating in the Parisian press that month.[4] The headline related to the discovery in a Parisian basement of a headless female corpse, lubriciously described as being bathed in a pool of blood. Previously dismissed by Vuillard scholars as a humorous response to the painting's cloisonnist technique (Cogeval 2003: 79), I believe Mirliton's cartoon and caption are rather more profound than this. They recognize that Vuillard's *Sleep* helped to kill off the fantasy of the inadvertent corporeal and psychological revelation of the bourgeois female body proposed by paintings like Zandomeneghi's *In Bed*; in return, they sought their own bloody revenge on the sleeping female figure that is just that—a sleeping female figure.

BEDSIT SUBJECTIVITY

If the bedroom scene of Zandomeneghi's era staged a veiled feminine corporeality, the early twentieth-century bedsit scene enacted the bedroom body's displacement. Here, *bedsit* is broadly defined as a single-occupancy, single-room tenanted dwelling, likely to be one of several in a multi-occupancy house and where certain daily practices such as washing and dining ordinarily take place in communal rooms. Known in France as a '*chambre meublée*', or furnished bedroom, and in early-twentieth-century Britain as a 'bed-sitting room' or 'bedsitter', the bedsit operated as the combined site for a range of domestic practices including work, sociability and sleep. Whilst tenanted single-room dwellings have always been a feature of urban domesticity, the bedsit became a concerted motif of interior design discourses in the early twentieth century, perhaps as a response to the perception that, in a period of housing shortage, more single, young people were establishing themselves in lodgings prior to marriage, but also as part of a broader concern for the efficiency and rationalization of domestic space. The bedsit scene also became the focus of artistic representation, and this section will argue that, for female artists in particular, it held a new currency as a space of subjective experience and creative potentiality. However, not all artists chose to represent the woman's bedsit lifestyle in positive terms. Harold Gilman's *Tea in the Bedsitter* (1916) specifically represents the bedsit as the site of failed feminine sociability. A member of the Camden Town Group and associate of Walter Sickert, Gilman offered a damning assessment of an independent young woman's attempt to maintain the middle-class social ritual of taking tea. In a room dominated by cool tones of pale blue, two young women are seated at a round table in the foreground. Each melancholic figure looks down to her left, avoiding eye contact. The table is laid with cups, saucers and plates for four, and at the centre resides a teapot and milk jug. However, neither figure has been served tea, whilst to the left an imposing ladder-backed chair, larger than any other chair in the room, remains oppressively empty, waiting to receive a seemingly endlessly absent presence. Adopting a trope familiar to the 'at the table' scene (Berry 2006: 173), the fourth table setting abuts the forward plane of the painting and thereby belongs implicitly to the viewer. However, the high viewpoint renders the viewer's imaginative presence ambiguous at best. Rather than engaging directly with the table and its occupants, the viewer's gaze floats above the figures and across the room, as if afforded a privileged view of a gathering to which the viewer had been invited but failed to attend. Amongst other elements, a window, a door and, directly behind the figures, a single bed are depicted—its eiderdown rendered in the coolest of all the painting's pale blue tones and presenting an icily smooth surface that offers little suggestion of corporeal satisfaction. Above the bed, as though to reinforce further the mute blankness of the scene's failed sociability, a painting loosely conveys the portrait bust of a female figure—without facial features.

Whereas Gilman's *Tea in the Bedsitter* might be interpreted as deflating the ambitions of independent young women, bedsit scenes by female artists, specifically foreign artists living and working in Paris, have been interpreted more positively. The most familiar of these scenes, Gwen John's *A Corner of the Artist's Room in Paris (with flowers)* (1907–9), of which an open window version also exists, has commonly been described as a sublimated self-portrait and, more specifically, as 'a self-portrait of a fulfilled and happy woman' (Borzello 2006: 49). Of course, the artist's body is visually absent, though implicitly present as the subjective author of the painting and its carefully posed flowers, parasol and shawl. Less familiar are Stella Bowen's *Ford's Chair* (1928) and Bessie Davidson's *The Green Armchair* (1937); both are paintings by Australian artists of armchairs in the interiors of their Parisian apartments. Locating these paintings within the broader phenomenon of early-twentieth-century women artists focusing on their bedsit and apartment interiors as metaphors of feminine independence, Georgina Downey has argued that Bowen's and Davidson's interiors similarly did not derive from a sense of exclusion from urban space (2004: 88, 94). And despite their domestic subject matter, nor are these and related paintings a matter of obedience to conventional codes of feminine domesticity. Rather, by laying cautious (Bowen) and exaggerated (Davidson) claims to a concept of the specifically French interior and its furniture, these paintings invoke and attempt to resolve the expatriate artists' ambivalent sense of belonging in Paris (Downey 2004: 96–8).

A set of three naturalistic drawings of a bedroom, made by the unknown British artist Mary Eliott Brown whilst lodging in 1912 to 1913 in a house in the Parisian suburb of Passy (familiar to Impressionist art historians as the *arrondissement* in which Berthe Morisot lived and worked), offers its own tentative imagining of the artist's identification with Parisian urban modernity, if not its full representational realization.[5] As with the paintings by John, Bowen and Davidson, these drawings exchange the female bedroom body for subjective presence and locate that subjectivity within a specifically Parisian milieu. More than this, when taken together, as they were undoubtedly conceived, Brown's drawings constitute a visual journey around the artist's room that imaginatively signals, without directly representing, a capacity to inhabit external urban space. Brown's pictorial journey around her Parisian bedsit invites comparison with the literary journey conducted in 1790 by Xavier de Maistre and published in 1794 as *Voyage autour de ma chambre*. Confined to his bedroom for six weeks as part of an army punishment, de Maistre wrote a travelogue of his room: 'Next to my arm-chair, as I go northwards, my bed comes into sight' (1885: 12). Here, everyday items of furniture feature as significant landmarks of sensory and mnemonic inspiration, and so despite, or even as a result of, his enforced physical interiority de Maistre achieves subjective exteriority, identifying the bed, in particular, as the place in and from which to 'travel': 'I confess I do delight in these sweet moments, and prolong to the utmost the pleasure I find in meditating on the comfortable warmth of my bed. Where has the imagination freer play?' (1885: 12).

Brown's journey around her bedsit is less haphazard than that of de Maistre, but it treats everyday items of furniture with an equivalent level of interest and imaginative possibility. Brown directs her gaze and pencil into three of the room's corners, enabling an approximate reconstruction of its arrangement and contents that also facilitates an understanding of the physical and subjective place from which each drawing was made. *Towards the Chimneypiece, with a Hanging Shelf and Small Table* was probably drawn whilst sitting in a chair at the foot of the bed. In this drawing, Brown vaguely itemizes the numerous contents of a shelf and folding table. There are picture frames, postcards, vases, a crucifix and other *bibelots*; their acquisition in Paris by the artist hinted at by the two boxes placed on the seat of an armchair—waiting to be unpacked. *Towards the Window, with Wash-Stand* has been drawn at the head of the bed as it offers a view across the corner of the folding table towards a mirrored armoire and a curtained washstand and through the half-opened windows onto the balcony grille. Each of these components works hard to locate the artist *as an artist* in a room in France, but the latter, in particular, may have constituted for Brown a familiar pictorial trope (Berry 2006: 175) by which modern-life artists (including Morisot, Gustave Caillebotte and Paul Signac) signified 'being in a Parisian interior whilst contemplating the possibility of being outside'. Finally, *Towards the Bed, with a Hat on a Chair* (Figure 8.3) has been drawn in the vicinity of the window. From across the room, the pencil delineates a fragmentary slice of the edge of the fireplace, the corner of a table (quite possibly, the folding table), a bedside cabinet, a single bed, a chair and the edge of a door. Again, imaginative exteriority is signalled by the door and also, in a manner evocative of Gwen John's painting, by the hat and unidentifiable garment resting on a chair. But it is the bed that, in this instance, is of greatest significance. This is partly because John, Bowen and Davidson seem to have turned their gaze away from the bed as a pictorial motif with the potential to signify a foothold in artistic Paris, perhaps feeling it too compromised by associations with the bourgeois bedroom body. But it is also significant because of the reductive way in which Brown's bed has been depicted. Note the attention given to the hat and

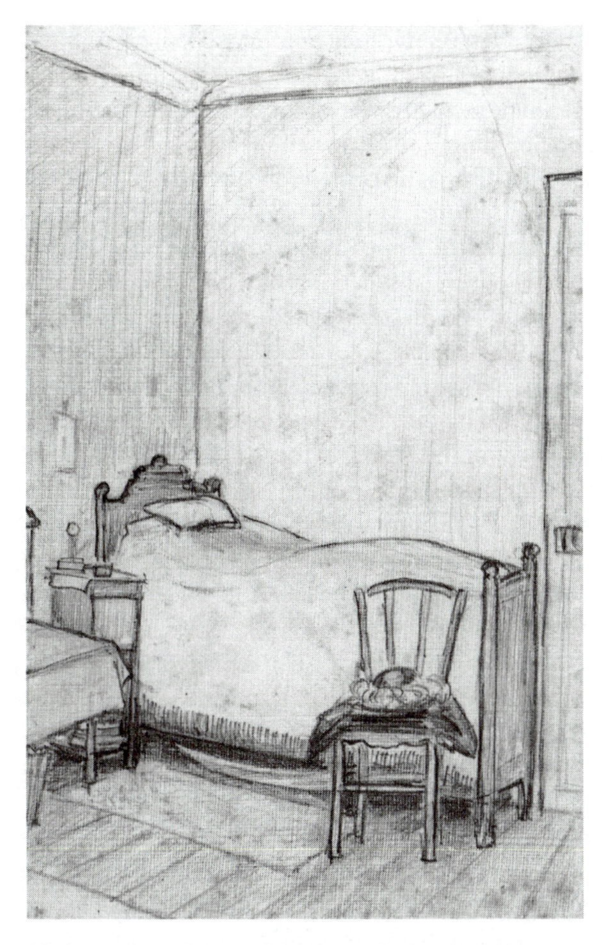

8.3. Mary Eliott Brown, *Towards the Bed, with a Hat on a Chair*, c. 1912–1913. © Victoria and Albert Museum, London.

garment, and to the shadow under the bed. Note, by contrast, the faintest pencil line that delineates where the bed meets the wall and that fails entirely to delineate the bed's opposite edge. Granted, the pencil makes more of the headboard and footboard, if only to exaggerate just how narrow the bed is. This may be an accident of poor foreshortening, but it produces a bed of minimal physical presence that is, nonetheless, entirely consistent with the broader visual culture of the bedsit.

During the 1870s in Britain and elsewhere, articles and advertisements concerned with bedsit living began to appear in furniture trade journals such as *The Furniture Gazette*. Directed, in particular, at single, male readers, these articles and advertisements focused on the latest technology in single-occupancy one-room living: the folding bed. Whether a bed was disguised as a cupboard or, more ingeniously, as a piano, furniture manufacturers such as the Standard Folding Bed Company recognized that those 'choosing' middle-class bedsit living wanted to distinguish their lifestyle from the necessity of one-room living for working-class families and identified the spatial and temporal marginalization of beds and sleep as the means to do so. Accompanying illustrations present the bedsit as though it were a middle-class salon—the bed safely tucked away behind an imposing piece of furniture and all democratizing (and feminizing) intimations of sleep repressed.[6] And when, in

Britain, the London furniture retailer Heal & Son developed a 'bed-sitting room' ensemble that was photographed and reproduced in Heal & Son's 1900 bedroom catalogue, a single, iron bed (normally the preserve of children and servants) was relegated to a curtained alcove, barely visible amongst an expensive-looking dining suite, matching sofa, display cabinet and artfully arranged mantelpiece (Heal & Son 1900). It is my contention that, in choosing subjectivity and sociability over corporeal lassitude, both the artistic bedsit scene developed by female artists and the bedsit ensemble designed by furniture retailers tapped into a dominant conceptualization of the specifically masculine bedroom as a room of several functions, of which sleeping was the least admissible.

Despite shifts in prescription and practice towards the conjugal bedroom, the idea and ideal of the man's bedroom remained remarkably consistent across the design discourses of the Victorians and the moderns. Most consistently, architectural and interior decoration guides and modernist design magazines seemed concerned that the male body risked objectification in the bedroom. As such, the bed operates as 'the elephant in the corner' of the masculine bedroom, rarely achieving representational visibility, let alone substance, as a result of its association with (feminized) corporeal stasis. Ease of access and fleeting occupation dominated the respective concerns of Robert Kerr in 1864 and Hermann Muthesius in 1904. Offering little comment otherwise on the topic, each advised that the bedrooms of single men in large houses be located close to the service staircase in order, in the words of Kerr, to facilitate 'unceremonious access' (1864: 162; Muthesius 1987: 93). Writing at length on the topic in 1880s France, Emile Cardon insisted that a man's bedroom is completely 'other' to that of a woman's (1884: 31). Principally, Cardon envisaged the masculine bedroom as a place for intellectualism, homosociability (linked to smoking) and the display of individual subjectivity. Cardon argued that a man's bedroom should be furnished with a desk, a bookcase, a cabinet for the display of collections and, at the periphery, a single bed. Indeed, he claimed that it is only in the bedroom of a 'lazy, egotistical man' that the bed dominates (Cardon 1884: 32). Whereas, in the bedroom of an 'active man', the bed occupies the least space possible and often disappears completely behind drapery: 'instead of being the principal being, the bed will be just an accessory, more succinct, less apparent, more summary and is reduced to that indispensable for the rest needed for health' (Cardon 1884: 34). Ultimately, Cardon prescribed the maximum width of ninety centimetres to a man's bed; the only instance in his interior decoration guide that precise measurement seemed worthy of citation (1884: 99). Jumping forward to a 1929 French modernist design magazine article, a man called Bob is interviewed in *Art et Industrie* on the topic of the young man's bedroom whilst driving a sports car to his golf club. In response to the interviewer's request that he state what such a room 'must be like', Bob exclaims, 'I who am never in my room!' before drawing in the golf course sand a carefully conceived partitioned room that separately incorporates a bar, gramophone and corner sofa, a shower enclosure and, sharing the same compartment as a punch ball and weights, an unidentified, faintly drawn rectangular box—the bed (Maigret 1929: 48). Cardon's intellectualized, mature homosociability may have given way to informal heterosociability and youthful physical prowess, but the bed, sleep and corporeal stasis were no less an afterthought to the masculine bedroom's *a priori* display of individual subjectivity in 1929 than they were in 1884.

BEAUTIFUL BODIES, TIDY MINDS

In their respective 1884 and 1887 interior decoration guides, neither Emile Cardon nor Henry Havard envisaged their interiors accommodating a child's bedroom. Indeed, the child simply has no place in their interiors. This situation changed, however, in 1896 when Henri de Noussanne's *Le Goût dans l'ameublement* was published. Significantly, illustrations to this book featured young children playing and Noussanne used the English word 'nursery' to identify the child's bedroom, further stating that 'the dear young ones are furnished in the English mode' (1896: 177). Whilst Noussanne did not, therefore, distinguish between the day nursery and night nursery favoured in British interior decoration guides (Hamlett 2010: 112), he acknowledged the model provided by the British middle-class home's clear demarcation of child space from adult space that was established with the installation and decoration of rooms specifically designed for children. Whilst British and French homes had, of course, featured bedrooms for children prior to this moment (often, however, incorporating shared beds), from about 1850 British manufacturers began to produce child-orientated furnishings such as wallpaper (Hamlett 2010: 112) which signalled a shift in conceptualization of the child's place in the home. The child's bedroom, and its inhabitant, had become the object of specialized interior design and decoration. In the same period, the child also became a regular feature in artistic and visual culture, most notably emerging as the dominant motif in the expanding industry of children's illustrated books. This final section brings these two 'child-orientated' fields together. It focuses on the child in the child's bedroom as represented in illustrations for children. The focus, therefore, is quite specific, for a number of reasons: first, because, like the bedsit, the child's bedroom scene emerged as a distinct category of visual representation in the period studied. Second, because children's illustration forged close links between representation of, and design for, the child's bedroom. Finally, because it allows us to re-connect bedroom subjectivity to bedroom corporeality as the child's psyche and body were made the focus of reformist design.

Whether installed as a practical and symbolic means of protecting children from disease (Corbin 1990: 480) or adult sexuality (Musée des Arts Décoratifs 1995: 185), certainly individual beds and the child's bedroom can be considered a symptom of the Victorians' enhanced perception of childhood as innocence definitively 'walled off' from adulthood (Mavor 2007: 78). It might also be more generally symptomatic of the increased value attached to a home-centred childhood that resulted from legal prohibitions on child labour. The effect of the latter, certainly, was a re-conceptualization in the early twentieth century of children from producers to consumers, or at least, to the objects—as both recipient and motif—of adult consumption (Cunningham 1995: 177–8). Certainly, the child's bedroom, which in middle-class Victorian houses was prescribed to be located as far from the conjugal bedroom as possible, affected a different experience of night time including a fear of being alone in one's room (Musée des Arts Décoratifs 1995: 187). From this, a new culture of bedtime emerged featuring illustrated stories, soft toys, night-lights and maternal presence (for children raised by nannies this may have been one of the few daily points of maternal contact) (Musée des Arts Décoratifs 1995: 187; Corbin 1990: 480). Significantly, in relation to the illustrated children's books, the child's bedroom, as the site of reading and as the subject of illustration, was frequently combined, and still is.

Too expansive a topic to adequately summarize here, analysis of the bedroom motif in children's illustration will be limited to two key examples. Firstly, a significant but under-studied illustrator of children's books, Henriette Willebeek Le Mair. Of Dutch nationality but trained in Paris, Willebeek Le Mair illustrated children's books that sold well in both France and England during the first three decades of the twentieth century. She specialized in representing fashionably dressed children in upper-middle-class gardens and interiors, rendered in a lithographic mode whose sugary, flat colours outlined in black directly echo the look of contemporaneous *pochoir* print fashion illustrations such as those by Paul Iribe and Georges Lepape. And, as with pochoir fashion prints, Willebeek Le Mair maintained an insistently two-dimensional approach to the representation of figures, objects and spaces which, when combined with a limited colour palette, fuse elements such as child, bed and interior to each other as part of a seamless and coherent whole. Indeed, Willebeek Le Mair's bedroom scenes, including *Time to Rise* (1911), *Bed in Summer* (1912), *Lazy Boy* (c. 1912–14) and *Evening Prayer* (c. 1912–14) tend to share the same pictorial properties: a rosy-cheeked, wide-eyed child dressed in nightclothes seated or lying in a perpendicularly orientated and two-dimensionally rendered bed contained itself within a shallow alcove or curtained recess that dominates the pictorial space and that itself is contained within a decorative border. In effect, the beautiful, uncomplicated surface of the bedroom child is fixed within a series of equally beautiful, surface deep rectangles that constitute its bedroom. There are no psychological hidden depths to these children; they and their bedrooms are instantly knowable; the fashionable products of adult consumption. It is no coincidence that one of Willebeek Le Mair's books, a collaboration between the illustrator, A. A. Milne and the Colgate company, was entitled *A Gallery of Children*, or that one of the illustrations to this book, *Miss Waterlow in Bed* (Figure 8.4), presents a child in bed in the manner described above, but this time with a diaphanous curtain held back by a large

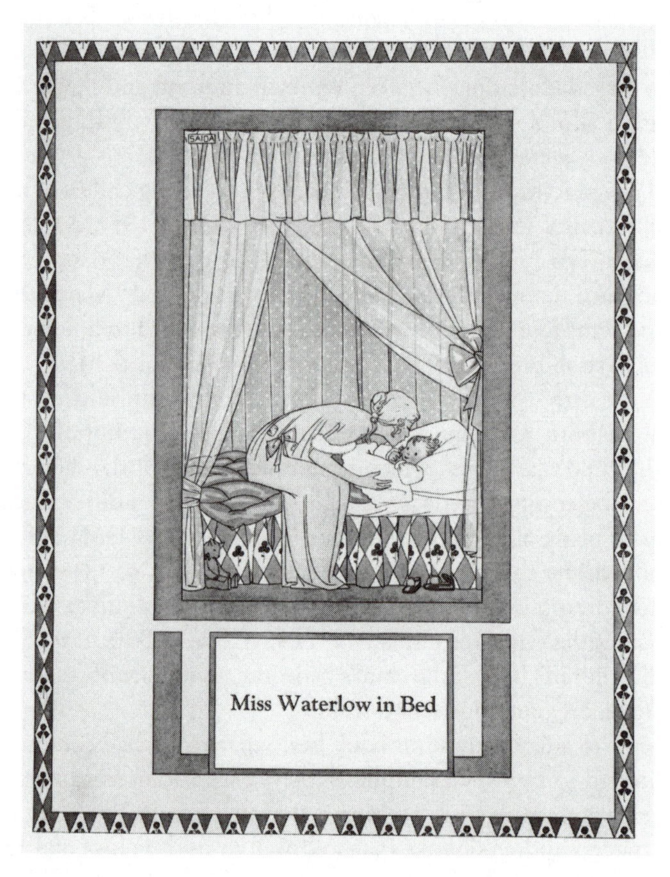

8.4. Henriette Willebeek Le Mair, *Miss Waterlow in Bed*, illustration from A.A. Milne, *A Gallery of Children*, 1925. Private Collection (Soefi Stichting Inayat Fundatie Sirdar/The Bridgeman Art Library).

pink bow that reveals the bedroom child as a deliciously wrapped gift and object of desire for its elegantly gowned mother who, in this instance, leans in for a goodnight kiss (Milne c. 1925: 27).

As Jacqueline Rose has argued, children's literature is rarely that—literature for children (1993: 1). The same may be argued of children's illustration, particularly the type of lavishly illustrated books that Willebeek Le Mair produced. Indeed, in 1897 *The Studio* magazine published a special issue, 'Children's Books and Their Illustrators', aimed directly at adult collectors of the new publishing phenomenon: expensive illustrated children's books (White 1897–8). Though children may be the dominant motif of children's literature (and illustration), Rose argues that 'it gives us the child, but it does not speak *to* the child' (1993: 1). Rather, children's literature speaks to adult desires for the child. Rose makes her persuasive general argument about children's literature in specific relation to J. M. Barrie's Peter Pan; one of the most enduring but problematic of characters for children.[7] This is not only because Peter Pan is a character that is not allowed to grow up but also because the first publication of the story of Peter Pan as a (illustrated) book for children, *Peter Pan in Kensington Gardens* (1906), was based on an extract from Barrie's 1902 adult novel about a man's desire for little boys, *The Little White Bird*. In fact, Peter Pan originated as part of a story told by the narrator of *The Little White Bird* 'to a boy whom the narrator was trying to steal' (Rose 1993: 5). A later chapter describes, from the subject position of the narrator, the overtly sensual experience of undressing, bathing and sharing a bed with a little boy that has been allowed by his mother to spend the night at the narrator's house (Barrie 1998: chapter 19). In other words, the many and enduring children's versions of the Peter Pan story emerge from 'an unmistakable act of censorship' in which the repressed problem of adult desire for the child continues to reside alongside a fantasy of childhood in which audiences continue to invest (Rose 1993: 5).

Rose's assessment of Peter Pan and, in general, children's literature has implications for how we might understand Willebeek Le Mair's presentation of bedroom children as objects of parental desire. Moreover, Rose's understanding of *Peter Pan in Kensington Gardens* as a repression of *The Little White Bird* bears upon my second example of a bedroom illustration 'for children', John Hassall's *The Darling Family Nursery: Peter Enters in Search of His Shadow and Wendy Awakes* (Figure 8.5), a

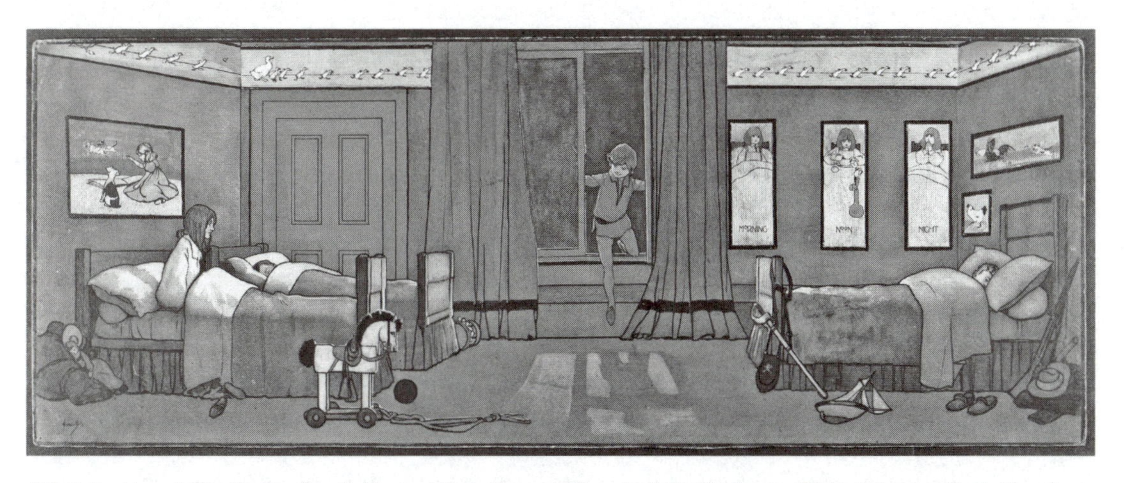

8.5. John Hassall, *The Darling Family Nursery: Peter Enters in Search of His Shadow and Wendy Awakes*, illustration from *Peter Pan*, c. 1906. Bristol City Museum and Art Gallery (Bristol City Museum and Art Gallery, UK/The Bridgeman Art Library).

poster sold as one of a set of six in the foyer of London's Duke of York's Theatre in 1907 where Barrie's *Peter Pan* was being performed (this play being the basis for Barrie's 1911 illustrated children's book *Peter Pan and Wendy*). It is my contention that Hassall's poster censored disconcerting aspects of the play's bedtime narrative, offering adults that purchased the poster on behalf of their children, perhaps for display in their child's bedroom, a tidied-up version. Much of the early narrative of the play centres on the bedtime routine of the Darling children, Wendy, John and Michael. In one scene, Peter Pan listens at the window to their mother, Mary, reading a bedtime story. But he is discovered and in the rush to escape leaves behind his shadow (Barrie 2008: 18). In a subsequent scene (represented in the Hassall poster), Peter Pan returns to retrieve his shadow, whereupon Wendy awakes and is persuaded by Peter Pan to leave, with her brothers, for the Neverland. The parents watch, helpless and distraught, as their children fly away (Barrie 2008: 35–58). Ostensibly, these elements of the play presented to parents a terrible prospect—that during the night their child might be stolen from their bedroom by a supposedly benign outside force controlling their minds. Indeed, struggle for control over childhood subjectivity constitutes a significant theme of the play. Whilst Mary Darling seeks to tidy her sleeping children's psyches, much as she tidies their bedroom each night, Peter Pan occupies their sleeping minds as an unconscious disrupting force.[8]

The anxieties that the play unleashed, Hassall's poster repressed. It is a deeply rational space that the poster presents, signalled immediately by Peter Pan's smiling entry accompanied, on the floor, by a naturalistic projection of his shadow (which, according to the plot, should be missing) and unaccompanied by the supernatural figure of Tinker Bell (which should be present). The bedroom itself is conventionally composed to offer the illusion of a three-dimensional, stage-like box for which the viewer constitutes the physically absent but scopically controlling fourth wall. Three beds, perpendicularly orientated and bearing the same muted blue-and-white bedding equally offer the illusion of a rational recession into space. Whilst two boys sleep in their individual beds, the inexpressive, certainly not fearful, figure of Wendy awakes in hers. Despite this being a bedroom shared by boys and a girl, the audience is made acutely aware that a sexually differentiated order is observed. Each bed is allocated a suitably gender-specific range of toys that includes a doll for the figure of Wendy and a drum and a rifle for the figures of her brothers. On the wall are a number of specifically child-orientated, brightly coloured pictures and decorations. These include a frieze featuring a mother goose and an orderly parade of goslings and, to the right of Peter Pan, a series of three pictures sequentially labelled 'Morning', 'Noon' and 'Night' that present a young girl dutifully observing the temporal order of her domestic life by waking in bed, eating lunch at midday and praying at bedtime. Whilst seemingly insignificant to modern viewers, these pictures and the frieze may have been highly familiar to contemporary middle-class children and their parents who would have been able to purchase them for their own child's bedroom. Indeed, in his 1904 analysis of *The English House*, Hermann Muthesius twice made approving reference to Hassall's decorations for children and reproduced two photographs of children's rooms, designed for exhibition and sale by Story & Co, featuring the same wall decorations including the *Morning*, *Noon* and *Night* series.[9] Muthesius's analysis of Hassall's child-orientated nursery decorations formed part of a broader discussion of the value of nursery furniture to 'nourish the childish imagination' (1987: 233). A few years earlier, the French interior decoration expert Henri de Noussanne had engaged in a similar discussion of the impact of bedroom design upon childhood subjectivity. Noussanne argued that children's bedrooms should be decorated with brightly coloured pictures of flowers and animals as a means to develop children's imagination and sense of taste (1896: 177). More than this, Noussanne suggested that appropriate decorative stimuli could actively control the behaviour of disruptive children by calming their nerves (1896: 177).[10] In other words, through the combined visual and design culture of the child's bedroom, Muthesius, Noussanne and Hassall offered to parents the illusion, at least, of control over the corporeality and subjectivity of their children. Finally, Hassall's circular approach to the bedroom scene (in which a poster, featuring a child's bedroom decorated with purchasable pictures of a child's bedroom, that was itself available to purchase as part of the merchandise for a child's play centred, in part, on the child's bedroom) demonstrates the extent to which, in the early twentieth century, the child became, though certainly not unproblematically, *the* modern means of staging the body and subjectivity in bed and *the* modern object of domestic desire.

NOTES

1. Translation of the following: '*La chambre, il ne faut pas l'oublier, est avant tout l'asile des actions mystérieuses, des grands et des petits secrets, le refuge des souvenirs. C'est dans le logis un véritable sanctuaire; et aussi le lieu fatal où le plus puissant comme le plus humble se trouve seul à seul en face de soi-même, où la vérité si souvent trahie, fardée, bannie, se révèle brusquement dans son déshabillée parfois peu flatteur, où pendant la nuit, qui porte conseil, l'esprit se recueille, l'imagination vagabonde, revit le passé, evoque les images évanouies, calcule, suppute, cherche à prévoir, combine, arrange, décide et finalement prépare l'avenir.*'
2. The German architectural historian Hermann Muthesius best expressed this in his 1904 analysis of English domestic architecture: 'In English opinion the bedroom belongs essentially to the woman and it might almost be said that the man merely enters it as her guest, as we have seen him doing in the drawing-room, the main living-room of the house. No man, surely, will find fault with this state of affairs. The woman often remains in the bedroom for some time after she has risen, so she usually has a little desk in the room and the fire-place is comfortably appointed' (Muthesius 1987: 92).
3. Translation of the following: '*Dans l'usage habituel, et dans les convenances les plus strictes, la chambre de madame est un lieu sacré ou nul ne pénètre et qui rest fermée, même alors que les invités trop nombreux ne peuvent plus respirer dans les autres pièces . . . Si hermétiquement fermée que soit la chambre de Madame, entrons-y cependant un instant.*'
4. See, for example, 'La Femme coupée en morceaux', *Le Voltaire*, 1 November 1892, 1; 'Le Crime de la rue Botzaris (Une femme coupée en morceaux—Découverte du cadaver)', *Le Petit Journal Illustré*, 12 November 1892, 1; 'Crime rue Botzaris', *Le Petit Parisien Illustré*, November 1892, 1.
5. An accompanying curatorial note states: 'Mary Hunter (née Brown) lived in Paris for some time in 1912–13 in the house of M. and Mme. Diemer at 14 Blvd Emile Augier, Passy 16e.' Victoria and Albert Museum, Prints and Drawings Study Room, E.323–1985; E.324–1985; E.325–1985.
6. See, for example, the anonymous article featuring an engraving of an 'Interior Furnished with a Sideboard and Folding Bed Combined', 'The Standard Folding Bed', *The Furniture Gazette*, 26, 129.
7. '*Peter Pan* stands in our culture as a monument to the impossibility of its own claims—that it represents the child, speaks to and for children, addresses them as a group which is knowable and exists for the book, much as the book (so the claim runs) exists for them. Where or how such a claim originates in the first place will be one of the questions asked here, but the question will be focused on *Peter Pan* in so far as *Peter Pan* is the text for children which has made that claim most boldly, and which most clearly reveals it as a fraud. *Peter Pan* has never, in any easy way, been a book for children at all, but the question it throws back to us is whether there can be any such thing' (Rose 1993: 1).
8. 'Mrs. Darling first heard of Peter when she was tidying up her children's minds. It is the nightly custom of every good mother after her children are asleep to rummage in their minds and put things

straight for next morning, repacking into their proper places the many articles that have wandered during the day. If you could keep awake (but of course you can't) you would see your own mother doing this, and you would find it very interesting to watch her. It is quite like tidying up drawers. You would see her on her knees, I expect, lingering humorously over some of your contents, wondering where on earth you had picked this thing up, making discoveries sweet and not so sweet, pressing this to her cheek as if it were as nice as a kitten, and hurriedly stowing that out of sight. When you wake in the morning, the naughtinesses and evil passions with which you went to bed have been folded up small and placed at the bottom of your mind; and on the top, beautifully aired, are spread out your prettier thoughts, ready for you to put on. . . . Occasionally in her travels through her children's minds Mrs. Darling found things she could not understand, and of these quite the most perplexing was the word Peter. She knew of no Peter, and yet he was here and there in John and Michael's minds, while Wendy's began to be scrawled all over with him. The name stood out in bolder letters than any of the other words, and as Mrs. Darling gazed she felt that it had an oddly cocky appearance' (Barrie 2008: 7–8, 10–11).

9. 'A few furnishing firms, Story & Co. in London in particular, have recently taken up nursery decoration with enthusiasm; they showed two nurseries at an exhibition that aroused great interest among the public and went much of the way towards starting a movement to transform the already neat and pretty nursery into one of unmistakable beauty. They commissioned the celebrated draughtsmen Cecil Aldin and John Hassall to do the decoration. Most of the designs by these artists, who are famed far beyond England's shores for their delightful illustrations to children's books, consisted of friezes of animals and similar subjects, which stood out with redoubled charm from the otherwise undecorated walls . . . In addition to the fixed wall decorations, movable pictures play a large part in nurseries. A number of English artists deserve credit for having painted pictures suitable for children's nurseries, by far the most important being again Cecil Aldin and John Hassall. But even before them, good artists, especially Heywood Sumner, had painted excellent nursery pictures, though they were possibly a little too serious and pious for the youngsters. Aldin's and Hassall's paintings are not guilty of these sins. Children find their gaiety and exuberance quite fascinating and they can, furthermore, be considered almost model wall-decorations with their simple treatment of contour and colour' (Muthesius 1987: 232–4).

10. '*Je voudrais pourtant aux murs, sur la peinture claire,—vert pâle si possible, c'est la teinte qui convient le mieux aux yeux délicats des enfants,—je voudrais accrocher des gravures simples, des dessins de fleurs d'un vivant coloris, d'animaux familiers, d'oiseaux. C'est un moyen précieux autant qu'infaillible de développer d'abord l'imagination des enfants, et plus tard le goût.*

    Des bébés de six mois sont attirés par les figures, par les couleurs; leurs yeux brillent, leurs menottes se tendent. Il n'en faut pas davantage souvent pour calmer leurs cris. Au lieu de secouer les enfants ou de mener tapage, ce qui ébranle les méninges dans leur cerveau délicat, ingéniez-vus à fixer leur attention par une impression de la vue. C'est moins malaisé qu'on ne l'imagine. Ne vois-je pas autour de moi une adorable fillette, qui a bel et bien sept mois des gravures coloriées, surtout des gravures de modes! Elle trépigne, rit, souffle, balbutie. Impossible de nier que les figurines l'intéressent. Grand Dieu, que sera-ce dans quinze ans d'ici?' (Noussanne 1896: 177–8).

REFERENCES

Anon. (1892a), 'La Femme coupée en morceaux', *Le Voltaire*, 1 Nov.: 1.

Anon. (1892b), 'Le Crime de la rue Botzaris (Une femme coupée en morceaux—Découverte du cadaver)', *Le Petit Journal Illustré*, 12 Nov.: 1.

Anon. (1888), 'The Standard Folding Bed', *The Furniture Gazette*, 26, 1 April: 129.
Anon. (1892), 'Crime rue Botzaris', *Le Petit Parisien Illustré*, Nov.: 1.
Auslander, L. (1996), *Taste and Power: Furnishing Modern France*, Berkeley: University of California Press.
Barrie, J. M. (1998), *The Little White Bird*, <www.gutenberg.org>.
Barrie, J. M. (2008), *Peter and Wendy*, <www.gutenberg.org>.
Barthes, R. (1975), *The Pleasures of the Text*, tran. R. Miller, New York: Hill and Wang.
Berry, F. (2006), 'Lived Perspectives: The Art of the French Nineteenth-century Interior', in J. Aynsley and C. Grant, eds., *Imagined Interiors: Representing the Domestic Interior Since the Renaissance*, London: V&A Publications.
Borzello, F. (2006), *At Home: The Domestic Interior in Art*, London: Thames & Hudson.
Brisset, J. (1853), 'La ménagère parisienne', *Les Français peints par eux-mêmes*, 2: 249–53.
Cardon, E. (1884), *L'Art au foyer domestique*, Paris: Librairie Renouard.
Cogeval, G. (2003), *Édouard Vuillard*, exhibition catalogue, Montreal: Montreal Museum of Fine Arts; Washington, DC: National Gallery of Art.
Corbin A. (1990), 'The Secret of the Individual', in M. Perrot, ed., *A History of Private Life: From the Fires of Revolution to the Great War*, tran. A. Goldhammer, Cambridge, MA: Harvard University Press.
Cunningham, H. (1995), *Children and Childhood in Western Society Since 1500*, New York: Longman.
de Maistre, X. (1885), *A Journey Round My Room*, tran. E. Goldsmid, Edinburgh: Privately Printed.
Didi-Huberman, G. (2003), *Invention of Hysteria: Charcot and the Photographic Iconography of the Salpêtrière*, tran. A. Hartz, Cambridge, MA: MIT Press.
Downey, G. (2004), 'Armchair Tourists: Two "Furniture Portraits" by Expatriate South Australian Women Artists', in E. Hartrick, R. Hogg and S. Supski, eds., *Write/Up Journal of Australian Studies*, St. Lucia: API Network and UQP: 80, 87–98.
Guerrand, R.-H. (1990), 'Private Spaces', in M. Perrot, ed., *A History of Private Life: From the Fires of Revolution to the Great War*, tran. A. Goldhammer, Cambridge, MA: Harvard University Press.
Hamlett, J. (2010), *Material Relations: Domestic Interiors and Middle-Class Families in England, 1850–1910*, Manchester: Manchester University Press.
Havard, H. (1887), *L'Art dans la maison (grammaire de l'ameublement)*, Paris: Ed. Rouveyre et G. Blond.
Heal & Son (1900), *Bedsteads, Bedding and Bedroom Furniture, Heal and Son's Illustrated Catalogue*, London: Heal & Son.
Kerr, R. (1864), *The Gentleman's House; or, How to Plan English Residences, From the Parsonage to the Palace*, reprinted in B. Miller Lane, ed., *Housing and Dwelling: Perspectives on Modern Domestic Architecture*, New York: Routledge.
McLean, J. (2008), *Impressionist Interiors*, exhibition catalogue, Dublin: National Gallery of Ireland.
Maigret, F. G. de (1929), 'La Chambre d'un jeune homme', *Art et Industrie*, 9: 21–24, 48.
Martin-Fugier, A. (1990), 'Bourgeois Rituals', in M. Perrot, ed., *A History of Private Life: From the Fires of Revolution to the Great War*, tran. A. Goldhammer, Cambridge, MA: Harvard University Press.
Mavor, C. (2007), *Reading Boyishly: Roland Barthes, J. M. Barrie, Jacques Henri Lartigue, Marcel Proust, and D. W. Winnicott*, Durham, NC: Duke University Press.
Mesch, R. (2009), 'Housewife or Harlot? Sex and the Married Woman in Nineteenth-Century France', *Journal of the History of Sexuality*, 18/1: 65–83.
Milne, A. A. (c. 1925), *A Gallery of Children*, London: S. Paul.
Mirliton (1892), 'Troisième exposition des peintres impressionistes et symbolistes', *Le Journal*, 26/Nov., supplément littéraire, 1.
Musée des Arts Décoratifs (1995), *Rêves d'alcôves: la chambre au cours des siècles*, exhibition catalogue, Paris: Union Centrale des Arts Décoratifs.
Muthesius, H. (1987), *The English House*, tran. J. Seligman, Oxford: BSP Professional Books.
Noussanne, H. de (1896), *Le Goût dans l'ameublement*, Paris: Firmin-Didot et Cie.
Rose, J. (1993), *The Case of Peter Pan or the Impossibility of Children's Fiction*, Philadelphia: University of Pennsylvania Press.

Sidlauskas, S. (2000), *Body, Place and Self in Nineteenth-Century Painting*, Cambridge: University of Cambridge Press.

Silverman, D. (1989), *Art Nouveau in Fin-de-Siècle France: Politics, Psychology and Style*, Berkeley: University of California Press

Walton, W. (1992), *France at the Crystal Palace: Bourgeois Taste and Artisan Manufacture in the Nineteenth Century*, Berkeley: University of California Press.

White, G. (1897–8), 'Children's Books and Their Illustrators', *The Studio*, winter, special issue.

9.

HIDDEN SPACES: CAVITIES, ATTICS AND CELLARS—MORBID SECRETS AND THREATENING DISCOVERIES

mark taylor

Histories of rooms, artefacts and spaces of the domestic interior tend to include patterns of inhabitation, the public/private divide and gendered readings of the inhabitants and their spatial arrangements. Many Victorian treatises on domestic architecture characterized women as the arbiters of taste, creating a neat, comfortable home for the returning male. Bound by a set of abstract moral codes, the home was argued as a refuge and place of repose for the family, a nurturing environment for children, and a safe place for visitors. This chapter discusses occasions when the domestic environment breaks this code, becoming the site for murder and the location for concealing bodies. The macabre spectacle of home as mortuary, characterized by violence, terror and the killer's physical and psychological interaction with the interior, shares a number of similarities with realist novels and gothic fiction that engaged hauntings, spectres, ghosts and the paranormal, indicating that the domestic interior can be examined as a psychological and topographical encounter, and a place where the inanimate is made animate. Within this genre, the ordinariness of everyday life and modes of inhabitation are unfolded as horror stories that include hidden rooms and secret passages that reflect the lair of the protagonist's mind. This chapter examines this relationship by initially discussing house and room as metaphors of the mind and their subsequent mirroring in physical space. Within these metaphors are notions of secrecy, particularly the places where things are hidden, and the structures necessary for exposure. The identification of the mind with space is further examined through the self-exploratory literary devices of nineteenth-century novelists including Honoré de Balzac and Charlotte Brontë. These authors are selected because of their particular observational accounts of life and the use of metaphor, homology and reciprocal relationships between people and their environment. The final section focuses on several situations where Victorian moral characteristics of home are questioned, and any reciprocal relationship is profoundly disturbing. In these examples where inhabitants are murdered and hidden in the home, the domestic ideology of self-sacrificing women and protective males no longer applies. Within an overcrowded urban environment, the home as lodging house with its itinerant occupants is also the private space of female danger.

While much has been made of the late-nineteenth-century domestic interior reflecting a nurturing and caring environment governed by the 'angel in the house', not all domestic environments conformed to this ideal. In some cases, the fear of other occupants' behaviour and the home's spatial arrangement of locked areas, hidden rooms and secret passages induce a state of fear. For some people, escape was made by hiding and suppressing their movements as well as reducing their contact with those they fear; for others, there was no way out. In 1893, Herman Webster Mudgett, alias Henry Howard Holmes, built a large multi-story building in the Chicago suburb of Eaglewood. Occupying a city block at the intersection of Sixty-third and Wallace Streets, it was constructed to capitalize on the Chicago World's Fair (1893), and featured shops, offices and private rooms for rent. The conspicuous castellated elevation with large bay windows was described in the press as the 'Holmes Castle', and the architectural treatment resonated with the nineteenth-century domestic ideal of 'a man's house is his castle'. The metaphoric use of the fortress, a place of defence against attack and violence, also amplified the power relations between the 'lord' and his subjects, as well as signalling a secure and safe interior. Unbeknown to his tenants, the primary purpose of the building was not their safety and security; it was to be a place where he could murder and dispose of his victims without fear of capture. To achieve this, Holmes devised a complex spatial arrangement of hidden rooms and secret passages and pathways that enabled him to move about unnoticed and dispose of his dead (Figure 9.1).

The idea of architecture housing hidden rooms and spaces has in literary narratives been argued as both a real and metaphoric means of understanding the complex relationship between the person and his or her mind, spatialized through narrative structures. In her analysis of hidden rooms in the poems of Isabella Valancy Crawford and P. K. Page, Wanda Campbell argues that both authors make a claim to 'a hidden room for women's intellectual and creative work' (Campbell 2002: 2). Drawing upon Irigaray, she notes that these spaces reflect 'a new respect for and representation of complex female space away from the traditional locations of kitchen and bedroom where women's use-value as "a commodity" has been most evident' (Irigaray 1991: 31). Campbell proposes that, while Crawford interpreted the entire house and posed the question as to the 'existence of a secret inner sanctum' (Campbell 2002: 2), Page, writing over a century later, focuses entirely on the hidden room. For Page, the hidden room is the 'complex structures of knowledge and power traditionally prohibited to women' such as the Bodleian Library at Oxford University (Campbell 2002: 3). Campbell argues that the hidden room is within the architectural structure of the poet's mind, and access must be by invitation, by permission, with mutual consent, and will recede if

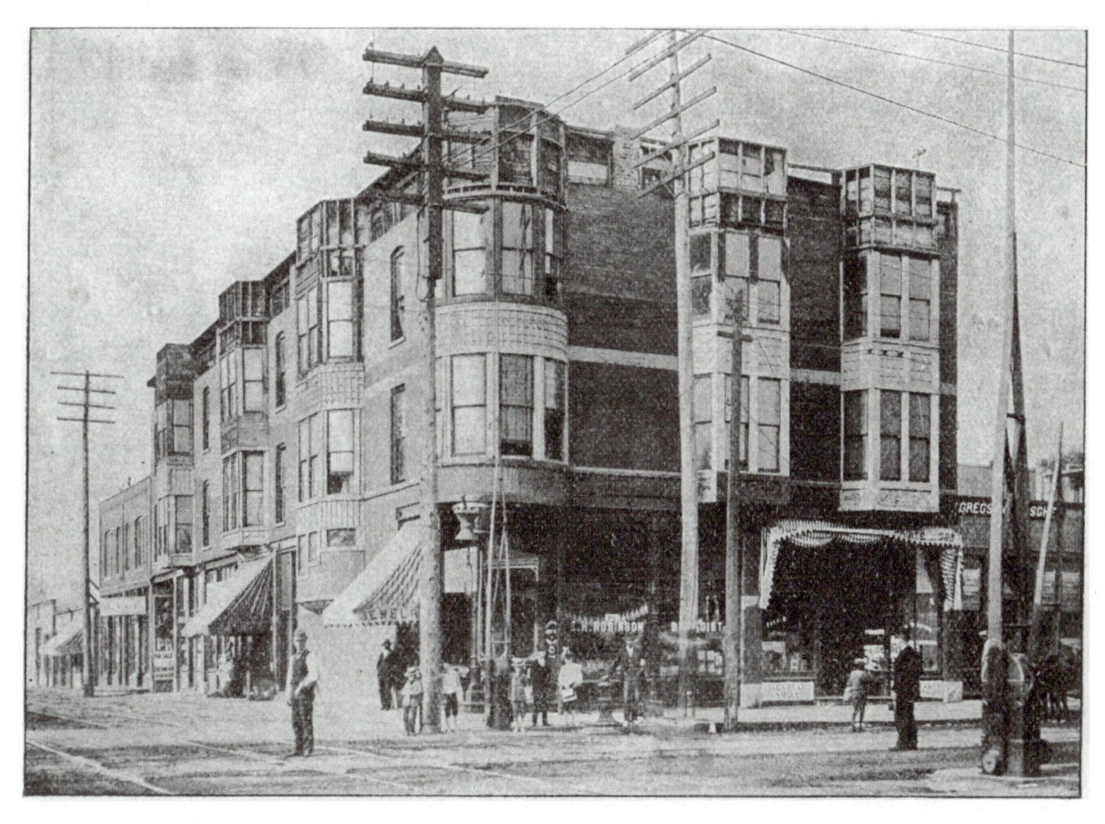

9.1. The Holmes Castle. Image ICHi-27827, Courtesy of the Chicago History Museum.

the approach is unbidden. The invitation to enter the hidden room of the poet's imagination is *not only* to experience architecture through words but also to *engage* the power relations in their spatial structures, thus the power relations are 'real'. While Campbell never explicitly refers to these women having a room to write their thoughts, at the heart of her essay is recognition that the history of architecture, as a gendered history, has promoted the spaces of men, many of which women were excluded from, or they were made to feel uncomfortable. She notes that, while the first 'closet' was developed in the fourteenth and fifteenth century interior, the man's study was the first truly private space. It is a space she refers to as 'the hidden room of male intellectual activity'.

This shift into physical spaces that mirror the activities of the mind or to some extent signify the intentions of the inhabitant, whether by these Canadian poets or more familiar Victorian novelists, is a psychological act of self-exploration. The nineteenth-century French novelist Honoré de Balzac's realist fictions are both topographical and psychological and include descriptions of persons or of interiors such as those in *Le Père Goriot* and *Eugénie Grandet.* In the former novel, Balzac described how 'the whole person, in short, explains the pension [boarding house], as the pension implies the person' (Balzac 1897: 13), suggesting a connection between Madam Vauquer and her establishment, as both a topographical and psychological exchange. Moreover, William Stowe suggests, 'The reader may not know exactly what it means that Madame Vauquer's person explains her establishment, any more than he understands how the ladies knitted petticoat sums up her salon, her dining room' (Stowe 1983: 28). Stowe argues that the technique is to provide a series of 'indisputable statements' and then follow this with a series of apparently related but 'logically dubious statements that gain credibility by contagion' (1983: 28). He suggests that the character's situation is made evident by a series of statements that in themselves are intelligible even if not uniformly logical. In the latter novel, *Eugénie Grandet*, the home of the miser, M. Grandet, serves meagre breakfasts that echo the rigid economic measures performed by Grandet's character. Balzac's ability to convey the intensity of the situation is probably due to his own early struggle against poverty, and hence the novel in some way reflects Balzac's own character and experiences.

Discussing the novelist in his age, literary critic Martin Turnell proposes that Balzac had an 'interest in crime and a highly personal form of melodrama' (1950: 211), that violence is enjoyed 'because it is somehow never real' (Turnell 1950: 214). More recently Owen Heathcote also argues that violence and murder are 'more explicitly linked to struggles over territory, from the early text of *Les Chouans* to the much later *Les Paysans*' (Heathcote 2009: 127). This view is also confirmed by Felicity Edholm's analysis of Paris in the 1880s, which indicates that while alcohol featured heavily in the lives of the poor 'there was a great deal of violence and the close proximity in which people lived, the sharing that was necessary, the lack of privacy and sanitation, caused all kinds of interpersonal tensions' (Edholm1993: 163). Sharon Marcus, in her analysis of home and city in the nineteenth century, notes that in Victorian London crowding brought with it the problem of many bodies in too small a space, as the single family dwelling was 'segmented into several parts (set of rooms, a single room, a single room divided by a screen)' (1999: 105). Victorian urban explorations equated lodging houses with overcrowding and high rates of mortality, where dead bodies lay alongside newborn infants and 'sensational anecdotes recurred throughout the literature of urban exploration concerning dead bodies that mouldered in tenements and lodging houses and made those residences "tainted" sites of "decomposition" ' (Marcus 1999: 128).

The connection between violence and hidden spaces is performed not only relative to a disintegrating urban condition but also in the nineteenth-century home, particularly relative to the imprisonment of women under the guise of insanity or to confirm a power relationship. While there are a number of documented accounts, and as many explanations for 'madness', the hidden room/space or room/space for hiding within has been the subject of many English Victorian novels. Karen Chase argues that in Charlotte Brontë's novel *Jane Eyre* (1847), the text is spatially articulate and depicts several houses with multiple rooms, many of which are in continual upheaval as characters open and close doors and windows, ascend and descend staircases, and cross thresholds (Chase 1984: 47–65). As these houses preoccupy their inhabitants and rooms take on distinct personalities, the protagonists' mental qualities come into play, altering their behaviour. The interior as a formal spatial (designed) arrangement is replaced by one that constructs new relationships through patterns of movement and inhabitation that occurs with each occupant's actions. Chase argues that in negotiating the five principal residences, Jane declares rooms to have personalities, and constructs the houses relative to her mental state, as in one instance when Jane attempts to avoid other people in the house and 'engages in architectural contortions in order to remain the unobtrusive governess' (Chase 1984: 59). The ability of the body to respond to spatial conditions and influence the narrative is further reinforced by Charlotte Brontë's lavish descriptions of rooms above those of the inhabitants, and utilization of a number of devices to depict layers of containment, whether physical shells of enclosure or psychical descriptions of 'dangerous' emotive energy. She portrays rooms within rooms, containers within containers, and the house as an outer shell for routes to intricate spaces.

In one passage of the novel, Jane narrates the occasion when she 'mounted into the window seat: gathering up my feet, I sat cross-legged, like a Turk; and, having drawn the red moreen curtain nearly close, I was shrined in double retirement' (Brontë 1996: 20). With the folded drapery to one side and clear panes of glass to the other, Jane was protected, but not separated from either the garden or the library. For Jane, the window niche was a secret place that enabled her imagination to be played out in the spatial structures of the house. As a woman of impoverished circumstances clearly attempting to educate herself despite the problems of her gender, she was not safe from her abusive cousin John Reed, who, upon discovering she had borrowed a book, attacked her and locked her in the Red Room. Again, Jane was hidden in the home though this time in a violent manner, and not of her own accord. This action repeats Edward Rochester's treatment of his first wife, Bertha Antoinetta Mason, though it is she who is violently insane and moved to Thornfield where she is locked in the attic. In both these events, it is not the room that is hidden from view, but incarceration removes the room from participating in the normal domestic practice, and, by being 'off-limits', it is effectively hidden. The difficulty with incarceration is that it deprives not only liberty but also the ability for self-determination and self-governing, since the victim is subject to another person's control.

Susan Sherer (1996) argues that the impulse to hide in a secret space is a wish for autonomy, and she observes that many Victorian novels began as a retreat from an increasingly urban world (with all the attributes of speed, change, overcrowding, sanitation and so on). In Shearer's analysis of Lewis Carroll's novels *Alice in Wonderland* and *Through the Looking-Glass*, she states, 'The spatial imagery and objects that fill Wonderland and the Looking-Glass world are similarly misleading. Hidden doors, dark tunnels, ungraspable keys and dense woods all create an architecture crowded with secret spaces and hence suggest an atmosphere of concealment and discovery' (Sherer 1996). She argues that to hide an object, a person, a story, a memory, 'implies that there is a constant, an unwavering signifier that can be hidden, which is to say, a floating signifier eludes concealment' (Sherer 1996: 5). To this extent Sherer proposes that 'in the forward motion of a sequacious, progressive logic: A must exist before B can hide it' (Sherer 1996: 5). In a narrative fiction, the hidden space or person requires contextualization which might include an observer or witness to the possibility of a secret. The same is true for a real event, though in the case of the American H. H. Holmes (1861–96) and others, contextualization includes the illegality and moral outrage at their activities inside the architecture, particularly when these activities challenge ideas of 'home'.

The representation of Holmes provides some indication of the hatred and disgust that he aroused. Born on 16 May 1861 in Gilmanton, New Hampshire, Holmes studied medicine at the University of Michigan in Ann Arbor (Mudgett 1895: 7–8), where he took an excessive interest in dissection and corpses. Although there are no known cases of murder during this time, he used disfigured corpses to fraudulently obtain insurance monies, suggesting that that handling the dead was not morally repulsive. Although raised in a strict religious family, Holmes's life of crime was characterized by self-obsession and money. While working for a widowed drugstore owner in the suburb of Englewood, Chicago, he contrived her disappearance at the time he acquired the business and property. Following this easy acquisition, he developed other 'businesses' and purchased land across the street from the pharmacy where he built his three-story hotel with ground-floor shops, and, as he noted, 'Here my real troubles commenced' (quoted in Mudgett 1895: 12).

The interrogation of Holmes by the police following his arrest on 17 November 1894 shifted from the horse stealing charge to an insurance swindle involving his friend Benjamin Pitezel. Uncertain whether Pitezel was alive or dead, Philadelphia policeman Detective Frank P. Guyer began tracing Holmes's movements in an effort to find Alice, Nellie and Howard Pitezel, all of whom had been left in his charge. Holmes stated that the three children had travelled through several towns, en route to England, in the care of Minnie Williams. Detective Guyer was not convinced they had left the country and painstakingly recreated the children's journey (Guyer 1896). Following his investigations, the two girls decomposed bodies were found hidden under the earthen floor of a very small and low cellar at 16 St. Vincent Street, Toronto, and the burnt and charred remains of the boy were found in a small cottage in Irvington, Indiana. During questioning, attention also turned to No. 701 West 63rd Street, Chicago, the building that became known as the Holmes Castle. Holmes occupied most of the rooms on the upper (third) floor, rented flats to parties who came and went, and had control over the second floor. He also ran a number of small businesses in the building and employed a number of young ladies as stenographers and typists, several of whom, including Mrs Conner and her daughter, Pearl, Miss Kelly, Emily van Tassel and others, were never seen again (Corbett 1895: 388).

Journalist Robert Corbitt entered the building as soon as bones were found (Corbitt 1885: 368). He described the building as being beside four railroad tracks and comprising 'high, red bricks walls and windows of curving contour whose stained glass of variegated colours make it strikingly attractive' (Corbitt 1895: 368). The result of a fire upstairs meant there remained only six tenants, whereas the ground floor was still occupied by stores, the corner one Corbitt described as 'a beautiful piece of work [with] a massive pillar topped with an elaborate and elegant composite capital, radiant with harmonious colors', and above the octagonal entrance was 'a beautiful cupola' (Corbitt 1895: 368). The interior comprised frescoes in mild colours and black-and-white floor tiling in a diamond pattern. Behind this store was a winding staircase leading from the outside to the charred and broken remains of the upper levels. Corbitt described how the stairway was enclosed by a 'grand oriel-window projecting from the outside wall' (Corbitt 1985: 368). Corbitt's unusually meditative and elaborate reconstruction of the 'public' face contrasts with his description of the interior as 'strangely labyrinthine', a view confirmed by others: 'At the south end of the floor was a space in which a person could wander several different ways on an account of the irregular walls' ('Holmes' Den Burned' 1895: 1). Despite the poor quality workmanship, the external physical appearance assimilated into the urban fabric, whereas the interior challenged floor-planning conventions (Figure 9.2).

Many descriptions of the hotel are, as Mark Seltzer argues, reasonably reliable but necessarily speculative and fragmentary; he describes the guest floor unfolding 'in mazelike fashion, incorporating corridors leading nowhere, with concealed passages behind walls, sliding panels, secret staircases, peepholes into the rooms through the backs of pictures and trapdoors concealing metal chutes that communicated with the elaborately designed basement' (Seltzer 1998: 206). The sense of order on the outside compared to the chaos within figures a condition of repression, the apparent good surrounding the evil. The absence of an architect or delineator was not an eccentric act to enable the romantic 'natural architect' but a deliberate effort to hide interior activities. As if to confirm the spatial ambiguity, several sketches of the interior and floor plans produced for newspapers contained a number of discrepancies and departed from the familiar spaces of 'bedrooms', 'sitting rooms' and 'libraries' such that their annotation betrayed criminal intentions. Rooms labelled 'asphyxiation chamber', 'room of three corpses', 'closed room', dummy elevator for lowering

From the outset, the purpose of the rooms on the second and third floors was quite baffling, 'one peculiar feature about the thirty-five rooms on the second floor was the number and location of the fifty-one doors which were cut in the walls in every conceivable place' ('Modern Bluebeard' 1895: 40). The sensational interest in the boarding house geography and Holmes's psychology recognized that the number of doors in each room would allow a person with knowledge to pass easily through the building and leave others lost. The *Chicago Tribune* reported that a hall at the south end of the second floor was disorientating due to irregular walls and narrow passages, and police had found 'secret rooms without light or air, a sealed chamber, a hidden trapdoor leading to a hanging secret room, and a steel-bound room built into the wall' ('Modern Bluebeard' 1895: 40). This hanging room 'about seven feet by five feet' was suspended between the first and second floors and accessed by a stair from the trapdoor, and a further two sets of stairs. One set descended to a shop, but at the time was closed off, and the other descended only six feet and ended abruptly in a blind partition ('Modern Bluebeard' 1895: 40). From this low partition was a route to the dummy elevator shaft, the only way out, which 'drops to the cellar'. This secret space was designed to aid the disposal of bodies, by forging a direct connection to the basement.

Corbitt's detached description of the main staircase leading through long halls and corridors to a windowless room, and his observation that on the next floor 'there is a false vault made of steel which is placed against the wall and covered with plastering, and also solidly packed with mineral wool' (Corbitt 1895: 369), contrasts with other impressions that allude to fate of the occupants. The vault was false; beyond the large heavy outside door with combination lock and regulation inside door, 'there is nothing but a plaster wall packed with asbestos. The space between the two sets of doors is about two feet, allowing room enough for a person to stand and have the outer door closed upon him, in which he would in short order be suffocated' ('Footprint is Found' 1895: 2). The *Chicago Tribune* reported that a woman's bare footprint was found on the inside door of the blind vault provided some grounds for speculating that 'Holmes' victims or some of them were inveigled into the vault between the two sets of doors and there they were smothered to death' ('Footprint is Found' 1895: 2). Although the investigators were convinced the footprint was that of a woman, the text refers to the space being sufficient to suffocate a male. While this might be a problem of a patriarchy, it nevertheless shifts the emphazis away from the female murder victim. To account for the footprint, which could not be removed, the police proposed that Holmes placed acid on the floor to accelerate the suffocation and the victim, having trodden in the liquid, placed her foot against the door in an effort to force it open, leaving an imprint eaten into the enamel. From the vault, it is supposed 'the victims were carried around the winding hallway to the bathroom, which contained the secret entrance to the hidden stairway that led to the basement. Here the police think, they were laid upon the dissecting table, which bears evidence of blood . . . and dissected into parts small enough to allow a ready disposition of them' ('Footprint is Found' 1895: 2).

In the basement, 'large qualities of human remains' were discovered, and 'two large vaults of quicklime, one containing some human bones, have been found beneath the floor' ('Modern Bluebeard' 1895: 40). During their investigations, workmen broke through a false wall that led under the alley to discover a large tank with pipes leading through the basement wall. From this tank came an overpowering 'nauseous' gas with a strange odour that exploded injuring the labourers ('Not Human Bones' 1895: 2). The *Chicago Tribune* article also noted that beneath the dirt floor were found quicklime pits and traces of acid, as well as a crematorium furnace built into one wall that was 'neither for heating purposes nor for boiling water' ('Modern Bluebeard' 1895: 40). Mark

Seltzer proposes that dummy elevator shafts from the top floors, 'large enough to accommodate a body, evacuated corpses into the vats of quicklime and acid in the basement, the literalised space of Holmes's voracious id, so that they disappeared without a trace' (Seltzer 1998: 209).

Holmes's preferred method of killing his victims did not include the bloodied mess of another contemporary serial killer, Jack the Ripper, but involved gassing, suffocation and burning alive. All of these methods were conducted at distance, without Holmes needing to be near his victims. For example, during their search of the room on the second floor where Holmes used to sleep, workmen found a gas pipe that 'turns down and into the floor and beneath the boards is a cut-off' ('Modern Bluebeard' 1895: 40). This cut gas pipe was argued to be one of Holmes's instruments of death: 'Sitting in his room he could turn on with ease a flow of gas that would fill the dark sleeping apartment and asphyxiate the occupants' ('Modern Bluebeard' 1895: 40); this observation was echoed in Boswell and Thompson's account in *The Girls in Nightmare House* (1955). For the hotel guests, terror was only evident once they realized their entrapment, such as when sealed in the vault or when gas and flame were introduced into their rooms, but for other guests, asphyxiation occurred when they were asleep. Even if the victims thought themselves safe from Holmes, the house acquired a murderous agency. This act reflects the structure of the nineteenth-century horror novel, which Anthony Vidler identifies as 'the apparently homely interior that gradually turns into a vehicle of horror' (Vidler 1992: 36).

In the nineteenth-century novels discussed above, the narrativization of the individual's bodily and spatial identity present a profile of the inhabitant. In Holmes's case, the fragmentary and misleading spatial and material hotel as a physical and psychological profile is brought to bear on the domestic interior. All normal or conventional interpretations of the domestic space as a safe nurturing environment are both present and absent, in that the bedrooms, bathrooms, halls and closets are recognizably domestic, yet duplicate as killing spaces and disposal chutes. This American gothic 'castle', with its simultaneous pretentions to history and absorption of technology, and Holmes's antifamilial violence 'epitomized the conflation of private and public spaces in the home/factory of the Holmes Castle itself, and beyond that, in the rival genres of bodily violence in his career' (Seltzer 1998: 223). Holmes's monomaniacal delineation of space included rooms for morbid sleep and intolerable torture, and a network of openings and confusing corridors. Monitoring was also performed at a distance through the use of 'electrical devices which warned him . . . when anybody walked over the floors of either the second and third story' ('Modern Bluebeard 1895: 40).

The house as a kind of machine sealed the fate of all who were within. Only Holmes was able to freely cross between the benign (open) and violent (hidden) sides of the hotel. Fundamentally, the murder house offers a spatial doubling, the ordinary rooming house and offices set alongside secret rooms and hidden trapdoors, and the psychological doubling of the personable and friendly employer/lover assisting a number of young women with work, who is also the calculating murderer who lured them to their death. The two worlds remained apart and while some visitors moved from one to the other and never returned, the true horror was never exposed until the secret was contextualized through the revelation of the parallel chambers. To some extent, this doubling of life and the consequent doubling of the floor plan is also reminiscent of Rachilde's novel *La Jongleuse* (1900), where the strange 'double house' of the female protagonist, Eliante Donalger, comprises the 'decadent side and a rather conventional bourgeois side' (Watson 1999: 188). Although the two zones are seen as separate, Eliante's uncle and niece live on the courtyard side of the house where conventional bourgeois life is performed, whereas her private quarters are on the decadent garden side. Like Holmes, she is able to traverse both sides and, in the case of the novel, conducts herself in a different manner and in different dress. With Holmes, there is little evidence as to how he performed in the sinister enclave of the mansion; none of his confessions describe how the rooms were used or what became of his victims. In the drama played out in the Holmes mansion, the realms of nurturing domesticity were deliberately confused. Inappropriate constructions restructured domestic, sexual and social order.

The mid-twentieth-century spectra of Reginald Christie's domestic murder victims did not carry the same attention to disposal that Holmes reached half-a-century earlier. Christie rented the ground floor rooms of a three-story terrace house at 10 Rillington Place, London, and was able to observe movements in and out, and to the shared toilet in the rear yard. Although he never had spatial control, he managed to move through the house quite silently in his plimsolls, as Timothy Evans sister testified: 'One of the worst things about Christie was that you could never hear him coming' (Kennedy 1971: 65). When Christie was finally caught by the police, forensic evidence revealed that two bodies were buried in the garden, one under the floorboards, three in a concealed cupboard off the kitchen, and two in a dark wash house accessed from the garden (Figure 9.3). The latter two bodies, of Beryl and Geraldine Evans, were victims of Christie, but due to a number of false confessions by Timothy John Evans, Christie evaded discovery and Evans went to the gallows. Each body was bound and tied with cord and hidden behind some old wooden floorboards stacked

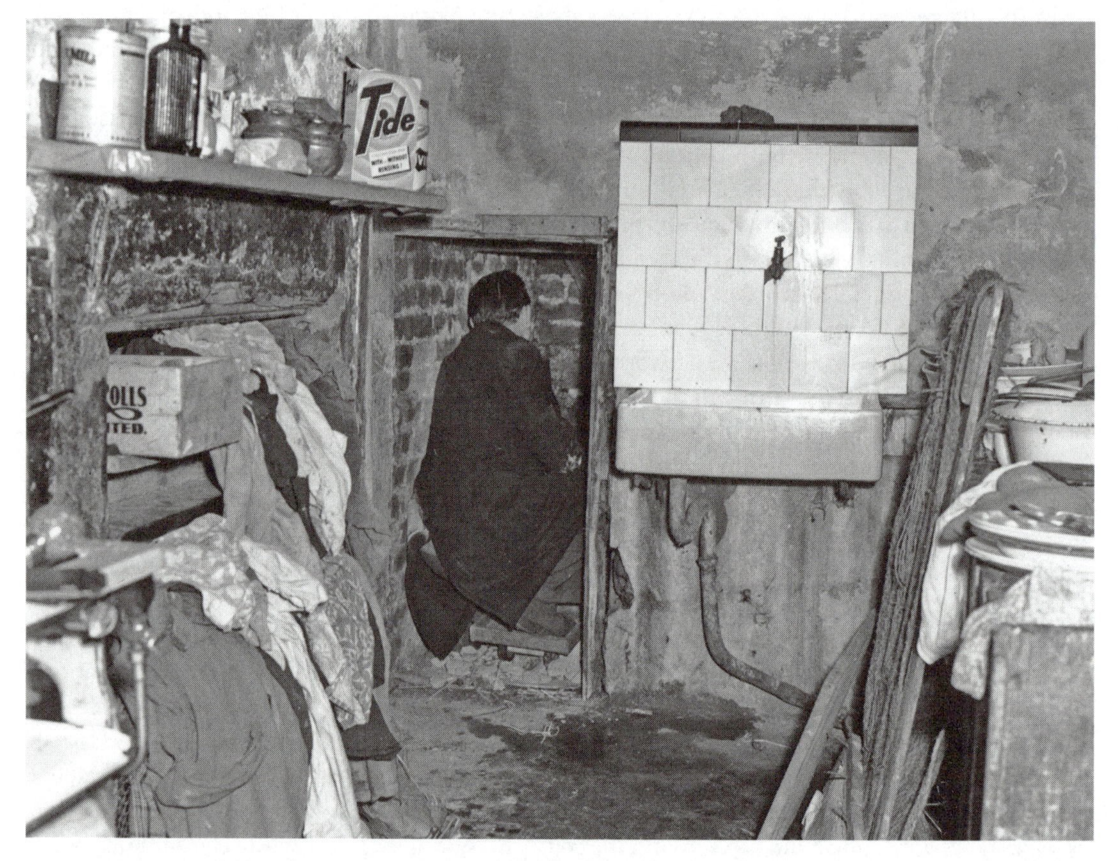

9.3. 10 Rillington Place. © Mitchell/Hulton Archive/Getty Images.

against the wash-house wall. When found, the 'packages' were removed and upon inspection were found to contain corpses. The fact that there was no smell was attributed to it being a cold November when 'refrigeration conditions were perfect' (Kennedy 1971: 113). The initial search of the house failed to locate the corpses, and, although this may be due to police uncertainty as to what they were looking for, it also suggests that while the spheres of murder and domesticity might interact, their unusualness prompts at least the hope of their separateness. In December 1952, Christie strangled his wife and hid her body in a shallow grave under the floorboards of his front room; in the early months of 1953 a further three victims were gassed, strangled and hastily concealed in a kitchen alcove that extended behind the wash house. Broke, without a job, and his home resembling a miniature mortuary, Christie left the flat and wandered around London for several days until the discovery of the bodies and his eventual arrest. Unlike Holmes, who carefully planned all his murderous encounters, Christie acted on impulse to, firstly, protect himself and, secondly, for immediate sexual gratification through necrophilia.

Whereas Reginald Christie's victims were concealed in an alcove and a wash house, Fred and Rose West's nine murdered females were recovered from under the concrete basement floor, beneath the bathroom floor, and in the garden covered over by a paved patio. Their three-story home at 25 Cromwell Street, Gloucester, was excavated in 1994, when police began a search for a missing child rumoured to be buried in the garden. Despite their early protests regarding damage to their property and police harassment, any allegiances to the home as a place for family and nurturing were soon dispelled when one body was identified as Fred West's daughter, Heather, and interviews with the West's and their remaining children revealed a life of torture, rape and prostitution. During their twenty-year occupation, sections of the house where Rose West entertained clients were locked and off limits to all children, and any transgression into their parents' area resulted in beatings (Sounes 1995: 195). The children's soundproof basement 'playroom' was accessed through a concealed trapdoor and was used for incestuous torture and rape, which mirrored the bondage, torture and killing that occurred in the 'adult area' on the first floor. Fear and a strict spatial structure created autonomy for the West's by isolating the family and allowing control over its own 'plot of land'. With the discovery of the female murder victim, the home's autonomy is thrown into doubt.

The familiar nineteenth-century cultural construction of the home as a refuge, a place that separates the safe from the unsafe and the tame from the wild is disrupted through the actions of the occupant. A paradigm of nurturing domesticity symbolized through the hearth is confronted by violence and death that revolves around the offering and then withdrawing of a safe spatial enclosure. The multi-tenanted home with an intensification of close proximity living and transient occupancy alongside permanent residents suggests a different strategy for 'private existence' than the autonomy of the single-family house. Holmes's spatial autonomy was conducted through his occupation of most of level three, control over the rented rooms and movement through a network of hidden rooms, whereas Christie's complex shared arrangements meant the ground floor was not exclusively his own, but the garden and wash house were available for hiding bodies. Fred and Rose West shared their home with lodgers and their young children at the time most killings occurred, but through fear they instigated a spatial separation between adult and child areas, while utilizing the basement and garden for disposal of victims.

The discussion of the poets and literature suggests that the hidden is shown to be something anticipated or wanted, whereas the hidden rooms and spaces of the murderer are not desirable. To some extent, this offers confusion; this is not just a spatial confusion of intimate inner space isolated from the outside, but a collapse of traditional occupation. The disposal and concealment of bodies is a violence on the domestic, in that it disrupts and transforms home to mortuary. When the house is invaded by death, the murderer's techniques and technologies transform the interior into an instrument of control; rather than excluding violence, the architecture shields and protects from neighbourly observation. Although the perpetrators of the crimes are in some sense acting out their desires as a form of self-exploration, any psychological connection between inhabitant and space that is revealed as 'personality' (as in the literary examples) is overwhelmed by the crime, and architecture's complicit relationship is made apparent. Ultimately, the violation of the boundary between persons and spaces violates the boundaries of the domestic interior and, to some extent, the familial social order.

REFERENCES

Boswell, C., and Thompson, L. (1955), *The Girls in Nightmare House*, New York: Fawcett Publications.

Campbell, W. (2002), 'The Hidden Rooms of Isabella Valancy Crawford and P. K. Page', *Mosaic: A Journal for Interdisciplinary Studies of Literature*, 35/4: 69.

'Castle is a Tomb' (1895), *Chicago Tribune*, 28 July.

Chase, K. (1984), *Eros & Psyche: The Representation of Personality in Charlotte Brontë, Charles Dickens, and George Eliot*, London and New York: Methuen.

Corbitt, R. L. (1895), *The Holmes Castle: A Story of H.H. Holmes Mysterious Work*, Chicago: Corbitt and Morrison.

Edholm, F. (1993), 'The View from below: Paris in the 1880s', in B. Bender, ed., *Landscape Politics and Perspectives*, Oxford: Berg.

'Footprint is Found' (1895), *Chicago Tribune*, 28 July.

Guyer, F. P. (1896), *The Holmes-Pitezel Case: A History of the Greatest Crime of the Century and the Search for the Missing Pitezel Children*, Philadelphia: Publishers' Union.

Heathcote, O. (2009), *Balzac and Violence: Representing History, Space, Sexuality and Death in 'la Comedie humaine'*, Bern: Peter Lang.

'Holmes' Den Burned' (1895), *Chicago Tribune*, 19 August.

Irigaray, L. (1991), *Philosophy in the Feminine*, London: Routledge.

Kennedy, L. (1971), *Ten Rillington Place*, London: Panther.

Marcus, S. (1999), *Apartment Stories: City and Home in Nineteenth-Century Paris and London*, Berkley: University of California Press.

'Modern Bluebeard' (1895), *Chicago Tribune*, 18 August.

Mudgett, H. W. (1895), *Holmes' Own Story*, Philadelphia: Burke and McFetridge.

'Not Human Bones' (1895), *Chicago Tribune*, 21 July.

Seltzer, J. (1998), *Serial Killers: Death and Life in America's Wound Culture*, New York: Routledge.

Sherer, S. (1996), 'Secrecy and Autonomy in Lewis Carroll', *Philosophy and Literature*, 20/1: 1–19.

Sounes, H. (1995), *Fred and Rose: The Full Story of Fred and Rose West and their Gloucester House of Horrors*, London: Warner Books.

Stowe, W. W. (1983), *Balzac, James, and the Realistic Novel*, New York: Princeton University Press.

Turnell, M. (1950), *The Novel in France*, London: Hamish Hamilton.

Vidler, A. (1992), *The Architectural Uncanny: Essays in the Modern Unhomely*, Cambridge, MA: MIT Press.

Watson, J. (1999), *Literature and Material Culture from Balzac to Proust*, Cambridge: Cambridge University Press.

INDEX

Page numbers in **bold** refer to illustrations.

C

D

Y

Z